The Shanghai
Stars and Stripes

ALSO BY ALFRED EMILE CORNEBISE

*The CCC Chronicles: Camp Newspapers of the
Civilian Conservation Corps, 1933–1942* (McFarland, 2004)

*The United States 15th Infantry Regiment in China,
1912–1938* (McFarland, 2004)

The Shanghai *Stars and Stripes*

Witness to the Transition to Peace, 1945–1946

ALFRED EMILE CORNEBISE

McFarland & Company, Inc., Publishers
Jefferson, North Carolina, and London

LIBRARY OF CONGRESS CATALOGUING-IN-PUBLICATION DATA

Cornebise, Alfred E.
 The Shanghai Stars and stripes : witness to the transition to peace, 1945–1946 / Alfred Emile Cornebise.
   p. cm.
 Includes bibliographical references and index.

 ISBN 978-0-7864-4756-5
 softcover : 50# alkaline paper ∞

  1. Stars and stripes (China ed.)—History. 2. World War, 1939–1945—Journalism, Military—United States. 3. United States—Armed Forces—Periodicals—History. 4. World War, 1939–1945—China.   I. Title.
 D731.S728C67   2010
 079'.51—dc22   2009049968

British Library cataloguing data are available

©2010 Alfred Emile Cornebise. All rights reserved

No part of this book may be reproduced or transmitted in any form or by any means, electronic or mechanical, including photocopying or recording, or by any information storage and retrieval system, without permission in writing from the publisher.

Cover images ©2010 Shutterstock

Manufactured in the United States of America

McFarland & Company, Inc., Publishers
 Box 611, Jefferson, North Carolina 28640
  www.mcfarlandpub.com

For Sofia Carlene Janice Cornebise

Acknowledgments

First of all, I wish to acknowledge the considerable assistance of the staff at the Special Collections Branch of the Hamilton Library of the University of Hawaii at Manoa, in particular Dr. Karen Peacock, head of the Collections; Bronwen Solyom, curator; Lynette Furuhashi, Pacific Specialist; Dore Minatodani, librarian; and Ann Rabinko, library assistant. Their help has been indispensable in getting access to needed materials and obtaining reproductions and permissions to use the Arthur Goodfriend Papers central to my efforts in writing this study. Their insights about Goodfriend, whom some of the staffers knew well, have also been a great help to me.

A former staffer at the Shanghai *Stars and Stripes*, Alpheus "Bill" Jessup, provided me with invaluable information about the newspaper and its operations, notably pointing out the importance of the Arthur Goodfriend Papers and their location.

The staff of the New York Public Library provided me with microfilm of a full run of the Shanghai *Stars and Stripes* and of the paper's *Magazine Supplement*.

At the Hoover Institution Archives, I received substantial assistance in procuring a portrait of General Wedemeyer from Carol Leadenham, Assistant Archivist for Reference, and Janel Quirante, Assistant Archivist for Visual Collections.

At the U.S. Coast Guard Headquarters, Deputy Historian Scott Price assisted me in obtaining a needed photograph. Members of the Naval History and Heritage Command helped me to obtain official U.S. Navy photos essential to this study.

In France, at the University of Lyon, Christian Henriot, editor of the Institut d'Asie Orientale's Virtual Shanghai Project, forwarded images of Shanghai to me.

In Shanghai, Graham Earnshaw and Derek Sandhaus, of Earnshaw Books, provided me with information regarding *Tales of Old Shanghai* and images of the city.

Finally, I wish to thank my wife, Jan Miller Cornebise, a writer in her own right, for her careful reading of the manuscript and for the many suggestions and corrections of my inevitable mistakes. Her firm support throughout this endeavor is greatly appreciated.

Table of Contents

Acknowledgments	vii
Preface	1
Introduction	5
I. Origins, Foundations and Early Operations of the China (Shanghai) Edition of the *Stars and Stripes*	11
II. The Home Front: The View from Afar	28
III. The Chinese Conundrum	34
IV. Growing GI Unrest: Ferment, Furor, and Occasional Favors	38
V. Japanese Problems: Repatriation and War Crimes Trials	49
VI. The China Scene Changes	61
VII. Two Redoubtable Staffers: Arthur Goodfriend and Franc Shor	64
VIII. Going Home	80
IX. The Worldwide Collapse of GI Morale	95
X. The Effects of Soldier Unrest on the Soldier Press	112
XI. The Marines	120
XII. The Conduct of Servicemen in Shanghai	132
XIII. The Marshall Mission	136
XIV. The Shanghai *Stripes*: Later Developments and "30"	147
XV. Conclusions	161
Chapter Notes	171
Selected Bibliography	187
Index	193

Preface

The Shanghai *Stars and Stripes*, officially known as the China (Shanghai) Edition of the *Stars and Stripes*, was published from September 28, 1945, to April 13, 1946. It was established at the instigation of Lieutenant General Albert Coady Wedemeyer, the commander of the China Theater of Operations, to enhance morale. Unlike the other editions of the *Stars and Stripes* of the World War II era, which mainly supported Army GIs, Wedemeyer's bailiwick included sailors and Marines whom the new paper also served. By the closing of the China Theater in May 1946, it had ceased operations, its mission accomplished.

To launch this venture, Wedemeyer shrewdly drew upon the abilities and judgment of the editor-in-chief of the European editions of the *Stripes*, Lieutenant Colonel Arthur Goodfriend. Though published for only a few months, its lively venue was packed with momentous scenarios, developments and events. Certainly, American fighting men, recently released from armed conflict following the Japanese surrender on August 14, 1945, could be excused their exuberance, incessant high jinks and sheer relief at having survived the war. These emotions were strongly intermingled with tantalizing, delicious tingles associated with their anticipation of an early swift return home. For many veterans, their dreams were rapidly gratified. For others, a time of waiting for weeks and then months unfolded with some dire, unforeseen consequences.

To be sure, the magnitude of the task of getting everyone home was enormous. Ships, so long engaged in combat and the supply of the combatant forces, had to be rescheduled, sometimes renovated, and directed homeward. Crews had to be assembled. The vast distances involved and other logistical matters posed other difficulties. The sheer size of the Army, which attained numbers of over eight million by mid–1945, was daunting. Most soldiers were draftees desiring instant passage home and prompt discharges. Having only contempt for Regular Army ways and ideals, these citizen-soldiers had a burning desire to leave the service. The Navy and Marines, and other combatant forces, added their large numbers, unique needs and requirements.

These factors were played out on a demanding and complex stage. China was unimaginably chaotic, the consequence of the protracted struggle with

Japan beginning in 1937. Furthermore, the nation was sharply divided between Chiang-Kai-shek's Nationalists — themselves hobbled by intrigue and warring factions — and the Chinese Communists. Both of these contenders strenuously sought political and military advantage with little hope of reconciliation. The problem as to what American attitudes should be in these circumstances defied easy solution. In certain official quarters the answer lay in employing American manpower and resources to support Chiang — a doomed venture — but this caused much controversy and often strong reaction from the Communists.

Meanwhile, U.S. soldiers, sailors and Marines were used to secure the country and repatriate millions of Japanese soldiers and civilians. Time and energy were also expended in bringing Japanese war criminals to trial. Yet additional Americans were needed to maintain the peace so recently won and much lend-lease materiel had to be guarded or disposed of. Clearly, the nation's diplomatic and military needs were in conflict with the urgencies of the vast majority of its armed forces overseas. The home front also intruded, adding more pressure to the cauldron.

The Shanghai *Stars and Stripes* therefore emerged onto a ready-made, intense journalistic beat. Fortunately, its founder, Colonel Goodfriend, was well qualified to launch and manage the paper in its early weeks. A thoroughly professional staff was rapidly assembled and the paper was soon fully up to speed. Armed with supportive directives from Wedemeyer, it developed as a clear true voice of its readership. By means of a lively letters-to-the-editor column — the "B-Bag" — it manifested the spirit and letter of an ideal soldier press as formulated and developed by the paper's predecessors in the Great War and in World War II. These publications reflected the dicta of the high command, such as General Eisenhower, the Supreme Allied Commander in the European Theater of Operations in World War II, who once reminded Colonel Goodfriend that *Stripes* was to be a free, decent paper, run by soldiers, for soldiers. The only censorship and restrictions were those that might be imposed for security reasons. In fact, the Shanghai edition was the last open and relatively free U.S. soldier paper. Subsequently, as the "Good War," i.e., World War II, and its accompanying "good soldier papers," i.e., the *Stars and Stripes*, passed from the scene, soldier papers were steadily reduced in the postwar years to mere house organs. Much more rigid, and reflecting conservative "Regular Army" ways and ideas, they became pale imitations of their venerable forbears. In this regard, Churchill's "years of the locusts" ensued for soldier journalism and much else regarding American military ventures in this era.

Beyond these considerations, the Shanghai edition is perhaps best viewed as functioning within a time and place characterized as transitional, dimensions of which it duly recorded and analyzed. The years 1945 and 1946 were those of rapid change from war to peace, and from another perspective, extending from a shooting "hot war" to an equally dangerous "Cold War." For the average GI the transition was especially profound, catapulting him from the battlefield to the home front. In China, the transitional dimension bore the mystique of the classic East-West encounter, though now in rapidly changing circumstances.

The author, who has chronicled the history of several doughboy and GI newspapers, was eventually attracted to this last significant official Army publication and the times and site of its setting. The primary sources were readily available, including a complete run of the paper and its weekly *Magazine Supplement* in the New York Public Library. Many additional papers, plus archival and primary materials, supplemented these two major lodes. One important source was the vast collection of papers of its founder, Arthur Goodfriend, located in the Special Collections archives of the University of Hawaii, which generously allowed full access.

A close study of the Shanghai *Stars and Stripes* provides a unique opportunity to examine a pivotal time and place in the history of the world: the end of hostilities in World War II in Asia, and immediately following. Affording a means of probing some of the parameters and meaning of those times, by extension, such an endeavor can provide some perspective regarding significant dimensions and problems of our present age, with an emphasis on encounters between East and West in yet another challenging era.

Introduction

"Tell me the story; there's always a story."
— Anonymous neurosurgeon

In May of 1945, VE Day was proclaimed in Europe; in August, VJ Day followed in Asia. On the face of it, World War II was over and the world had entered another era: the postwar years. The long search for Churchill's elusive "sunlit uplands" then ensued, with mixed results. The consequences of the struggle that had produced sixty million dead and so many other dire and depressing conditions could not be put right in short order. A catalog detailing everything that was out of joint would be a massive tome indeed. Reconstruction efforts would engage millions of people and billions of dollars for many years to come.

As was the case during the war, events were clearly distinct between the European Theater of Operations (ETO) and theaters in the Pacific and Asia. For students of the era, one rewarding source worthy of investigation is that of the armed forces newspapers. Among the most important are the various editions of the famous *Stars and Stripes*. The European theater boasted many of these, among them the London, Paris, Rome and Naples papers. In the Pacific, there was the mid–Pacific edition published in Honolulu. In Asia, the Tokyo paper was launched in October of 1945. It failed, however, to develop as its European counterparts had because of the heavy hand of General Douglas MacArthur, whose empire was never a favorable venue for a relatively free soldier press. Much better situated was the China (Shanghai) edition of *Stripes*, which served all American military personnel in the China Theater, the only version of the paper to embrace all branches. The others mainly focused on the U.S. Army.

The Shanghai *Stripes* was founded not long after the cessation of hostilities in August of 1945, by which time American forces were arriving in considerable numbers in the important centers of eastern China. These included the cities of Peiping, Tientsin, Tsingtao and Shanghai, where the West had been established in the 1920s and early 1930s before the arrival of the Japanese, especially after 1937, progressively ended the Western presence. The paper's prime mover was the U.S. Army's commander in chief of the China Theater, Lieutenant General Albert Coady Wedemeyer, who recognized the need for a soldier, sailor and Marine paper to help boost morale. It seemed obvious to him, therefore, to establish a version of the ETO's successful *Stars and Stripes* in China.

For the vast majority of military personnel of whatever country, at war's end one major morale issue was the matter of returning home, a subject that was a natural for a soldier paper to address. Unfortunately, the solutions were hardly simple and efforts to work them out would engage the brains and energy of countless officials and administrators at every level. The problems were compounded by the massive crowds of refugees and the flotsam and jetsam of war with the dislocations this debris occasioned.

Many Americans on active duty in the midst of the chaos surrounding the precipitous ending of hostilities following the employment of the atomic bombs would have been gratified to learn that Army Chief of Staff General George Catlett Marshall and Henry Stimson, the Secretary of War, among others, possessed a clear view of what was then immediately required. On August 15, 1945, the day after the Japanese surrender, a Memorandum for Chiefs of All War Department and Special Staff Divisions was issued. This addressed the subject of "War Department Policies for the Period Following V-J Day."[1] The War Department's mission now, the document stated, was to focus on demobilizing the Army, and the elimination and curtailment of the activities of the Department to the maximum extent consistent with providing the occupational forces in conquered and liberated areas. It was also to make "reasonable provisions for fundamental post-war military requirements," providing that these did not interfere with demobilization and curtailment programs. Throughout, the document went on, "every member of the Army will be treated as an individual. Primary emphasis will be placed upon the rapid discharge of military personnel in their order of priority as determined by their critical scores," based on a points system. This had earlier been devised by the U.S. Army to provide for the return of veterans to the United States as quickly and as equitably as possible. Other branches of the service adopted it in theory, but in practice set up their own formulas to suit their separate needs. Marshall explained that "in considering the interests of eight million men it is naturally impossible to find a solution satisfactory to all, equally just to all." The system that was adopted seemed to be the best that the War Department could devise, and was established "on the basis of the greatest good for the greatest number." It was prepared following a year or more of analyses of Gallup polls taken in all theaters, "where every phase of the matter was considered." The interest of the War Department was "solely directed to the rapidity of an orderly demobilization with every consideration that is possible to give the individual when dealing in terms of millions."² According to the system, the Army awarded one point for each month of service between September 16, 1940 (when the draft was instituted), to May 12, 1945, just after VE Day. Another point was awarded for each month of overseas service during the same time. Five points were recorded for each award, such as the Distinguished Service Cross, Distinguished Flying Cross, the Purple Heart, and others. Five points each were counted for campaign stars worn on theater ribbons. Twelve points were awarded for each child in the soldier's immediate family, up to a limit of three. A cutoff was initially established at eighty-five points, the first "magic number," though these were steadily reduced as the perceived "needs of the service" dictated.³

What is striking, despite the many limitations, failures and drawbacks, is the considerable success in realizing these goals. The official documents serve to identify the parameters of what was intended by officialdom and military planners regarding them. They reveal the philosophy stemming from the ideals and heritage of the United States as a nation and of such leaders as Marshall and Stimson and many others.

Nevertheless, in the hurly-burly of the intense activity, and the to-and-froing, much fell through the cracks. The points system, which worked reasonably well, and was generally well-received, could nonetheless be abused. The soldier papers, such as the China (Shanghai) Edition of *Stars and Stripes*, describe the extent to which official plans were carried out, or failed. These were affected by many factors, including inertia, as well as the traditions of an established military universe and many untoward developments inherent in ongoing military operations and their usual "fog." In addition, there were logistical problems involved with the transporting of millions of people. Human nature and natural events, not to mention time and space considerations, such as those inherent in traversing thousands of miles of ocean, notably in the Pacific, also intervened to produce less than officially desired ends and results. In the upshot, many servicemen, having exhausted their patience awaiting their shipment home following an already long and arduous war, sometimes reached their breaking point, which resulted in worldwide GI demonstrations and protests and even riots for a few weeks in January of 1946.

Related to some of these developments was a perennial concern with the military caste system. The extent to which the Army, especially, even in the midst of intense military operations from 1943 to 1945, sought to assess opinion on this subject is remarkable. Letters to the editor in the many editions of *Stripes* in World War II were a fair indication of ongoing interest in these matters and certainly one of the reasons why many high-ranking commanders were less than enthusiastic about free and open servicemen's papers.

As is usual with troop publications, the Shanghai paper revealed much about the everyday life of American military personnel in the China area immediately following the end of hostilities in 1945. Many other themes surfaced as well, such as how this particular military newspaper fared, with some discussion about the proper role of a military paper and issues of censorship and other related matters. In addition, readers learned about pressing concerns among servicemen everywhere at that time. While many of the troops there manifested relief at their not having to invade Japan — and the majority were hardly opposed to the dropping of the atom bombs— the news of this awesome weapon so recently released created its own fallout among the U.S. military personnel, though not to the extent that might have been imagined.

The China situation was further compounded and confused by the intensifying civil war between the Communists and the Nationalists of Chiang Kai-shek. In this regard, America's precise attitudes and roles were frequently debated. Some insight into East and West relations, at this time and in the decades to follow, for good or ill, can be garnered by the more astute from the pages of the Shanghai *Stripes*, even if dimly. General Marshall's ill-fated year-long mission of late 1945 to early 1947, which sought to resolve China's internal difficulties, was also closely reported in its earlier months— the paper ceased publication in April 1946, and Marshall was there until early in 1947. In addition, when finding themselves immersed in the appalling physical conditions among the Chinese, many Americans sought to ease their suffering, though many were simply repelled and ignored what they saw with little appreciation of what it all portended for China's future. Then, too, many GIs had recently been in combat and the undoubted relief that they felt about simply being alive, and their lusts and longings for certain familiar creature comforts, which they found readily available in newly liberated Chinese cities, could not be ignored. The pursuit of these forms of "happiness," however, often produced their own tensions and woes.

In addition, the China scene was complicated by the presence of over a million Japanese civilians and troops, many of the latter still armed. How would these be repatriated without any untoward incidents occurring? Also, how could this be done with the transportation available, all the while meeting the needs and ever-more-vocal demands of American military personnel so bent on their own return home? Then there were the Japanese war crimes trials also closely followed in the paper.

Because of the many transitional aspects of this time, this book focuses on some of these topics as they were developed in the pages of the Shanghai *Stripes*. As it has been observed, all times are transitional but, with a nod to George Orwell, some times are more transitional than others. This study is, first of all, transitional between the era of World War II and the postwar age. At another level, this includes a forecast of a longer period which witnessed the waning of Western influence in Asia by the twenty-first century. Thus, while some of the editions of the *Stars and Stripes* were witnesses to war, especially in Europe, the Shanghai edition was rather a spectator to the early postwar era with emphasis on Asia.

Another transitional path which the paper described in great detail concerned service personnel in that tenuous, agitated state between military service and the return to the States where the home front was winding down, another area of considerable interest. The conditions and events of this sometimes lengthy interlude — far too long, as many perceived it — provided much grist for the paper's mill.

The rapidly emerging Cold War provided further fodder. This too is another transitional factor, when the world moved from a stance of armed conflict to another kind of confrontation demanding differing and complex responses as nations sought new footings in the drastically changed circumstances. The Shanghai *Stripes* did not neglect these momentous developing patterns.

The Shanghai *Stripes* was the last major exemplar of an authentic, bona fide American GI paper in the hands of the men themselves. Finally, therefore, this study is transitional in that it describes and delineates the gulf between a provocative and informative soldier paper and the much more innocuous sheets that have characterized military papers during the postwar period extending to the present. This bipolar differential accelerated in late 1945 and early 1946 partially as a result of the worldwide unrest in the American military services and the overt, sometimes violent, response of servicemen to the redeployment problem. Eisenhower and Marshall — to which the name of Wedemeyer should be added — had considerable influence in allowing such as the *Stars and Stripes* to remain soldier papers in the hands of the men themselves. Formidable forces, however, within the conservative establishment, especially in the Army, had always deplored the existence of a relatively free and open soldier paper. By patience and perseverance these forces eventually substantially diminished the soldier press. These factors were abetted by the fact that many of the staunch proponents of publications such as the *Stars and Stripes*, and the magazine, *Yank*, had returned to civilian life, leaving an unfettered GI press undefended and vulnerable. The departure of Eisenhower and Marshall from their positions of command was an additional factor.[4]

As a record of major events worldwide, and more specifically regarding China in 1945 and 1946, this study seeks to provide scenarios about a time when West met East in a significant way in a turbulent era of great confusion, uncertainty and change. All in all, therefore, the venue of the China Edition of the *Stars and Stripes* proved a lively if chaotic milieu. This the paper did not fail to mirror and describe with a measure of verve, vivacity, and, on occasion, acute insight in the best traditions of its predecessors in World War I and World War II and those of American journalism in general.

I

Origins, Foundations and Early Operations of the China (Shanghai) Edition of the *Stars and Stripes*

"Hail to thee, blithe Spirit!"
— Percy Bysshe Shelley, "To a Skylark" [1819]

Sometime in early September of 1945, the editor-in-chief of the European editions of the U.S. Army's troop newspaper, the *Stars and Stripes*, Lieutenant Colonel Arthur Goodfriend, flew from Paris to Shanghai via Chungking, Nationalist China's wartime capital. His new assignment was a three-month tour of duty during which he was charged with establishing a China edition of the *Stripes*. It was to be set up in Shanghai, recently liberated from the Japanese, who had been there since 1937.[1] There were already several troop papers in the China-Burma-India Theater (the CBI). One of these was the *China Lantern*, which was published as a triweekly in Calcutta, India, though it also maintained editorial offices in Kunming, China. It was not regarded, however, as sufficiently attuned to developments in China, which was by then, as of October 25, 1944, detached from India and Burma as its own separate Theater. Nor did the *Lantern* possess the *Stripes*' cachet. Shortly after the new paper began publication, the *Lantern* ceased operations.[2] In Chungking, Goodfriend met with Lieutenant General Albert Coady Wedemeyer, the commander of U.S. Forces in the China Theater, a man of redoubtable stature and renown, and around whom considerable controversy swirled, especially later in his career. He was born in Omaha, Nebraska, in 1897. Entering West Point in 1917, he graduated in 1919, as a result of the abbreviated wartime curriculum. The usual tours of duty were interspersed with travel abroad, and in the early 1920s, he was in the Philippines. In the early 1930s, he served with the 15th Infantry

Regiment in Tientsin, China. Returning to the United States in 1934, he attended the Army's Command and General Staff school at Fort Leavenworth. In 1936, he was an exchange officer with the German *Wehrmacht* and spent a two-year tour at Germany's historic *Kriegsakademie*. There he witnessed Nazi Germany's rapid rearmament and noted the development of the *Blitzkrieg* doctrines soon to be unleashed upon Europe. Returning home, Wedemeyer briefed the Army General Staff, including the chief of war plans, Brigadier General George C. Marshall. At his own request, he was then assigned to troop duty at Fort Benning, Georgia.

Meanwhile, World War II had begun in China in 1937, and in Europe in 1939. In September 1940, Wedemeyer was recalled to the War Department as a major, and in the spring of 1941, he

Lieutenant Colonel Arthur Goodfriend, founder of the Shanghai *Stars and Stripes* (from The Papers of Arthur Goodfriend, Special Collections, University of Hawaii Library, by permission).

was assigned to the War Plans Division of the General Staff. In July of 1941, Wedemeyer was charged with drafting a comprehensive war plan that FDR had requested. His handiwork became famous as the "Victory Plan," which emerged as the basic document for America's conduct of the war against the Axis powers. This envisioned moving first against Germany, aims that were not appreciably altered by Pearl Harbor. It also emphasized the cross-channel invasion of Fortress Europe as soon as possible, a view which Wedemeyer strongly championed. Wedemeyer rapidly rose through the ranks and, by the summer of 1942, was a brigadier general. Becoming chief of the Strategy and Policy Group in the War Department's Operations Division, he played a key role in the early management of the war. Though he hoped for a field command in Europe, this was not forthcoming. Meanwhile, Roosevelt and Churchill decided to establish a new command in Southeast Asia to better coordinate operations in the China-Burma-India Theater — the CBI. Headquartered in New Delhi and called the Southeast Asia Command (SEAC), it was headed by British Admiral Lord Mountbatten. Wedemeyer became head of plans in the new entity. In this regard, he learned much about the Asian area of operations which would shortly stand him in good stead. When, on October 24, 1944, General Joseph Stilwell was relieved of his duties as commander of the CBI, Wedemeyer found himself in Chungking as head of the newly-created China Theater of Operations.

(An American command, Burma and India were no longer joined to the Chinese area.) By now a lieutenant general, Wedemeyer soon stemmed a major Japanese offensive in China, improved the effectiveness of the Chinese armed forces, and completed plans for final operations against Japan which were not needed in the wake of the atomic bombing of Japan in August of 1945, bringing an end to the war. The struggle wound down with less attention to China because the Asian war's final path lay in another direction under the management of Admiral Chester Nimitz and General Douglas MacArthur.[3]

Back in Chungking, as their meeting unfolded, Wedemeyer informed Goodfriend that troops were scattered throughout China, and admitted, "[M]orale is bad. We need a newspaper. How long must we wait?" Goodfriend promised that, "with a press in working order, supplies, priority in personnel and a little luck," the paper could be launched in as little as two days. Wedemeyer was delighted, and together he and Goodfriend worked out the details of the *Stripes*' philosophy and modus operandi, producing a document subsequently known as the paper's "Magna Charta."[4] Agreed to on September 11, 1945, the Charta was largely based on Goodfriend's proposals worked out in advance. Its preamble stated that the China edition of the paper would "probably [be] the last edition of the servicemen's newspaper to be published in this late, unlamented war. We hope its life will be short and sweet," and he declared that "rarely has a newspaper so earnestly aimed at going out of business at the earliest possible date." Basing his views on the traditions of the *Stars and Stripes* of World War I, and the subsequent editions of World War II, he vowed that it would extol "honesty and liberty," and maintain "an

Lieutenant General Albert Coady Wedemeyer, commanding general of the China Theater of Operations (Official U.S. Army Signal Corps Photograph).

awareness of its responsibility to the nation, the Armed Forces and the serviceman reader." Its aim, he went on, "is to deliver daily a piece of democracy in print." To these ends, as was true of the *Stars and Stripes* worldwide, the paper would give the news, good or bad, as completely and accurately as possible, with no more censorship than applied to civilian newspapers. Servicemen old enough to fight, he insisted, "were old enough to know the truth." The paper further intended to "dish up" the comics, sports, poetry, pictures and features that Americans liked to see in their newspapers back home. In addition, there would be brief essays labeled editorials, which would be unofficial, and accordingly could not be "blamed on the White House, the High Command or anyone except the editor." He would therefore take the credit, though he would also "take the rap." Finally, there would be the traditional "B-Bag," a letters column in which readers could "agree, disagree, gripe, bitch, bark and holler — and give his personal recipe for curing the ills of the world."[5]

Wedemeyer endorsed the Magna Charta, and accordingly allowed much latitude in the paper's operations. Goodfriend was pleased to note that the new edition of *Stripes* was therefore "lucky in its Supreme Commander." Wedemeyer concurred that it would be purely a soldiers' paper, devoted to their GI interests and desires, and promised that there would be no impediments of the paper's operations by any headquarters, including his own. He, too, wanted a column to accommodate soldiers' letters to the editor and wanted them printed even though they criticized the general himself, his headquarters, or the Army in the China Theater. He would also tolerate letters containing views or news that criticized officers. He even admired cartoonist Bill Mauldin's *Willie and Joe*, he declared. He did hope that the paper would seek to raise the level of taste among the GIs, and therefore, it might avoid too much suggestive "cheesecake." Even here, these remained his own views, he admitted, which must not color the paper's conduct and judgment in such matters. While Wedemeyer perhaps later had some reservations about his "blank check," as Goodfriend acknowledged, "until April 13, 1946 when the *Stripes* signed off '30 and out' he never flinched."[6]

The establishment of the Shanghai *Stars and Stripes* was thus assured, but its launching within only a few days required considerable ingenuity, effort and not a little good fortune. Goodfriend departed Chungking accompanied by Sergeant Edmund Hogan, "a stocky black Irishman from Albany, New York," and Sergeant John Clift, a "tall blue-eyed Texan," who meanwhile had joined him in Chunking. Hogan had been the editor of the Rome and Naples editions of the *Stars and Stripes* and Clift was the sports editor for the same papers.[7] Goodfriend later recalled the harried flight to Shanghai:

> A ramshackle C47 flew Hogan, Clift and me to Shanghai. We stopped at Hangkow to refuel. The airstrip had been abandoned. We pumped in 700 gallons by hand. Airborne again, a puzzled pilot groped over mountains through monsoon rain with nothing to guide him but a little radio station broadcasting Chinese opera

I. Origins, Foundations and Early Operations 15

from a studio in the *Shanghai Evening Post and Mercury* building near the Bund, the future site of *The Stars and Stripes*. To that beacon we owed our lives. It took three blind passes over its transmitter and some quick computation in the cockpit to locate the bombed-out runway [of Kiangwan airport.]⁸

They obtained a car and made their way to the Cathay Hotel on Nanking Road. This had been requisitioned by the U.S. Navy but their mentioning the name of the *Stars and Stripes* convinced a Navy lieutenant to sign them in as "five-striped Admirals of the Fleet." A bus boy was summoned who "arrived with caviar, a magnum of Mumms [champagne] and three slit-skirted sing-song girls."⁹ The next day the three went by rickshaw to the plant of Shanghai's equivalent of the *Paris Herald Tribune*, the *Shanghai Evening Post and Mercury*, owned by a legendary American expatriate journalist, John W. Powell. It was located in a mid-Victorian edifice on Avenue Edward VII. Goodfriend, rather jocularly and with a bit of exaggeration, described what the men found:

> Entering the composing room in the rat-ridden cellar Hogan almost wept. The Chinese had invented printing. Here, as in an untidy museum, were arrayed the original machines—linotypes of dynastic vintage verging on scrap, a flatbed press circa Genghis Khan, a stereotype foundry in which the type of Confucius' *Analects* might have been formed—fossils encrusted in rat-droppings and rust. Only the primeval processes remained intact. To make plates for the press the Chinese crew started with a single sheet of rice paper, placed it over the Chase, brushed it with flour and water, piled on more paper and paste until it reached the thickness of a mat. Then dusting the packet with another fistful of flour they locked Chase and paper into an iron frame and baked it in a wood-stoked oven. The product came out smoking and smelling like a hot-cake. Clift nibbled on a piece. "'Add a few raisins,' he admitted, 'and it wouldn't be bad!'"¹⁰

Upstairs, in the editorial offices, the situation was in equal disarray. There "a Sikh family camped. Bearded men in turbans dozed on the desks. In the corners sari-clad women cooked pungent curries over charcoal stoves." As to other members of the family, "a horde of naked children played with the remains of ancient Remingtons. Stuck in glue, babies bawled an accompaniment to the endless twanging of fiddles, the banging of cymbals and drums from the radio studio occupying an adjacent office."

In the midst of these conditions, Goodfriend despaired of keeping his promise to Wedemeyer. But as if by magic, help began to arrive. Victor Senichenko, a White Russian composing room foreman at the plant, rallied the Chinese crew. By cannibalizing the linotypes, they were able to make one work, but the press was hopeless. Into the breach stepped Lieutenant Maurice Pernod, who had appeared rather mysteriously from the staff of the *Chinese Lantern*. He announced that he had found a "spanking new super-speed Japanese rotary press" located at the *North China Daily News* a few blocks away on the Bund. He and Hogan thereupon "forged Chiang Kai-shek's chop [i.e., seal], stamped it on a requisition, and acquired the press together with a stereotype foundry and a week's supply of coal, Shanghai's rarest commodity." Pernod proved to be a production genius and with him in charge of output, those problems "were largely licked, except for paper." Meanwhile, Clift uncovered a hoard of newsprint hidden in the basement of the United States Marine Barracks on Bubbling Well Road, as well as several barrels of ink.[11]

Subsequently, in short order, matters began to fall into place and the staff was rapidly recruited. Among those was surely the paper's most colorful "character," described by Goodfriend as "an entire staff," who "appeared in the person of a swashbuckling replica of Errol Flynn, a Sergeant of the 14th Air Force. Dressed in cavalry breeches and boots, Franc Shor ambled in without orders, swept a slumbering Sikh off the top of a desk, set up a portable [typewriter] and banged out half the copy for the first edition, including the lead story on Shanghai itself. For good measure he threw in a humor column and a feature soon famed as 'Yank about China' ... [and] a poetry column called 'Barracks Bards.'"[12]

Almost overnight, Hogan, named the new sheet's managing editor and armed with Wedemeyer's promise of top priority of available personnel, assembled a team of crack correspondents and newsmen. Among these were Austin C. Wehrwein, later a Pulitzer Prize winner with the *Milwaukee Journal*; Howard Brotz and Abe Rosen of the *Philadelphia Inquirer*; and Bill Smock of the *Pittsburgh Press*. Jim Becker, formerly with Associated Press and later a columnist with the *Honolulu Star Bulletin*, took over the news desk. Lou Miller of the *New York World Telegram* edited sports. Ham Goode was the paper's staff photographer and John Blew of Oregon drew cartoons.

Six officers "matched the GI staff in verve and vigor." In addition to Pernod, these were Levan Shreve; William Sturdevant; Bob Randolph of the *St. Louis Post-Dispatch*; Alpheus ("Bill") Jessup; and Charlie Leong.[13]

Another American journalist, Irene Kuhn, a well-known war correspondent and radio commentator who had been in China before the war, also arrived in Shanghai from Chungking and was immediately recruited by Goodfriend, though she did not remain long.[14] She and Goodfriend attended to the billeting of the staff. For this, they journeyed to the Ward Road Prison, where they "dis-interened [*sic*] an old friend, Christine England," a white-haired English lady who had survived the Japanese occupation of Shanghai. Before the war, England was the proprietress of one of Shanghai's plushest boarding houses, famous for its cuisine and cocktails. Meanwhile, to house the staff, Goodfriend had commandeered a palatial Chinese official's residence on Yu Yuan Lee Road in the French Quarter of the former International Settlement. England became the housemother of the establishment, making sure that her charges were well fed and properly cared for with clean sheets and pressed uniforms. To these ends, she employed sixteen servants and soon boasted a fine table and bar. The bar quickly proved its worth; Major General D.L. Weart, commander of the Shanghai Base Command, was among those entertained. When he complained that the house was cold, the response was that coal was in short supply. Weart

Lieutenant Colonel Arthur Goodfriend and Irene Kuhn. Ms. Kuhn was a civilian correspondent for the Shanghai *Stars and Stripes*. She lived in China in the 1920s and 1930s, working as a newspaper correspondent and radio commentator (from The Papers of Arthur Goodfriend, Special Collections, University of Hawaii Library, by permission).

promptly signed a chit "releasing coal for the billet, plus enough for the stereotype foundry and all the *Stripes*' other needs."[15]

Despite the success in getting things underway, Goodfriend missed keeping the promise to Wedemeyer, though only by three days. The first copies of the *Stripes*' edition came out on Friday, September 28, 1945, five days after he had arrived in Shanghai. It was destined for a run of six months, two weeks and two days, closing up shop on April 13, 1946. Initially a four-pager, by October 8, it was an eight-page sheet.[16] Though Goodfriend was a bit late with getting the paper out, Wedemeyer was "overjoyed" by its appearance, as were "cheering soldiers, sailors and marines as newsboys peddled the first papers on the Bund, Bubbling Well Road and Nanking Road." The first issue featured Wedermeyer's photograph on the front page and his salute and warm welcome to the new *Stripes*. He pledged that the new publication was dedicated to all American servicemen in the China Theater, and would see to it that they were among the best-informed GIs in the world. He further declared that the sheet

Lieutenant Colonel Arthur Goodfriend and *Stars and Stripes* correspondent Irene Kuhn, in front of the paper's offices at the press building of the *Shanghai Evening Post and Mercury,* #19 Avenue Edward VII, near Shanghai's Bund (from The Papers of Arthur Goodfriend, Special Collections, University of Hawaii Library, by permission).

would be a free newspaper, in keeping with the rights of every free American to have a press curtailed by no one. Styled the "Newspaper of the U.S. Armed Forces in the China Theater," it was the only all-service edition of the *Stripes*, being for the benefit of all military personnel in the Theater. Other editions of the *Stripes* in World War II were primarily for the Army. The paper was published by the *Stars and Stripes* Detachment of the Information and Education Section, Headquarters, U.S. Forces in the China Theater (USFCT). Printed daily, Monday through Saturday, at the *Shanghai Evening Post and Mercury* press located at 19 Edward VII Street, near Shanghai's famous Bund, it was routinely vetted by both U.S. Army and U.S. Navy censors.

Ten thousand copies of the paper were delivered by sampans to warships up and down the Yangtze River. The Marines flew papers to their major bases in Tientsin and Peiping. For GIs scattered throughout China's vast interior, Goodfriend noted, "[W]e set up a delivery system unmatched anywhere." Before dawn each day trucks carried the papers to Kiangwan airfield and were then flown to Kunming, Chungking, Chengtu, Hangchow, Chekhiang, Tsingtao and Nanking along with food and medical supplies. A shuttle service then took over and lifted them to smaller bases.[17]

Much of the news flowed in via the USS *Rocky Mount*, the flagship of the Seventh Fleet, anchored in the Whangpoo River. Soon, the Army Signal Corps, the United States Information Service, the Associated Press, the United Press and Reuters set up offices in Shanghai, and these became other sources for copy. The paper cost two cents in American money and $30 in Chinese National Currency (CNC). Other forms of currency used included "puppet money" (CRB, sometimes called the "banana dollar"), $10,000 being required in these funds to purchase an issue of the paper. The office of the *Stripes* had to attend daily to the receipts. As Goodfriend described it, "a dozen deadpan clerks sorted out the money, stacking the paper in gigantic bundles and bagging the coins. Then, lining up behind Shor, they carried the cash to the money-changers where Shor's trading talents guaranteed the best going rates in converting ... [puppet money] to CNC with which we paid off our employees and other expenses." With the rates changing daily, this matter deserved close attention. Indeed, the CNC rate "soon soared out of sight" as the Nationalist government began flooding the country with bank notes, totaling about 40 billion dollars daily. Consequently, a large black market grew in old editions of the *Stripes*. As Goodfriend sadly observed, "In a city jammed with ten million refugees, thousands of them dying of hunger outside our door, a scrap of paper was worth a human life."[18]

Regarding the modest charge of two cents, some readers argued that the paper should be free, but Goodfriend made it clear in a later editorial that it was a true newspaper and not a mere handout. The distinction was important, he explained, observing that a newspaper was generally sold, while a handout was a publication that somebody wanted read for perhaps some ulterior motive and accordingly it was free. In short, people generally respected what they paid

View of Shanghai's famous Bund, the center of Shanghai's life, then and now (courtesy The Virtual Shanghai Project [http://virtualshanghai.net], Image ID 126).

for. Goodfriend believed, therefore, that servicemen would rather have a free, untrammeled press for which they paid than an official flyer which they got for nothing.[19]

The Shanghai locale, where the paper found itself, was fascinating. The city, which in the 1930s had a population of approximately three million Chinese, also included over 100,000 foreigners, who styled themselves "Shanghailanders." In the 1930s and the 1940s, some of these were Jews who had fled Europe before and during World War II. The Nazis desired that they be eliminated, but the Japanese, who had begun the war in Asia by conquering Shanghai in 1937, consigned them in 1943 to a ghetto. The city had long been dominated by foreigners. From the time of the First Opium War with the British in the 1840s, Shanghailanders steadily gained control of much of the city, as they did in other locations in China, obtaining extraterritorial rights to try their citizens in their own courts. In 1843, Shanghai became one of several Treaty Ports, where foreign ships could use the facilities and conduct trade with few restrictions. The several treaties of the nineteenth century exempted foreigners from most Chinese taxes; they could post their troops in China and missionaries were free to propagate the Christian faith. These opened the floodgates, and Western culture, business, banking, and influence inundated China. In consequence, most

I. Origins, Foundations and Early Operations 21

aspects of Chinese political and social life were soon dominated by Westerners in what would be known in China as the "Century of Shame," extending from the 1840s to the mid–1940s. The Americans and the British only relinquished extraterritorial rights in China in 1943 in the midst of World War II.[20]

Specifically, as to Shanghai, the British and American communities were joined in 1863, creating the International Settlement. The Shanghai Municipal Council was formed to administer it. The Council even organized its own small military force for defense, the polyglot Shanghai Volunteer Corps—the S.V.C. The French also had a large settlement—or Concession—which developed independent of the International Settlement, though contiguous to it. These foreign powers, and several others, such as the Italians, the Japanese, and the Germans—until World War I—also maintained entities, some with military and naval contingents. Altogether, Shanghai became modernized along Western lines, and developed into a lively center for culture, business and enterprise.

As to the American military establishment, the U.S. Navy maintained a China force, which in 1835 was called the East India Squadron. Further developments led, in 1910, to the creation of the Asiatic Fleet. Gunboat patrols on the Yangtze River began operating in 1854, though it was not until 1921 that the Yangtze River Patrol became more formally organized as part of the Asiatic Fleet. Also, as to permanent forces, the U.S. Army stationed its 15th Infantry Regiment in Tientsin, southeast of Peking, from 1912 to 1938, when it was replaced by U.S. Marines from Peking. These were drawn from the U.S. Legation guard detachment which served from the late 1890s and again from 1905 to 1941. In 1927, because of unrest threatening the International Settlement, the 4th Marine Regiment was stationed permanently in Shanghai. In 1932, during the so-called Shanghai Incident, when Shanghai was assaulted by Japanese forces for five months starting in early February, the city also felt the tread of soldiers of the U.S. Army's 31st Infantry Regiment, dispatched there to shore up the defenses of the Settlement. They were withdrawn in June 1932, when things calmed down in Shanghai, returning to their permanent base in Manila. Because of Japanese conquests in eastern China following 1937, the 4th Marines departed Shanghai in November 1941. Shortly thereafter, following the attack on Pearl Harbor, Marine units still in China were made prisoners of war. In 1945, following the defeat of Japan, American forces returned once more to eastern China, with a focus on Shanghai, which became the headquarters of the China Theater of Operations.

By the time of the arrival of American forces in Shanghai in 1945, it was, therefore, long since a storied place with a colorful past, and still today seems destined to project its mystique into the 21st century. Within China, the city had a reputation for decadence, cosmopolitanism and pluralism, not to mention its "instincts for contrarianism."[21]

Traditionally, one of the most famous commodities that Shanghai had to sell was its night life. The city's scene at about the time of the launching of the *Stars and Stripes* was well described in the first issue of September 28 by Franc Shor. The key word, he maintained, was "crazy." This was equally applicable to one and all: soldiers, sailors, Russian, Chinese, French and German girls. In addition, the shopkeepers, the bartenders and rickshaw boys were similarly affected. Indeed, this was all wonderful, Shor asserted, and there were no holds barred. For the GIs who had been sweating it out in Chungking, Kunming and dozens of other Chinese cities and towns, eating native food, supplemented by K rations, and almost never seeing a white woman, it was sheer heaven.

Shor further affirmed that the city was indeed "no lady," and never was. While many had tried to describe it in terms running the gamut from sinful, sinister, and wicked to beautiful and romantic, none had succeeded completely. Shanghai had also been featured in songs, poems, stories, plays and movies, yet no one had been able to take her full measure. Among those who tried was Aldous Huxley, who wrote in his diary in 1926 that he had been to many places as "busy and as thickly populous as the Chinese in Shanghai, but none that so overwhelmingly impressed me with its business and populousness. In no city, West or East, have I ever had such an impression of dense, rank richly clotted life. Old Shanghai is [Henri Louis] Bergson's élan vital in the raw, so to speak, and with the lid off, it is Life itself."[22]

The reveling that Shor describes had begun with the deliverance of the city from the Japanese yoke a few weeks before, and Goodfriend alleged that "compared with the frenzy that gripped Shanghai [on that occasion], Paris' deliverance [in August of 1944] had been a wake."[23]

Also in the paper's first issue, Irene Kuhn sought to inform readers about the city's character and appeal for Westerners in the 1920s and 1930s which she had witnessed firsthand. She described the easy-money situation with a favorable exchange rate and the methods of payment. One did not need much ready cash, she explained, except "small money," i.e., the twenty-cent pieces, the dimes, the copper coins and the strings of punched brass discs commonly called "cash," which were principally used for rickshaw fares and the like. What one did require was a pencil to sign chits for every kind of expenditure, even tips. Chits were normally paid on the first day of the month, though one need not pay for months at a time. On the Chinese New Year, however — which usually fell in late January — the Chinese traditionally paid all of their debts if possible, and Westerners did likewise.

A romantic aura permeated the atmosphere and time proceeded in "a graceful and gracious curve," Kuhn remembered, and Westerners lived a champagne existence on a beer income. One could rent a fine house with modern fixings and plumbing and a garden and servant's quarters for about thirty dollars a month. As many as eight servants came with the deal and their combined wages equaled the house rent. Shoes could be made to order by a shoe-tailor who came to the house and measured and fitted one for about three dollars a pair. Another tailor made women's clothes of the finest silks. One had only to give him a picture of a garment clipped from *Vogue* or a Paris fashion magazine and order him to copy it. This he did to perfection, complete with fancy hand work, all for about six dollars. Alcohol of all varieties was plentiful and cheap. Though there were few nightclubs, they were excellent, especially the original Del Monte, where one could buy an American breakfast at 4 A.M. after the gambling houses had closed.[24]

When spring came to Shanghai, Kuhn recalled, it came softly as though on tiptoe, and the soft green sheen of the misty streamers that veiled the willows along Siccawei Creek was duly appreciated. In the city, the Chinese ponies padded around the race course and the big sweepstakes fever was on. Every year someone drew a lucky ticket and won $100,000 or more. Among other diversions, houseboats floated up the canals and waterways bound for Soochow, a city renowned for its beautiful girls. Indeed, love also bloomed among the willows, and flourished under the soft spring moon, Kuhn observed. Altogether in those far-off days of yore, everything was lovely: the world, the times and the city of Shanghai itself.[25]

During those years, Shanghai was also a "Navy town," Kuhn remembered, and the American sailors came roaring in when the fleet sailed up from Manila. She remembered the grey destroyers anchored bow to stern in the Whangpoo River just off the Customs jetty. The Marines came down from Tientsin in the late 1930s on occasion to join the festivities. Unfortunately, the coming of the Japanese and World War II spoiled it all, and, though long lamented, the good times for Westerners would never return.[26]

Just after the war, Shanghai became once more a Navy town. In late September 1945, Admiral Thomas C. Kinkaid, Commander of the U.S. Seventh Fleet, announced that his ships were to assume the duties of the prewar Asiatic Fleet, which was the dominant U.S. naval power in the area before 1941. He had been invested with the command of the Western Coastal Forces, and his territory extended along the coast of China, from Hainan north, and included the Yellow Sea and the western Korean coast. The Seventh was to be headquartered in Shanghai, and initially had considerable strength, with about 75,000 men and numerous heavy warships, such as carriers, battle cruisers, heavy and light cruisers and many smaller craft. The Admiral's quarters were afloat on the flagship, the USS *Rocky Mount* (AGC-3), an Amphibious Force Command Ship.[27]

Shor agreed with Kuhn's assessment regarding the U.S. Navy, asserting that Shanghai especially appealed to the sailors who had manned the Navy's ships along the long, hard road of American conquest past Iwo Jima, Okinawa and all the way to Tokyo. For them, it was paradise because it was their town as it had always been. Shanghai natives knew Marines also, and had even heard of soldiers, but everyone truly waited only for the Navy. When the fleet was in, the massed white caps took on the aspects of a snowstorm hitting the city. Soon the streets were filled with uniformed sailors setting out in rickshaws and pouring into the bars and cafes. As for the rickshaw boys, the results were both heaven and hell — the greatly increased business being the heavenly part. But drunken sailors sometimes jumped between the rickshaw shafts and raced around corners on one wheel. This was the hell part. Even with the other attractions in Shanghai, one remained outstanding: a traditional American-style hot-dog stand complete with rolls and mustard.[28]

Unfortunately, as Shor admitted, while Shanghai was still a sailor's town, profiteering and a booming black market compounded its financial difficulties. To be sure, the shops were full of beautiful things. The Japanese had successfully used Shanghai as a major exhibition site for their "Greater East Asia Co-Prosperity Sphere." In the postwar age just dawning, however, the nightclubs had been transformed into crowded clip joints, complete with loud music and foul air. Though the liquor bottles had fancy labels, most were filled with spirits from Shanghai's Hongkew district, where many distilleries were located. Their contents were characterized by an indescribable taste and a steep price. Therefore, a sailor could get just about what he wanted in Shanghai but had to pay dearly for what the city in former times simply gave away.[29]

From the first issue, the Shanghai *Stripes* had a poetry column, "Barracks Bards," which encouraged would-be poets with the exhortation "If you woos the Muse, it's news." Its offerings, however, were more accurately described as mere verse or doggerel rather than significant poetry. Naturally, love was a subject pursued by many soldier-poets. One example was titled "Ode to a Memory," by Lieutenant M. Torosz, who could not remember the name of his Chinese girl, though its meaning was "Spring Lotus Flower," and he could still hear the sound of her soft voice intoning it which lingered in his ear. Nor did he recall where her home was in old Kunming, though he did remember the pleasant lane leading to it and the tiny gate near the door. He could still see the smile and the light in her eyes when he came late. As to her lips, they were the source of moth-winged kisses, and though the couple soon had to part, he declared that he would always bear a lotus blossom in his heart.[30]

Lieutenant Pat Frank, in his poem "Theme for Tonight," revealed that he had fallen in with an altogether different sort of woman, reflecting a diversity which was characteristic of the Shanghai scene. He said that he would sing her a song of the Shanghai moon, though undoubtedly others had done it before and would do so again, and soon. But for one night at least, he was going to have his fun while he could. He had served in the Chungking heat, not to mention in many dirty holes, and endured rough duty in Yunnan, and elsewhere in China's interior. Thus, he wanted a bottle and a blonde, who would be true to him as long as his money held out, and he would take a rickshaw ride with her by his side (and her hand in his pocket, no doubt). They would also take in a nightclub on Bubbling Well Road, and when the morrow dawned, he would certainly be broke, and the girl would be gone, but he was determined to enjoy to the full his one night to yell.[31]

The many temptations that the men found in Shanghai could result in second thoughts and pangs of conscience, as was the case with John C. Moynihan, the paper's feature editor, as he recorded it in the poem, "Bankrupt in Shanghai." He experienced a great deal of mental anguish and had the feeling that he somehow did not belong to the wild Shanghai scene, where things were frequently tawdry, tacky, trite and vile. Though it was a convivial place, and many were cordial to him — the headwaiter even knew his name — something was sorely lacking and he was only aware of it and what it meant when a lonely air came from the bandstand. Then he was deeply saddened, and in spirit was carried back to the one who bore him a changeless and undying love, had ensnared him, and gained the custody of his soul.[32]

One of the paper's writers, Lieutenant A.L. Crouch, was the very personification of the "Barracks Bard" column. He wrote poems which seemed omnipresent after his first appeared in the October 20, 1945, issue. This led T-5 Harry Louis to state in a verse that every time he read a poem by Crouch, he said "Ouch," and wished that the lieutenant would design to "declare one single verseless day." A defender of Crouch, T-5 H.H. Boynton, responded in his own poem, however, that the lieutenant's detractors were cursed with obtuse, dense and dull minds and possessed no esthetic sense.[33]

Hardly deterred by controversy, Crouch continued diligently to write for the paper, and published two books of poems illustrated by *Stripes*' cartoonists, notably Sig Reinhardt, which were sold in Shanghai area PXs. One was titled *China Sketches* and the second *Ding How*, the first appearing in February 1946 and the second in April of that year. Crouch had begun writing poetry in college and had previously published in the *Saturday Evening Post, Judge, Yank, Army Times* and other publications.[34]

As promised, another column, "B-Bag. Blow It Out Here," appeared, a veritable "chat room" of its day for the China Theater. This invited readers to blow off any excess steam, provided that they kept their missives clean, short, and clearly focused. Because many of the men had time on their hands as they awaited the boat home, and often harbored deep grievances, the "B-Bag" was heavily patronized. One of the first of the letters received was from Major General D.L. Weart, the commanding general of the Shanghai Base Command, in which he congratulated the new paper and praised it for its prompt appearance.

Elsewhere, the editor apologized that the comic feature *Blondie* was the only one then appearing but promised others shortly. These would include Bill Mauldin's *Willie and Joe*, without which the new edition of the *Stripes* would hardly qualify as a bona fide Army paper. By the October 9 issue, *Terry and the Pirates*, by Milt Caniff, and *Joe Palooka*, by Ham Fisher, were being published, as well as *Dick Tracy*, by Chester Gould, and Al Capp's *L'il Abner. Moon Mullins*, by Frank Willard, put in an appearance a bit later. Other features also appeared, one being *It Sez Here!*, a sports column by John Clift.

From the outset, numerous concerns surfaced in the paper's pages. One was the skyrocketing prices present on every hand. In the October 1 issue, the editor counseled the men that the problem was theirs to control: They could simply refuse to pay them. By October 5, General Weart had ordered that a fair-price list be devised and that establishments that charged more than the prescribed price be placed off-limits. Shanghai business concerns and municipal officials were also enlisted to cooperate. To further assist in managing financial difficulties, various PXs in the Shanghai area became money exchanges where gold was swapped for all of the currencies then in circulation on a non-profit basis. This was to counter the plague of money changers everywhere apparent. In shops, in bars and on the curb, hundreds of chiselers plied their mysterious racket, producing victims who were only aware that somehow in the process they were being short-changed.[35]

To be sure, the gaiety for many of the soldiers, sailors and Marines, styled by one observer as the "Shanghai saturnalia," continued in the city. Nonetheless, "the city also festered with starvation, sickness, beggary and crime. All night in bars, hotels and brothels revelry reigned." But emerging in the morning, carousing GIs "stumbled over dead bodies that littered the streets. Corruption was rampant." Goodfriend noted that "rare was the day when an official failed to arrive in our office with a proposition," seeking all manner of privileges or some advantage.[36]

Far more serious was the situation that arose after the atomic bomb had been dropped and the Japanese had collapsed. Goodfriend wrote that "before our eyes, in China, the fruits of victory withered. Instead of great victories, the *Stripes* bannered stories of starvation, inflation, corruption and crime. Readers were aghast as amid misery on a scale unimagined by Americans, civil war squandered the people's pitiful resources." Fighting was intense between the Koumingtang and Communist forces. Backed by American arms and planes, Chiang's forces were making gains in the Peiping-Hankow area on the north shore of the Yellow River. In Suiyan Province, however, the Communists were counterattacking. The presence of U.S. Marines in North China, mainly in Peiping and Tientsin, and the transfer of Chinese National troops into the Communist zone south of the Manchurian border by the U.S. Army Air Force, were both protested by the Communists' headquarters in Yenan as interference in China's internal affairs. These views were intensified by news that unaccountably American forces were even cooperating with Japanese as well as Chinese troops to prevent the spread of Communism. This aroused grave suspicions that a most unwelcome American involvement at a more pronounced level was imminent.[37]

In the event, Goodfriend soon left China, and as the tides of civil war rose ever higher, he became disillusioned, and wrote his last editorial, which was published in the November 12 issue. Titled "Not Fit to Print," the very short piece indicated that, while Goodfriend was supposed to commemorate Armistice Day, 1945, he was simply too depressed to come up with anything fit to print. He, as was true of just about everyone else, desperately wanted to go home, and, as he concluded, "I went." He left behind, however, a flourishing military newspaper which, undiminished by his absence, would continue on its unabashed way for months to come, and would bear the imprint of his image to the end.[38]

II

The Home Front: The View from Afar

Since You Went Away (1944 movie)

In wartime America, as the war continued month after month, it became increasingly difficult for the folks at home and those serving overseas to maintain meaningful contact. As one war correspondent has noted, "The hardest thing for people at home in wartime is to transfer themselves imaginatively to the front where their fighting men are engaged." Then, "when the unknown element of battle comes into the equation, it seems nearly impossible for those at home to realize what war is like." They could not comprehend, for example, that though many were killed, wounded or missing, "the first characteristic of war is not its hardship nor its danger, but the overpowering monotony." As he also astutely observed, the typical GI was "fighting the war for a picture. The picture may be a stained photograph of his family, or of his fiancée, wrapped and re-wrapped in a waterproof tobacco pouch at the bottom of his kit. Or it may only be a picture printed in his memory, changing and growing sharper or fading as he is buffeted about by the fortunes of war." Censorship of the mails further isolated both parties.[1]

The men abroad, in their turn, steadily lost a sense of reality as to conditions on the home front, and on their daily rounds the States took on a "glow" at variance with the country's true condition. Perhaps to placate these stressed men, or to interpose a sense of the true state of affairs at home, the *Stripes* reminded them that while the United States was certainly the wonderful place they all longed for, there were problems and changes—often vast in scope—there as well. The returning vet would find that after his first exuberant welcome, it would soon be necessary to get to work because the nation's main interest in the returning soldier would then be how soon he would resume his normal workday routines. No doubt, there would presently be strong hints to this effect, with an early breakfast on the table and a lunch pail packed and waiting by the door. Another editorial warned that indeed there would be no bed of roses at home. In fact, all would have to pay more taxes, endure inflation, work harder, play less, all with fewer luxuries, which were scarce. All Americans would have to tighten their belts until the war was paid for.[2]

For various reasons, therefore, from the beginning, the Shanghai *Stripes* kept up a drumbeat calculated to focus attention on the many forms of responsibility that returning GIs should consider. An editorial in the November 15 issue, for example, placed some of the blame for Pearl Harbor on the shoulders of "Mr. Plain American Citizen," who before the war had little understanding of world affairs and was mainly preoccupied with isolationism and entertaining prejudices of other peoples on the globe. These conditions made the attack virtually inevitable. On November 20, another agreed that while a vacation was in order for the homeward-bound men, leaving the world to its own devices over the long haul was a real danger, as it had been in the 1930s. The postwar era required that much more was demanded of citizens beyond the bearing of arms against an enemy. All citizens were responsible for keeping themselves informed about world events, as well as demanding and getting honesty in political office. In addition, all must be willing to participate with others to solve the nation's problems. An enlightened citizenry would assure that, as it had been forthrightly stated at the end of World War I, this time surely the world could be made "safe for democracy."

To these ends, the Shanghai *Stripes* closely followed the Pearl Harbor attack investigation launched by a congressional committee chaired by Senator Alben W. Barkley. This body sought to review events and determine, if possible, who might have been negligent in foreseeing and preventing the attack. *Stripes* saw this as opportunity to lecture veterans further as to their civic duties. In the 1930s there had been widespread failures on the part of Americans to take the dictators seriously. Furthermore, the draft act was nearly killed by Congress a few weeks before Pearl Harbor, but the average citizen was not alarmed. The public likewise paid little heed when Roosevelt appealed in 1937 for policies to quarantine aggressors. Therefore, U.S. indifference must bear much of the responsibility for the coming of war to the U.S., he concluded.[3]

Veterans may have decided that they were being subjected to unfair allegations and pressures, and if these were not enough, "Dear John" letters further soured home-sweet-home for some of the troops. A poem by one recipient, Sergeant Peter Wanger, titled "Good Recovery," suggested how the sting might be mitigated. Indeed, there were few reasons for the men to feel sorry for themselves. GIs in Shanghai could simply take advantage of the presence of the innumerable White Russian women, and others, who graced the city's clubs and bars.[4]

There were problems undreamed of overseas. For example, some returning veterans discovered that there were clothing shortages of some magnitude which might take months to resolve. One issue — that seemed crucial to some —

was the shortage of nylon hose. Several articles, some amusing in character, recounted the suffering of deprived females who often went to great lengths to resolve matters. The men were advised therefore to save their ODs, as they would be needed in civilian life.[5]

Finding a place to live was another difficulty because the nation also faced a severe housing shortage. The paper was filled with accounts of how many ex-servicemen were managing. Some "Seabees" (U.S. Navy Construction Battalions, or CBs), for instance, were using their construction skills to build their own homes. In Woonsocket, Rhode Island, an Army paratrooper, recently returned after three combat jumps and with six battle stars, advertised in a local newspaper that he would demonstrate his jumping skills from any altitude if someone would help him find a place to live.[6]

Regarding jobs, another matter of concern, in the first issue of the *Stripes*, Brigadier General George Olmstead, the Assistant Chief of Staff, G-5, the U.S. Forces in China, urged GIs to seek employment in China because jobs were in short supply in the States. One of his jobs was to coordinate U.S. Army activities with the Chinese, and it had occurred to him that while China might not appear to be a likely place to work, he was reminded that American soldiers following the U.S. Civil War had been beckoned to the American frontier. Present-day China, he declared, was similar to what the American West was then.

Olmstead informed readers that Japan had built many large industrial installations in China. With Japan forced out, the Chinese had inherited this giant industrial complex but lacked the technicians and management personnel to operate it. Chiang Kai-shek had asked for U.S. assistance, requesting specifically a substantial number of experts in engineering, transportation and communications. Another avenue of employment would be the United Nations Relief and Rehabilitation Administration (UNRRA), which was already processing applications. In addition, many American firms which had representatives in China before the war were returning and would also need personnel.

Another consideration was that for every GI remaining in China, there was one less place required in the hard-pressed transportation sector struggling to get everyone home. Nonetheless, while a few American servicemen remained in China, the vast majority were simply not interested.[7]

Also as to the home front, psychiatrists and other medical personnel frequently publicized warnings about returning service personnel, often focusing on their morale and their readjustment to civilian life. But these were usually roundly rebuffed by the men. One poem described how one returning serviceman saw his prospects. This imaginative rhyme, titled "Victus," which borrowed from William Ernest Henley's "Invictus," concluded that all challenges that might lie ahead would simply find him "unafraid." The poet, a "Pvt. Kilroy," wrote that he and many of his buddies would gladly sell their souls to leave China and the prospects of their futures back home held few terrors for them.[8]

When a medical officer in China advised the home folks to quit inquiring about the men's return because it was contributing to their low morale, one "Tough Sarge" writing in the December 20, 1945, "B-Bag," suggested that he go sit on one of his hypodermic needles. While this "brass-plated psycho" might be endangered by returning to the States, the "Sarge" asserted that most of the GIs hardly feared their becoming unhinged by their families' asking questions.

Overall, much of the pessimism proved unfounded. America, in fact, was to experience a boom, a consequence in part of the GI Bill of Rights, and ironically of the emergence of the Cold War, which kept much war production on line. As to the GI Bill, the novelist James A. Michener once wrote that he judged it to be "one of the best expenditures of public money made in my lifetime, for it helped an entire generation of bright young people improve themselves.... The burst of achievements in all fields that the United States saw in the decades following the end of World War II stemmed in large part from the flood of energy released by the G.I. Bill."[9]

Nevertheless, if greatly buoyed up by the GI Bill, which had generous provisions for educational opportunities, veterans were often informed by the paper that those fortunate to get home were swamping the nation's colleges and universities creating an educational jam of historic proportions. The effect in the short run, therefore, was to increase the anxieties of some of those overseas, who recognized that they must get home promptly if they were to capitalize on enrollment possibilities lest they be curtailed.[10]

Meanwhile, at home a focus on frivolous matters was also reported in the Shanghai paper, no doubt as antidotes for the grim war news prevalent for so long. These also cast some light on contemporary domestic social and cultural scenes. One example was an ongoing story concerning the case of the "Vargas Girls," the brainchildren of the artist and cartoonist, Alberto Vargas. His iconic pinups appeared in *Esquire* magazine — often on the cover — and were widely circulated in the war years, often adorning barracks walls and lockers. This matter attracted considerable attention, at least among GIs in Shanghai. Indeed, as the story unfolded it became regarded as important enough eventually to appear before the U.S. Supreme Court. Subsequently, one Charlotte Hess, a well-known physical culture expert, and a consultant to the well-known beauty firm of Helena Rubenstein, declared that the Vargas Girl had a serious case of lordosis — i.e., she was sway-backed. Also, her legs were three times the length of her body, and her thigh was one-and-one-half times the size of her waistline. It should be at least five to six inches smaller. This meant that she would have to use a mighty powerful girdle, of which few seemed available. Indeed, despite their being hailed as prime examples of pulchritude and glamour, no man would give a Vargas Girl a second look, she asserted. Vargas agreed, but defended her hips, noting that Venus De Milo set the precedent for "hippiness."[11]

Things may well have rested at this point, but in December 1945, Postmaster Frank Walker denied *Esquire* a second-class mail permit on the grounds that its covers graced by Vargas Girls were not "information of a public character." But the magazine obtained a federal appeals court decision granting the permit. In its own subsequent appeal to the Supreme Court, a Post Office attorney, Myron Taylor, argued that the legs of the curvaceous cartoon beauty are too long and that other bodily dimensions were out of proportion to the norms, and hence the covers were not "art" as *Esquire* had alleged. The Supreme Court took the matter under advisement and promised a speedy decision.[12]

Meanwhile, in Shanghai, in order to help pass the time before the Court acted, the Shanghai Special Services announced a Vargas Girl contest open to girls of the Shanghai area whose names were submitted by GIs. The results were not recorded, however.[13]

Moving expeditiously as promised, the Supreme Court ruled on February 5, 1946, that the Postmaster General had no right to bar *Esquire* magazine from second-class mailing privileges simply because he objected to the Vargas Girl and the magazine's sexy jokes. It labeled Walker's actions a case of arbitrary censorship by a government official who happened to be appointed to high office. The decision was widely regarded as new protection for U.S. freedom of the press, an issue having little to do with the Vargas Girl per se.[14]

Even racier was another matter discussed in the Shanghai *Stripes*. One issue included a photo of the actress Lili St. Cyr posing, with little covering her bosom, in the fashionable New York City restaurant, Leon and Eddie's. She was advertising a creation of a certain Renie, a Hollywood clothes designer who predicted that it would soon be the fashion. Though the photo was a bit risqué for its time, it perhaps did not merit the caption's claims alleging that the event was almost as important as the arrival of the atomic bomb.[15]

In the event, the sensation failed to live up to its billing. In the first place, few Hollywood actresses seemed disposed to become involved. Carole Landis, for one, thought that girls made a big mistake by revealing everything; it was better to leave something to the imagination. Neither did Paulette Goddard volunteer, explaining that she was just recovering from one cold and did not desire to run the risk of catching another.[16]

The servicemen in Shanghai, revealing an unexpected prim side, were also strongly opposed. The "B-Bag" soon recorded their displeasure. Two unnamed GIs thought the photograph was obscene and showed a lack of pride by American women. They themselves would be embarrassed to walk down Fifth Avenue with anyone so attired. A group of Marines from the 2nd Battalion, the 81st Mortars of the 5th Marine Division, thought that such Hollywood women were plainly uncivilized, and no one could respect them. They did not belong in decent society and the clothes designers involved were obviously sex-crazed.[17] The subject soon faded from public view and the press had to look elsewhere for sensations to report.

While many worried about the returning veterans and their various concerns, the *Stripes* was delighted to report that Christmas of 1945, for those who were fortunate enough to be stateside to celebrate, would find shops and shoppers alike in an agreeable state of frenzy, and bedlam was the order of the day. Long before Thanksgiving, the rush to shop early was apparent. Buyers were eager to splurge with their wartime earnings and the shops exerted every effort to satisfy their desires. Certainly, home, despite all of its difficulties, remained the goal focused on with unremitting vigilance.[18]

III

The Chinese Conundrum

> "These from the Land of Sinim."
> —Isaiah 49:12

The Chinese scene was enigmatic for most U.S. military personnel. Some of the confusion concerned the Chinese civil war, which was an unsettling event with various ramifications. It would also be deadly for some Americans, especially Marines, who sustained casualties in several armed clashes with Chinese Communist forces. The usual misunderstandings incurred by the meeting of contrasting cultures were also present, in this case, the classic encounters of East versus West famously evoked by the British poet Rudyard Kipling.

One matter involved language. Something of this was explained by a *Stripes* staffer, Austin C. Wehrwein, in an article in the paper's *Magazine Supplement*. One common Chinese term was "*Ding How!*" (*ting hao*). This iconic expression, meaning "excellent," was invariably accompanied by a thumbs up signal. It was the usual greeting, and it seemed especially appealing to children. When coupled with smiles or giggles, and other evidences of enthusiasm, it was calculated to evoke a favorable response from Americans, typically accompanied by pieces of candy or chewing gum, the universal currency on such occasions. Of course, "*Boo How*" denoted its opposite. The GI would use "ding a ding" (*teng yi teng*) for "stop" or "wait a while." He would say, "*may yo*" (*mei yu*) for "I don't have," or simply "no." The Marines especially adopted the term "*huba how*" (*hao pu hao*), which rapidly degenerated into "hubba hubba," a standard greeting or all-purpose term, though it meant more properly the question: "Is this good or bad?" Another Chinese expression which enjoyed a wide currency was "*cumsha, cumsha,*" a slang term used by beggars with the meaning of simply "gimme." It was usual to call lunch "*tiffin,*" a term which migrated from India, and newcomers "*griffins,*" or greenhorns. Because many of the servicemen in China had arrived from Burma or India, vestiges of slang from those parts of the CBI were still in vogue. These might include the word "*mallum?*" when they asked whether one understood. They also often had recourse to calling each other by the common Indian term for "sir," "*sahib*" (pronounced "sob"). English sufficed in many situations, such as expressions used in bargaining, one of the main diversions for soldiers in China. Therefore, one would commonly hear, "You say how much," and "last price," the first things a new China hand learned.[1]

The almost universal drinking scene employed the term "*jingbao* juice," or "jungle juice," to describe just about any brew. The term was said to have originated in Burma, where the natives brewed something by that name, but the word covered a multitude of possibilities. In Chungking, they drank "Chungking gin," or, as it was also called, "100 gin," which was a rather good Chinese product. But in Shanghai and all of North China, the standard drink was Russian vodka. In any case, no matter what the beverage, the universal "*gom bey*" ("*gan bei*") or "bottoms up," was employed while downing the libation.

As to the omnipresent females, street girls called "*gu ni*" ("*ku niang*"), or sometimes, especially in Chungking, "jeep girls," introduced a practical concept of love-making, that of the "long" or "short time" deal, usually phrased as a question as to how much for long or short time? Wehrwein explained its use as he had witnessed it employed by certain "sporting members" of Kweilin's female population. It took the form of a song, an ingenious sales talk, and went: "Hey, big horn, you luvva me, I luvva you. You say how much one time. Gotta jeep? Let's go!" Wehrwein opined that while Shakespeare might not have used those words, no one could deny that they were functional. Indeed, one scholar has written that "not the least of those benefitting from the presence of the free-spending Yanks were Shanghai's prostitutes, who were happy to be back in business big-time. Russian prostitutes were popular, but so were the Chinese, Eurasian and Korean girls, some of whom had even bleached their hair to 'wow their new overseas clientele with an image of the li'l girl next door.'"[2]

There were other terms in everyday use by GIs in China which, however, were not restricted to that Theater. These were common to U.S. servicemen worldwide, and included such terms as "sad sack," "snafu," and "sweating it out." It was also common to refer to each other, usually with a hint of derision, simply as "sergeant," even high ranking officers, though apparently rarely to their faces. The old retort to gripers, "You never had it so good," had a particular significance in Shanghai, where there was a widespread belief among enlisted men that a certain percentage of the officers there preferred what used to be called the "Paris of the Orient" to their hometowns. There was also some specialization as to branch of service in that soldiers generally referred to the U.S.A. as simply "Stateside," while the Navy preferred to call it "Uncle Sugar Able," derived from the familiar radio code for the letters of the alphabet. What was common in the CBI — itself sometimes referred to as "Confusion Beyond Imagination"— was to refer to the Himalayan "Hump" as the "Rockpile."

The Shanghai *Stripes* developed as a medium for informing its readers of details of Chinese civilization and ways of life, seeking to make the inscrutable scrutable. One topic discussed was that of the innumerable beggars who were common sights around and about the city. Indeed, as the paper explained, begging was a highly developed art form as well as a cold, calculated business which operated under numerous beggars' guilds. Each guild was usually ruled by a "Beggar King," someone on the order of the Charles Dickens character Fagin, as depicted in his novel, *Oliver Twist*. These men were often among the wealthiest in China. The guilds also held blocks of stock on the Shanghai Stock Exchange. They often provided transportation to get beggars to their begging sites, and money for funerals. Unfortunately, not all beggars were so well provided for and their suffering was real enough. There were numerous examples of people cutting off limbs to qualify for the beggar profession, and children were maimed or deliberately undernourished to make them appear more pathetic.[3]

Other sights, however, might have met the GIs' gaze, but remained elusive. The *Stripes* editor regretted that the fabled beautiful women and other delights of old Cathay were being withheld from American servicemen. He longed for the China of old travel brochures, or the Orient of the Burton Holmes' travelogues. He suggested that China make these treasures available to American troops and that her better families put out their welcome mats. In addition, her schools, museums, societies and other institutions might invite them in. In this way, soldiers and sailors with evenings free might have a chance to know the culture, hospitality and people of mysterious China. This could create a core of Chinese-American understanding and goodwill which would greatly enhance the chances of peace in Asia. This would be far better than their consorting with pimps, bawds and other disreputable characters. One wonders, however, how many American GIs would avail themselves of such opportunities, no doubt preferring precisely those unsavory sorts that the editor deplored. Furthermore, such ventures would hardly appeal to many Chinese, who scrupulously avoided contact with all foreigners. Certain Chinese, in any case, knew better how to appeal to the GI rank and file, shrewdly naming one brothel in Chungking "The Committee for the Advancement of Chinese-American Friendship."[4]

Marine Private First Class Nicholas D. Jackson, for one, however, was sensitive to what the Chinese routinely suffered. In his poem "Rickshaw Boy," he urged American GIs to seek to understand these boys, who pulled their vehicles through the city's dusty streets and along endless roads, all the while enduring aching feet, unceasing work, cold winds and other inclement weather while clad only in scanty clothing. What they really needed were simple words of kindness instead of the frequent curses that they received. Rather, Jackson hoped that the boys' passengers would treat them as suffering fellow human beings, an attitude which they would no doubt gratefully applaud.[5]

To help many of its readers better understand what service in China had meant, an editorial discussed the "Society of O.C.H. (Old China Hands)." This was not a formal organization, the editor admitted, but an invisible tie binding all men who had lived in China. Henceforth, wherever they went, for the remainder of their lives, they would be considered experts on the Orient. Consequently, their opinions and judgments on Chinese matters, such as food and artifacts, would be regarded as final.[6]

The veterans' expertise would undoubtedly especially be tapped when the subject of Chinese food arose. The editor wrote that it might be prudent to pen an ultimatum to "Chop Suey joints" in America. A "Chinowledge" feature explained to the men that the only "'chop suey" the Chinese were familiar with was a cheap hash eaten mainly by Cantonese beggars. Indeed, one American pilot, Flight Officer Kensley Robert Thompson, noted that when he attempted to order it in a Shanghai restaurant he was told: "So Solly, no Chinee dish, we do not have." What the Chinese did have was succulent roast Peiping duck and equally tasty shark's-fin soup made from cartilage of the fins of sharks. Similarly delicious was bird's-nest soup with pigeon eggs. The soup was made from a gelatinous substance found in and around swallows' nests sited on rocky cliffs along China's southern coast. In his estimation, he wrote, "I have never had such fine Chinese cuisine in America as I found in Shanghai."[7]

IV

Growing GI Unrest: Ferment, Furor, and Occasional Favors

"It is a tale told by an idiot, full of sound and fury...."
— William Shakespeare, *Macbeth* (1606)

Another story that simmered in the pages of the paper concerned the abuses of the brass and the military's rigid caste system. These issues loomed larger following the end of hostilities when the rank and file had time to brood about them and when they were being agitated by other pressures similarly magnified. Throughout the history of the American armed forces officers' privileges and the ever-present "chicken shit" were perennially discussed. No trivial matters, they weighed on that vital ingredient of any successful military enterprise: good morale.

To learn what the rank and file thought about various Army phenomena, it was revealed in Washington on April 2, 1946, that a series of studies had been made between December 1943 and September 1945, based on questionnaires submitted to troops in the various theaters. When enlisted men were asked, among other things, to assess their officers, the Army "got an earful." Their answers bore out views set forth in GI letters to editors and in numerous speeches and cartoons. Specifically, in the questionnaires' rankings, their preoccupation with officers' "differential privileges" was second only to their desires to get home. While the men in general did not object to the custom of granting prerogatives in line with extra responsibility, their resentment was aimed at what they considered excessive privileges or their abuses as traditionally accepted. This meant too strict or unnecessary military control and discipline and officers' general lack of concern for enlisted men's welfare. Specifics pointed to officers' taking unfair advantage of their rank and such practices as their using military vehicles for their own personal recreation, which, for some reason, especially rankled. As to what made for any unit's high morale, the most important was thought to be teamwork and pride in the outfit, closely followed by good officer-enlisted men relations.[1]

While there seemed to be little connection between the demobilization questions and those pertaining to the military caste system, they were, in fact, intertwined. This was explained by one of the *Stripes'* writers, Austin C. Wehrwein, in an article in the paper's *Magazine Supplement*. He noted that there was "a tremendous undercurrent of burning resentment against the military system as such." This had been held in check during the war because most of the men, many of whom were draftees who saw themselves as "citizen soldiers" and not professionals, had realized that protests would only aid the enemy. Furthermore, they also had concluded that they could leave it all behind them once peace had come. But "suddenly they discovered that they faced an indefinite period of service," and their deeply held democratic traditions "ran head on into the military system," one based on concepts of absolute authority. Because they seemed compelled to stay in the service, great numbers of them demanded reforms.[2]

These concerns were certainly present in the China Theater and the Shanghai *Stripes* devoted much space to them, and its "B-Bag" in particular was filled with the views of its readership. Indeed, a major reason why many within the military establishment were opposed to a free soldier press lay at this point. Typical complaints were contained in a letter in the November 14, 1945, issue signed by "T-5 Edward Brown (Nose)." In a letter titled "Corporal! Corporal!," Brown blasted the practice of enlisted men being made to "dog rob" for their officers, which, he contended, had reached epic proportions. Everywhere, enlisted men were sent on countless errands such as retrieving a pipe left behind in quarters, or running down to the PX to pick up a beer ration, or wrapping and mailing packages for their officers' wives. He hoped that the government would supply a Number One Boy for all officers who left the service. Their safest course, however, would be to remain in uniform, though they might be shocked to learn that Army regulations stipulated that such services in the peacetime Army had to be compensated.

Touching a much larger body of men was the Army's reverting to a spit-and-polish routine, as was customary in the "Old Army," when hostilities ceased. Sergeant Peter Swinton, for one, complained about the excessive drilling, lectures and similar duties. The men had had enough during their basic training and throughout their wartime Army careers, he declared, and it was now too far along in the game to start anew. The war was over and he, along with many others, regarded himself as strictly a civilian soldier. Drills were for career men and the "civilians" wanted no part of them. They wanted either to go home or be left alone. Private Neil Mellon concurred. If General Marshall and other brass hats liked the Army, that was their "little brown jug," he argued, which plainly did not include him.[3]

These matters became more pointed in Shanghai when it was announced in the October 22, 1945, *Stripes* that a "military courtesy drive" was being launched in Shanghai on that day. In other words, Shanghai was henceforth to be regarded "as a saluting area," the paper ruefully announced. In addition, proper uniforms, including ties, were to be worn on all occasions. Out-of-bounds regulations were to be strictly enforced. Curfew violators were to be picked up; there was to be no drinking of liquor or the carrying of opened bottles on the streets; and the fifteen-mile-per-hour speed limit in force in metropolitan Shanghai was to be strictly adhered to. Severe disciplinary action was to be imposed on those engaged in black market activities. GIs and officers were to be detained and reported to their commanding officers if in violation of these orders.[4]

Predictably, it was not long before the "B-Bag" registered complaints from readers. A tech sergeant griped about certain majors, called "Disciplinary Control Officers," who checked to see that uniform pockets were buttoned and salutes were properly rendered. It was, the sergeant went on, a hateful thing to squeeze the last ounce of tribute from the dwindling civilian army. He wondered when, if ever, the Army would recognize that they were dealing with adults and not children who could not be counted on to button their pockets. In rebuttal, Major General D.L. Weart, the Shanghai Base Commander, reported that there had been many violations of military discipline in Shanghai in the past few days by both officers and enlisted men.[5]

Central to much of the agitation surrounding the military courtesy drive was the matter of saluting, hardly a new concern. Lieutenant General George E. Stratemeyer of the U.S. Army Air Forces, acting commander of the China Theater while Wedemeyer was in Honolulu in conference with Admiral Nimitz, felt constrained, in a "B-Bag" letter, to elaborate. Saluting, he began, was a military custom that was hundreds of years old. It was, specifically, a signal of greeting and of mutual respect shared by those brought together by the customs, the privileges and the obligations of military service. Therefore, the act of saluting, when done properly, enhanced morale and a sense of dignity. In addition, saluting was a privilege, setting one apart from other people in the world who did not possess it. Accordingly, it should be jealously guarded as signifying pride, dignity and self-respect, as well as mutual respect between individuals of all ranks in the military.[6]

As might be expected, answers to Stratemeyer's letter were not long in coming. One "B-Bag" response was by T-4 Albert Lee, who agreed that the custom of saluting was indeed a hoary one which had originated long ago, perhaps as far back as when one caveman decided that he was better than other cavemen. Furthermore, if it was based on mutual respect, why was it that EM (Enlisted Men) were supposed to salute first and why were not EM required to salute each other, he asked. Also, clearly salutes were not only the prerogative of military personnel, but Boy Scouts and Girl Scouts also rendered them. Perhaps, Lee suggested, these absurdities might be made clear if EM began saluting everybody in uniform, including taxi drivers, doormen and even cops. The General had also stated that saluting sets the GI apart from the other people in the world. Lee could think of no more compelling reason for abolishing this pernicious habit because the last thing that U.S. military personnel should be encouraged to do was to see themselves as superior to everybody else. The consequences of this sort of thinking were clearly manifested in Nazi Germany, he concluded.[7]

Things were not much better in Chungking, where a routine Saturday morning inspection was in force. While admitting that it was according to regulations, one observer noted that it could be called by another name, and that there were many of the men who remembered Chungking under Uncle Joe Stilwell, when the only "chicken" came at Sunday dinner. They could also recall that under the command of General Wedemeyer the idea was primarily to get one's work done, and if a man kept his nose clean, he could enjoy what fun was available. There was at least one innovation instituted in Chungking to aid morale. A lottery permitted enlisted men to put their names in a hat from which seven would be drawn by Red Cross girls on each Monday. The winners received a three-day furlough in Shanghai the following weekend.[8]

Significantly, when Wedemeyer returned to Shanghai following his conference with Nimitz in Hawaii, he ordered, as of November 16, an end to saluting in the crowded streets of Shanghai, where it was a hardship. Henceforth only men on official business were required to salute.[9]

Undoubtedly, the Shanghai *Stripes* generally enjoyed a cordial relationship with Wedemeyer, though some GI readers sometimes looked askance at this, and occasionally charged that the paper was far too inclined to "brown nose" the General. Wedemeyer — no stern Patton or MacArthur — also attempted, despite his starchy military bearing and appearance and his obvious commanding presence, to be personable, and possessed a genuine desire to be fair in his relations with all the personnel under his command.[10]

If Wedemeyer's actions muted some of the complaints, other annoyances were plentiful enough for the arguments to continue. A "Corporal G.K." writing in "B-Bag" noted that certain officers went to extremes to get points they did not deserve. They often recommended each other for battle stars, and even awarded the Combat Infantry Badge, theoretically authorized only for actual combat operations, to officers who undoubtedly did not know how to load an M1 rifle.[11]

Some officers were concerned with privileges of even higher ranks. A letter in "B-Bag" in the November 12 issue argued that American democracy was probably best exemplified by everyone's taking his place in line and waiting his turn. He recounted that at the Capitol Theater he and a fellow officer sat down in a row occupied by two colonels and their two women companions. An MP informed him that the section was reserved for field grade officers and they would have to move to the junior officers' section. There were seats there, but the two went to the GI section to demonstrate their opinion of class discrimination as practiced in a place of amusement. In his view, when it comes to amusement, chow and the latrine, the motto should be "first come, first served." Rank had its privileges, he admitted, but not when they interfered with basic democratic principles. To be sure, he himself drew the line at calling his men by their first names, and kept proper distance in this regard. He was a rather strict military man with an artillery battery, and was sometimes known as an SOB. As an indication that complaints sometimes produced results, though it is not clear that this was in response to this particular letter, almost immediately Special Services placed seating at the Capitol Theater on a "first come, first served" basis, eliminating reserved seating for officers. This released more seats for enlisted personnel, who normally formed the bulk of the audience.[12]

The problem of some areas being off-limits for enlisted men but not for officers — one of Bill Mauldin's favorite cartoon topics — was present in the China Theater as well. A certain "disgusted 'civilian soldier'" undertook to sing once more the already well-worn tune about officers' privileges, though it irked him to think that after being repeated so often, the song was as relevant as ever. He complained that when he and other "lowly EM" planned a dinner party at the Cathay Hotel, they were told by an MP that the Cathay was for officers only and no enlisted men were allowed. A visit to his dictionary reassured him what "democracy" meant, and on every occasion, when he asked why officers had so many privileges, and enlisted men so few, he was informed that such was necessary to maintain discipline so that under combat conditions commands would be obeyed instantly. Nevertheless, this all seemed at variance with the true definition of democracy with its emphasis on equal rights.[13]

Of course, there was the officers' side of the argument, as one POed Lieutenant observed, pointing out that there were vast differences between the number of officers' points needed to get home, and the far fewer required of enlisted personnel.[14]

There was also a concern that the headquarters of the China Theater was over-endowed with brass, which was borne out by the fact that there were six generals there — and six privates. In addition, there were sixty-nine bird colonels, ten more than the tech sergeants who were there. These added to the brass carried by the sixty-three lieutenant colonels, the seventy-five majors and the 110 captains. The enlisted men were far fewer in number. One enlisted critic observed that the main reason some of these officers wanted to stay in China was they made good money and were fearful of prospective bread lines at home.[15]

Significantly, the propensities of certain officers to entrench themselves and in other ways perpetuate a rigid status quo following hostilities had been anticipated by General George C. Marshall, the Army Chief of Staff, in a Memorandum for Chiefs of All War Department and Special Staff Divisions. Concerned with "War Department Policies for the Period Following V-J Day," it instructed all involved to "combat natural tendencies to continue activities, demand services and retain personnel, supplies, equipment or facilities which are not clearly necessary to the announced mission of the Army and the War Department. This must be kept in mind in making all decisions." His exhortations, unfortunately, were not always heeded.[16]

Much of the problem with the brass was soon significantly addressed by Congress and the War Department. The first to act was the House Military Committee, which called various people before it to testify regarding the military establishment. One of these was retired Brigadier General H.C. Holdridge, a West Point classmate of General Mark Clark, both of the class of 1917, who called the army an undemocratic and un–American institution that was a carryover from the medieval era. Its prominent characteristic was a medieval caste system based on insurmountable obstacles between the officer aristocracy and the enlisted man. He characterized the Army leadership as class-conscious, ultraconservative and absolutist, which created a breeding ground for totalitarianism. His views were echoed in an article appearing in the Hawaiian *Stars and Stripes* charging the U.S. Army and Navy with fostering an oligarchical caste system inherited from Frederick the Great of Prussia and the 18th century British Navy. Treating enlisted men as "second class citizens" resulted in their returning home thoroughly hating and detesting military life.[17]

Farther reaching was a development which occurred on March 20, 1946, when War Secretary Robert P. Patterson named a six-man board, called the Officer-Enlisted Relationships Board — popularly called the "Gripe Board" — headed by Lieutenant General James Doolittle to investigate the Army's caste system. The board consisted of three other officers and two demobilized enlisted men who had fought in Europe. Deliberations began on March 29, and a parade of witnesses appeared before the board. These included Sergeant Marion Hargrove, author of the best-selling humorous book on Army life, *See Here, Private Hargrove*, and the GI cartoonist, Bill Mauldin.[18]

The Board's findings concluded that the roots of the "disease" resided in poor leadership, and the excessive official and social gap existing between officers and men. Partly to blame was a small body of inherently unqualified or inadequately trained officers who inevitably emerged in the swollen wartime military. It recommended a major overhaul of the officer corps. Envisioned was promotion by merit instead of seniority and the prompt dismissal or demotion of incompetents. A series of reforms to serve as safeguards for enlisted men against arbitrary acts of superiors were outlined. The military justice machinery should be modified to include enlisted men as members of courts-martial; sentences were to be progressively stiffened for higher ranks; and the inspector general's office was to be increased with the addition of more investigators. Bridges should be built across the officer/enlisted gap. Quarters and travel allowances, cumulative furlough time and terminal-leave pay were to be instituted for enlisted men as well as officers. In addition, some needless social discriminations should be expunged and off-duty saluting curtailed. Finally, the Board agreed that there was a need for a new philosophy in the military order: that of a full recognition of the dignity of man. One soldier writing in the Shanghai *Stripes* had earlier put the matter succinctly, stating that the enlisted man was not asking for the right to put his arm around an officer's neck or call him "buddy," but simply wanted to be treated as any other free American citizen who was doing a job for his country.[19]

Navy Secretary James Forrestal, however, pointedly asserted that the Navy would maintain its status quo. A few "stinkers" among officers did not justify junking a system in which most officers were fine, devoted, patriotic men, he declared. Forrestal also noted, on another conservative note, that though new Navy uniforms were contemplated, bell-bottoms would still be the official uniform because the new ones were not accepted by enlisted sailors, and what's more important, their girls did not like the new suits. The Navy would accordingly maintain its course as before.[20] As to the Army, though some changes were introduced to ease matters, for many decades its system would also grind on as before, and some of the abuses would continue or resurface in the future. This was anticipated by Robert C. Ruark, writing in the *Washington Daily News* on March 20, 1946, who saw fit to title his article "Army Tosses a Bone: Caste System Probe Just a Political Sop to Regain GI Affection." It would be difficult to argue Ruark's point, and the armed forces still continue to seek solutions for some of these problems.

Many other vexations plagued the men in China. One concerned clothing. At a time when the black market flourished, with military clothing being among the items hotly trafficked in, the rank and file often found it difficult to get replacements for worn uniforms. There were widespread suspicions of quartermaster personnel: Were they perhaps involved in black market operations? One aggrieved soldier, Jack Moynihan, addressed the matter in an "Ode to My Supply Sergeant," in which he deplored his frayed collar and cuffs and the fact that his buttons were missing, none of which seemed to qualify for a new issue of clothing. But the supply sergeant could be damned because Moynihan would soon be home and decked out in broadcloth and maybe even silk, all with no thanks to Army supply personnel.[21]

Another subject arousing some ire shared some of the paper's space during the Thanksgiving season. This addressed the fact that there would be no live turkeys for the men in China. In the November 22 issue, a photo of the bird was declared to be the only one that might be seen on Thanksgiving Day. A poem attached explained that, while the cooks could wield spoons and juggle pots and pans, they could not do much with sliced turkey that came from cans. One had to *see* the turkey in full form to appreciate it and anything less than the real McCoy would not suffice.

Undoubtedly, the roller coaster state of affairs, conflicting policies, and general frustration, uncertainties and vexation added to the stresses of service in the Chinese Theater. Also, in November, at the beginning of the winter season, the intensification of the Chinese civil war prevented coal transport ships from landing coal in Shanghai from the Chinwangtao area. The results were cold billets and no hot showers, causing much discomfort and consequent grousing.[22]

And things could be lethal. One problem concerned the consumption of poisonous beverages which led to several deaths. This prompted official warnings that serious dangers existed in buying both soft and hard drinks, particularly from street vendors. Consequently Army and Navy doctors announced a program to inspect all food and beverage establishments, and coincidentally would attempt to suppress prostitution. Almost immediately, further action led to the prohibition of buying from street merchants. This was a wise move because the Marines who had recently arrived in Tientsin also reported deaths from poisoned booze. The steps regarding drink were undoubtedly easier to accept when it was announced that all PX (Post Exchange) goods were no longer rationed except beer and cigarettes, but limits on these were extended so that each man could subsequently purchase up to three cases of beer per man per month and four cartons of cigarettes over the same period.[23]

To be sure, improvements were noted by some of the paper's readers from time to time. One soldier, while still agitated by uncertain mail delivery, which irked many GIs, noted that some conditions had gotten better. Apart from the obvious fact that men were steadily being sent home — if at far too slow a pace — other things made for greater peace of mind: The war was over and the ubiquitous Chinese women off Bubbling Well Road were not too bad, and on the base they now even had white tablecloths in the mess halls. The mail problem was also soon alleviated, in part by the men themselves, who were instructed to keep the Army Post Office (APO) informed of their addresses, because many transfers had been made in recent weeks. The mail situation was further eased in late November, when regular airmail service was instituted to the States by way of Tokyo and San Francisco.[24]

Military commanders in China were aware of the difficulties faced by all servicemen there. The *Stripes* therefore functioned as a bulletin board, delineating and describing plans, programs and innovations to distract them and ease the stress of the long waiting periods. Some of these ventures were routine as part of the Information and Education (I and E) programs regularly provided by the armed forces. Others were calculated to take advantage of China's specific attractions. In early October, the Army took over the Capitol Theater at 142 Museum Road and operated it as a free GI movie. A new GI nightclub, selling beer and meals and featuring an Army band and civilian entertainment, was created. It was located at the Race Club on the Race Course on Bubbling Well Road, in an upscale neighborhood opposite the famous Park Hotel and the Foreign YMCA, both well-known landmarks in prewar Shanghai.[25] Also in early October, the Armed Forces Radio System set up a station in Shanghai, with the call letters HMHA. In October, *Melody Parade*, the first USO show to appear, opened in Shanghai. On October 25, the Shanghai Base Command created the Shanghai Unit School, with courses in accounting, mathematics, spoken Chinese, sketching, and American political and social history being the first offered. Major General D.L. Weart, the Shanghai Base Commander, authorized section chiefs to release men from duty if they desired to attend. All classes that had been previously offered at Chungking were also to be resumed there. In addition, the American Red Cross opened the Embassy Club for enlisted men.[26]

Belatedly, a large enlisted men's club—called Enlisted Men's Club No. 1— was set up in Shanghai, at the British country club. It did not open, however, until December 16, 1945. The bar was the club's centerpiece and special efforts were made to supply it with liquor from the States. Dancing was featured twice a week. The club's presence deflected some of the complaints about proper entertainment sites for the EM.[27]

Also, for those still serving in Chungking, the local YMCA maintained a substantial program which featured recreation facilities, rooms, tours and lectures. In addition, there was an open invitation for soldiers to drop in most evenings for Chinese food. Thus, the men could get to know something more about China beyond the usual vitriolic mouthwash of Chunking gin.[28]

About the same time, a series of lectures was scheduled by the Information and Education staff in Shanghai on Tuesdays and Thursdays concerning China's politics, cultural history and industrial opportunities. One presentation, for instance, featured Dr. Kwei Chung-shu, a graduate of the University of Wisconsin and the editor of the *Shanghai Herald and China Critic*, who spoke on China's geopolitical position. Another was an illustrated lecture on Chinese art given by Mrs. T.G. Lin, the American wife of a prominent Chinese official, owner and manager of the Green Dragon Art Store and a recognized art expert.[29]

For those with highbrow inclinations, an article in the *Magazine Supplement* Issue Number 11, January 12, 1946, described the revived Shanghai Symphony Orchestra which, since liberation, was under the baton of Lieutenant Jonathan Sternberg of the China Theater Special Services Section. A music student at NYU and Harvard, he had been an assistant to Fritz Mahler with the National Youth Administration (NYA) orchestra in New York City. As a soldier, he was an assistant conductor of Irving Berlin's production of *This Is the Army*. He was one of the founders of the Stateside radio program *So You Think You Know Music*.

In early November, Shanghai's I and E Office also launched a series of educational and recreational excursions to Peiping, Nanking and Hangchow. Peiping was especially desirable as a tour destination because it was comparatively unspoiled by the Japanese and was consequently full of beauty as well as bargains.[30]

IV. Growing GI Unrest

Some of these were flight tours. The paper's editor strongly supported these ventures, observing that soon the men in China would be back home and tied down to their daily lives. Few would be able to travel, and certainly travel to China would only be a remote possibility. Therefore, now was the time for Americans to seek to know and understand the country. These ventures could consequently foster Chinese and American cooperation in seeking peace in Asia and around the world. Also, commanding officers should be generous with furloughs and leaves, he advised; there was still time before the boat ride home.[31]

These excursions were inaugurated on November 2, 1945, when the first Curtiss C-46 *Commando* troop transport carried twenty-six GIs from Shanghai to Peiping. Most active in this work was the 513th Troop Carrier Group. Subsequent flights were scheduled to Nanking and Hangchow; other tours went by rail to Soochow. Later Canton and Hong Kong were added to the agenda. Billets were supplied by the War Area Service Corps using some of the best hotels available.

The flights, however, had a downside for many crews. They often objected to flying the missions required by the Theater Education and Recreational Tours—known as TERT. The Troop Carrier Command strongly resented their outfit's being perceived simply as the "TERT Airlines." The flying that this entailed was also dangerous. One airman argued that each flight involved considerable work for the crews, in addition to which each had to be "sweated out." This was because, though the war was over, flight operations remained dicey and many of the aircraft had seen better days. Consequently, the safest place for an aircraft was on the ground. Some of the crews had no doubt read an article that had appeared in the paper reporting a high flight accident rate during the war. Some 26,000 lives had been lost and 22,000 aircraft of the U.S. Army Air Forces destroyed in noncombat accidents. Some of the troops who took the tours, were, by contrast, enthusiastic, finding the program highly desirable, pleasant and beneficial. Others chided crews for not wishing to fly fellow soldiers, many of whom had just emerged from hard duty in the backwoods of the interior, and were more than willing to risk flying to visit the historical and cultural sites of China. The Troop Carrier Command eventually won out, and after some successes, flying was suspended on February 11, because of a shortage of flight crews, bad weather and aircraft maintenance difficulties. The rail tours to Soochow and Hangchow, however, continued. Eventually, out of the 60,000 or so American troops in China during these months, some 3,466 took I and E excursions, which were terminated on April 20, 1946.[32]

While not touching the lives of the men in China directly, developments in Germany were frequently discussed in the paper's columns, providing readers with bases for comparisons. One matter highlighted was that the Army's commanders in Europe strongly emphasized official programs to keep GIs from fraternizing with the Germans, especially with the frauleins. For instance, in Bavaria, Lieutenant General Lucian K. Truscott, the commander of the U.S.

Third Army, mounted a major campaign—called in the *Stripes* the "Hate the Hun" program—to convince American troops that the Germans were still enemies and their failure to recognize this was endangering the peace. By means of films, lectures, photographic exhibitions and statistics, material was presented to emphasize these points. Calculated to dramatize the seriousness of fraternization, they were simply laughed at, and the men were thoroughly bored by the proceedings and turned deaf ears to them. Clearly, the average GI neither knew nor cared about the dangers of fraternization and only wanted to go home, or failing that, at least to find some feminine companionship. Undoubtedly, some of the motives both at home and abroad for getting the men home stemmed from the fears that fraternization would further undermine the morals of American servicemen.[33]

The paper did, however, warmly applaud the coming of the Nuremberg Tribunal, praising the fact that the traditional police court now functioned on the international level. Perhaps, the editor concluded, with a touch of optimism, this would make the outlawing of war, which many nations had agreed to in the 1920s, attainable at last. Elsewhere, the editor admonished his readers not to forget one of the greatest blots on the history of humankind, i.e., the wanton rape of the human mind and soul perpetrated by the totalitarian regimes. It was a duty, therefore, to hold the war criminals in an iron grip for many generations to come until they were again fit for civilized society.[34]

V

Japanese Problems: Repatriation and War Crimes Trials

"Whom the gods would destroy, they first make mad."
—Euripides, *Medea*

"And Only the Willows Will Weep."
—Anonymous

Closer at hand, how to treat the Japanese—invariably referred to as the "Japs"—remained a matter of immediate concern. Many of them had to be repatriated, others tried as war criminals. These considerations created uncertainties as to what attitudes should be embraced. The paper's editor sarcastically reflected that now that the shooting had stopped, new emphases, including a focus on cleanliness, suggested new standards. Consequently, new allies would now undoubtedly be required. The French, he began, were not only sloppy and lazy but tolerated manure piles in their front yards. They were also out to cheat one blind. The British had lousy plumbing, and their keen competition in the world's markets made them suspect. On the other hand, the blond and pink-cheeked Germans—who had sweet-smelling barnyards—and were generous with their beer, their women, and their smiles, were now regarded as a noble people. The Chinese were not only filthy, they were also greedy, as were the "Flips" (Filipinos). As to the Russians, only God understood their wicked hearts. Regarding the Japs, they were at once clean, honest, industrious and kind. Accordingly, the heroes of yesterday were the villains of today, and former foes were fast becoming friends. Where Goebbels had failed, the fraulein was making up for lost time; where Tojo stumbled, a geisha was cooking on the front burner. The editor suggested that Americans should choose up sides anew, only henceforth forget the ideals of the Four Freedoms and the dignity of humankind, and fight instead for "trains that run on time, a geisha in every bed, free

Munchner Brau and good old Lifebuoy soap." As the paper might also have explained, the editor was clearly "Peter Oboed."[1]

To be sure, such American leaders as General Douglas MacArthur seemed intent upon establishing a new Asia based on more flexible policies than many Americans, including GIs in China, were willing to accept. These differing views were well aired in the Shanghai *Stars and Stripes*. The first issue of the paper began the ongoing discussions. A visit of the Mikado—the Emperor Hirohito—was recounted. On September 27, the Emperor had left his palace for what was labeled a social call held in the American Embassy over which, since September 8, the Stars and Stripes had flown. Hirohito was dressed in formal clothes and MacArthur met him in his tieless khaki uniform with no medals, the same that he had worn for the surrender ceremonies aboard the battleship USS *Missouri* on September 2. The thirty-eight-minute conversation marked the first time that the Emperor had visited any foreign official in his career.

This step by MacArthur produced criticism worldwide, since it was widely interpreted as an indication that he had no intention of rooting out the clique that ruled Japan before and during the war. In fact, the General was being far too "soft" on the fallen foe, it was declared. Yet, one must acknowledge that MacArthur's views were sound. Had the Emperor been deposed, he would undoubtedly have become a martyr and the Japanese may have well continued the war at frightful costs for both sides. Countering the objections, in mid-October the General delivered a major address in Tokyo pronouncing Japan's obituary as a world power. He noted that about 7,000,000 armed men, including those in outlying theaters, had laid down their weapons in an extraordinarily difficult and dangerous surrender, on a scale never before been recorded in the annals of history. This had been accomplished without the loss of a single drop of Allied blood. Indeed, he went on, the usual swagger and arrogance of the former Japanese military leaders had given way to servility and fear. Nippon's armed forces therefore no longer existed and Japan had ceased to be a world power, either large or small.[2]

Further developments in Japan contributed to the democratizing of the nation. Colonel Ken Dyke, Chief of Civil Information and Education at MacArthur's headquarters, convened a meeting of all Japanese publishers and radio chiefs. He informed them that censorship was off, that thought control was gone for good, that every Japanese newspaper and radio must tell the Japanese people the truth no matter the consequences. News need not necessarily be favorable to the United States nor any of the United Nations. Neither was unanimity of opinion desirable. Each editor or producer was free to print and broadcast exactly what he thought. The war had been fought for precisely such freedom, and even the Imperial institution was not exempt from free discussion and criticism. Despite this evidence of progress, the editor of *Stripes* was still not satisfied. The idea also began to gain some ground that men were needed to remain overseas to present a stern mask toward Japan and Germany, forcing them to abide by the Allied war aims and thereby not lose the peace. Desires to go home needed to be tempered by a realistic look at the needs of the postwar world, a view strongly at odds with those prevailing among most GIs still in Asia.[3]

Another matter of concern was how the Japanese contrived to "dazzle" their conquerors. First of all, there were all those beautiful waitresses at the officers' mess in the Imperial Hotel in Tokyo. They wore brilliant kimonos and obis, and had faces and figures like dolls. Also, there were the Japanese kids, who lifted their thumbs in the victory salute as vigorously as liberated children in other lands did. Then there were the geisha houses. Some of these were set up initially by Japanese civilian entrepreneurs in the Ginza District in Tokyo, with the cooperation of MacArthur's headquarters. The organization which managed the undertaking was known as the Recreation and Amusement Association — the RAA. Its intended purpose was to provide geisha girls and other entertainments for GIs in Japan, notably in Tokyo. The girls were regularly inspected by Army doctors, who, if needed, provided them with medications and specific surgical operations. A sign, in fractured English, posted prominently on Tokyo's main street, proudly announced the organization's presence:

> Do you know R.A.A. Oh, you don't know? I'm so sorry. R.A.A. stands for recreation and amusement association that was established to console you, you see. Please come to the facilities of R.A.A. which she wait. Come to our gardens in R.A.A.[4]

According to a news report in the *London News of the World*, by the paper's Tokyo correspondent Thomas Noyes, quoting Minoru Tsuji, the organization's head, the RAA employed about 1,500 dancing girls and 600 geishas in ten geisha houses, three hotels and four restaurants. It had been ordered by the Japanese government six days before the first American troops arrived in Japan. Its founders, according to Noyes, were the directors of six long-established and notorious Japanese guilds which together controlled all the geisha girls, shady hotels and disreputable dens in Japan. Its object was to divert the attention of the occupying forces of the Allied nations from the respectable women of Japan. Thus geishas were cast in the roles of heroines, the vanguards of contact with the victorious Allied troops, sacrificing themselves on the altar of national purity.[5]

In addition to these consolations, there were symphonic concerts for GIs by Japanese musicians. There was also a "hot band" for officers at the Dai Iti Hotel. Everywhere, in Shinto shrines and elsewhere, there were floral arrangements, and one could warmly praise the "cutest customs" ever laid on for the tourist trade. The editor feared that the Japanese were trying to pull the neatest trick of the peace by suddenly becoming overly polite, and hence were now "good Japs." He also surmised that they were succeeding because many GIs and officers alike were greatly impressed by the pleasant, educational and wonderful experiences on every hand. Indeed, it was strange, he complained, that after the Allies had battled Jap aggression from Bataan to Guadalcanal and back, Americans were falling flat on their rears before a barrage of Nip culture and charm. It was also remarkable that human memory was so short and human comfort so precious that the horrendous war record of Japan could be forgiven and forgotten so quickly. Those who had fought the Japs, however, would never forget Pearl Harbor, he insisted.[6]

Sergeant Lazar Schenitz concurred, and wanted to know why the Japanese were being catered to. The one spark which had flamed America's offensive in the Pacific was the desire to exact revenge for such deeds as the Death March of Bataan. But now it seemed that Americans were only joking, he ruefully concluded. He was also disturbed that the Emperor was still enthroned, noting that while Hirohito might be widely regarded as the Son of Heaven, he could also be considered as another kind of son.[7]

One wonders what Sergeant Schenitz might have thought about an action taken by the Navy Department in Shanghai. There, Captain T.J. O'Brien, Director of Welfare — apparently sincerely — lauded Tokyo Rose for meritorious service which contributed greatly to raising the morale of American armed services in the Pacific by bringing them excellent Stateside music, laughter and news about home. Many veterans of the Pacific War would certainly have agreed with him.[8]

On the local scene, *Stars and Stripes* reported that in Shanghai some 5,000 unguarded Japanese were confined to a small island facing Shanghai's waterfront. These were Japanese Marines and Navy personnel who had been stationed in Shanghai when the war ended. Their imprisonment was enforced only by their own officers under the command of Vice Admiral Minoro Katsumo. They were kept busy growing vegetables on the Chinese mainland and doing construction work. They were also "sweating out" shipment home, as so many Americans were.[9]

Also, the collapse of the Japanese East Asia Co-Prosperity Sphere had repercussions. One result was that Japanese merchants, who had followed the flag into conquered lands, found themselves stranded and having to return home. In Shanghai, as Franc Shor reported in a "Yank About China" column, a rough collection of structures which reminded him of a midway of a country fair back home were in place. There on makeshift counters were colorful displays of Japanese goods, including kimonos, brass work, lacquerware, silks and brocades that were obviously the pride of the owner in the gone-forever days when the Japs walked the streets of Shanghai and flaunted themselves as the rulers of the whole of East Asia. Other goods featured in the rummage sale were from now defunct stores that had once existed in great profusion along the city's streets. While it was colorful, Shor noted that there was a funeral air about the place. Talking with one Japanese displaced merchant, who had owned a large store in Shanghai, Shor noted that he, and all of the Japanese there, were subdued, polite but also a little fearful. Now having to return to Japan, the merchant was saddened by his new lot. It would not be good to go back because the situation in Japan had greatly deteriorated. It was too bad, he further explained, that neither Americans nor Chinese understood the Japanese people who had not wanted trouble, but only peace and happiness and had also desired to help the Chinese people. Perhaps, he admitted, that this time around the Japanese had made a mistake. But next time the Japanese would make sure that everyone understood their motives. Shor agreed that they had indeed erred, but they would not make the same mistake again because there would be no next time.[10]

It also seemed clear that many Japanese were losing faith in their social and cultural underpinnings. This included hara-kiri and the Bushido code. Illustrating the point, the *Stripes* published an article based on a piece datelined Tokyo, November 26, 1945, by a Domei war correspondent, of an account of a Kamikaze pilot who seemed unable to manage to die. (Domei was the official Japanese News Agency.) According to this, Corporal Tomoharu Sasaki, a member of the Banda (first Kamikaze) unit, was sent out to die in a flaming crash against American shipping in Leyte Gulf in November 1944. He returned, "laughing," to his Carolines base and said his bombs had hit an American ship, so why should he dive? His staff officer, who had already reported Sasaki dead, thought of committing suicide himself to square things, but was dissuaded. Subsequently promoted four ranks, Sasaki returned from his second mission again "laughing heartily," reporting that he had obviously been deserted by the god of death. Escort fighters which accompanied him on his third mission were all shot down but not Sasaki. He returned, reporting a successful bombing, and therefore again saw no need to crash dive. This was no laughing matter to his superiors, who breathed easier when he failed to return from a mission against a U.S. warship off Luzon. What then occurred is not clear, but he was seen again in northern Luzon in January 20, 1945, and the Domei correspondent thought that it was his ghost, "until he laughed." Sasaki then confided that he did not believe that he would have a pleasant time of it were he to return to Japan. A living Kamikaze pilot there was simply out of the question.[11]

There was, however, little to laugh about for many Japanese soldiers returning from the war clearly suffering from a deep sense of disillusionment. In striking contrast to the enthusiasm of earlier times, they were met with little joy by citizens who often held them responsible for Japan's defeat. There was also little understanding of what they had suffered, and apparently most Japanese were too worried about their own problems to be unduly concerned about the veterans. Another complicating factor was that funerals had already been held for many of some 40,000 soldiers considered lost who had now returned to Japan. They were greatly shocked by scenes of damage in Japan because news of B-29 raids had been withheld from them. All military pensions and other relief measures had been eliminated. Only minimal aid was available. Upon their arrival, they were given a railroad ticket home, three or four days' food and a small amount of cash. They were jobless, with little prospects of work, because businesses were either closed or demolished, and many returned to find their homes destroyed and their families gone, often without a trace. Furthermore, black markets were in full swing and prices were sky high. More personally, Japanese women were more interested in the American GIs, and few wished to go out with the returnees. The Japanese children also eagerly followed jeeps begging for candy and chewing gum.[12]

Nonetheless, Americans manning the fleet of Navy LSTs engaged in repatriation duty noted that Japanese arriving home lost their passivity as the ships brought them into home harbors—as returning GIs would in similar circumstances. Private First Class Louis L. Newby, USMC, who had just completed a round trip voyage on an LST from Tsingtao, China, to Sasebo, Japan, reported that tears came to the eyes of the returnees, but learned that for many, such as Superior Private Summio Daguichi, these were shed only for the Emperor, and that all other emotions, strong as they were, could not erase the overwhelming feeling that "a god had been embarrassed." This attitude speaks volumes about their view as to what was at stake in the Pacific War and explains many of the actions of the Japanese Imperial Forces there engaged.[13]

One topic of continuing interest regarding the Japanese, and closely reported in the paper, was that of their war crimes trials, some of which were conducted in Shanghai. Others in Japan and Manila and elsewhere were also avidly followed. The tone was set in an editorial in late September in response to another appearing in the *New York Herald Tribune*. The New York editor, in a spirit of sportsmanship, suggested that Americans might now play baseball with the Japanese, who loved the game, noting further that lessons in sportsmanship might be good for them. The *Stripes* editor agreed, and suggested a lineup for the opening game. Why not let those who had murdered the Doolittle flyers "slug it out with a hot War Crimes Commission?" he asked sarcastically.[14]

Some of the interest in war crimes trials was awakened by the discovery of funeral urns in a Tokyo funeral parlor containing the ashes of three Doolittle fliers executed by the Japanese, as well as details of their deaths. About the same time, letters of the condemned Americans in which they expressed bewilderment over their impending executions, and which were never delivered by Japanese authorities, were discovered in a cave thirty miles from Tokyo by American occupation forces. Additional urns, containing the ashes of thirteen other U.S. airmen captured and executed on Formosa on June 19, 1945, were also recovered. The GIs' interest in the trials also stemmed from the fact that the Emperor was still on his throne, which continued to rankle: perhaps the trials would mete out justice to at least some of the guilty parties. In addition, a desire for vengeance against the Japanese, so pronounced during the war, had not entirely run its course, though it was fading in some quarters, as noted above.[15]

Closer to home, in Shanghai, it was reported that four Japanese officers who had presided over a court-martial which sentenced three of the eight captured American fliers on the Doolittle raid of April 18, 1942, to death by firing squad were still in the area. Following their arrest, war crimes trials were ordered at Shanghai's Ward Road Jail for the seven Japanese officers and men charged with the execution, though only the four were available for trial, the others having died in the meantime. The trial was conducted by a five-man United States Military Commission established by Major Willis A. West, chief of the China Theater War Crimes Branch. The Commission was headed by Brigadier General John W. Middleton, and also included four colonels. The four of the seven Japanese officers involved in the trial of the U.S. airmen were: Lieutenant General Shigeru Sawada, commander of the Japanese 13th Army at time of the executions of Doolittle raiders; Captain Rkyuhei Okada, a member of the court-martial; Captain Sotojiro Tatsuta, who carried out the executions; and Captain Yusei Wako, the prosecutor.[16]

Testifying for the prosecution, Captain Chase J. Nielson, a navigator on a B-25 involved in the April 18, 1942, raid on Japan when sixteen B-25 bombers flew off the deck of the aircraft carrier *Hornet*, recounted the ordeal of the Americans. For four years, Nielson had lived out the war in a Japanese prisoner of war camp. Released and since recovered, he flew to Shanghai in January from the United States to testify. Nielson related that his aircraft, piloted by Lieutenant Dean E. Hallmark, had crash-landed in the ocean off Lingpo, China. Only three of the five-man crew survived; they swam ashore and were then captured by a Japanese patrol. Taken to Tokyo for a fifty-day questioning ordeal, they were then returned to Shanghai with five members of another B-25 that also crashed in China. They were subjected to torture and interrogations for seventy days in Shanghai's infamous Bridge House Jail. There, on August 28, 1942, a mock court-martial was held. The court was made up of seven officers, and Nielson reported that there were no formal charges made against them and that they had no defense counsel and no witnesses. The whole affair, conducted entirely in Japanese, was over in about half an hour. The Japanese claimed that the eight fliers were being punished because they had bombed schools and had strafed civilians. The exact charges stated that while attacking Japan the American airmen had suddenly exhibited cowardice when confronted with both air and ground defenses, and had reacted by attempting to cow, kill and wound civilians by indiscriminate bombing and strafing. They had succeeded in causing the death and injuries of about ten civilians and the destruction of numerous residences which had no military significance. Nielsen testified that the charges were "absolutely untrue." They only bombed steel mills, factories and an oil field, and they had not used their machine guns at all. Initially all eight had been sentenced to death, but the sentences of five of the prisoners were commuted to life imprisonment. Two pilots, Lieutenants Dean E. Hallmark and William G. Farrow, and a gunner, Corporal Harold A. Spatz, however, were to be executed.[17]

At his trial in Shanghai, Captain Tatsuta, chief jailer of the military prison in Shanghai, indicated that the men were executed at dawn on October 16, 1942, at Public Cemetery No. 1 on the outskirts of Shanghai, by a fifteen-man firing squad. He had previously prepared crosses and boxes for their ashes and bones. Tatsuta claimed that he had only the kindest and most warm-hearted feelings toward the three fliers, and alleged that they had become friends, especially after the fliers had showed him pictures of their sweethearts. Though he had already been informed of their impending execution, he refrained from informing them, though he hinted "that something might happen," and persuaded them to write their wills. He testified that his warm feelings toward the airmen led him to decide only to tell them of their fate at the moment before marching them out to be executed. He said — quite improbably — that they told him that things were O.K., and that they had expected their fate. Once their arms had been bound to crosses, Tatsuta told them that they were dying heroic deaths and that their names would be remembered in American history. His warm feelings were reinforced by the fact that his own sons in the army might possibly find themselves in a similar situation some day. He described the victims as fine young men, but that they were weak and thin. After the execution, he stated that he burned all three bodies and put their ashes and charred bones into small boxes which were forwarded to his superiors. He assumed that they would then be sent to the men's homes in America.[18]

The five Americans who were not executed lingered in prison in Shanghai for a time and in April 1943, were sent to Nanking. There, on December 1, 1943, Lieutenant Robert John Meder died of beriberi and malnutrition as a result of being a prisoner of war. Conditions in the Japanese prisoner of war camps were such that many American prisoners died of disease and malnutrition. The remaining four were rescued by American soldiers in August of 1945.[19]

The U.S. Commission issued its verdict on April 12, 1946. The defendants were all found guilty; Sawada, Okada, and Tatsuta were sentenced to five years' confinement at hard labor, and Wako to nine years. The results of this trial caused a furor in the United States, where many felt that the penalties were far too lenient.

Another trial in Shanghai's Ward Road Jail was that of eighteen Japanese held responsible for an inhumane Hankow death march which resulted in continued beatings, torture and finally a horrible death by fire for three American airmen, identified as Lieutenant Lester R. White and Sergeants Henry W. Wheaton and James E. Forbes. This occurred on the streets of Hankow on December 16, 1944. These events followed when eight men bailed out of their disabled B-29 fifty miles north of the city, after it had bombed Hankow. All having survived, four walked to safety but four were captured, one of whom died later in a prison hospital. With no trial of any sort, the three remaining captives were forced to strip to their undershorts and were then marched in a five-hour-long ordeal through the city in bitter December cold. With rope halters around their necks, they were subjected to a grotesque humiliation parade, during which they were brutally beaten, and when they repeatedly passed out, were revived, and finally taken to a crematorium at edge of the city, doused with gasoline and set on fire. At least one of the men was apparently still alive during the cremation and was heard screaming by witnesses, though a Japanese Army private testified that he had choked the prisoners to death before they were burned. Afterwards, an eerie scene ensued when several Japanese prayed over the bodies of the three deceased airmen in a bizarre religious ceremony. Witnesses testified that these actions were perpetrated mainly by the 34th Japanese Army based in Hankow and that city's gendarmerie.[20]

After protracted proceedings against the Japanese defendants, the most important of whom was Major General Masataka Kaburagi, chief of staff of the 34th Army, the five-man American commission, also headed by Brigadier General John W. Middleton, together with four colonels, handed down five prison terms of eighteen months to life, and five were sentenced to hang. One of those executed was General Kaburagi, named as the formulator of the parade plan. One warrant officer, two sergeants and a private were also to be hanged because it was determined that they used ropes to strangle the three fliers to death. In his review, Wedemeyer approved the death sentences, though he reduced the prison terms of three of the men from twelve to six years. The executions were to be carried out on April 20 with only official witnesses at the scene.[21]

Much more significant was the trial of General Tomoyuki Yamashita, commander of Japanese forces in Philippines from October 9, 1944, to September 9, 1945, and the one-time feared "Tiger of Malaya," who, on February 15, 1942, had accepted the unconditional surrender of Singapore from the British commander, Lieutenant General Arthur C. Percival. The proceedings began on October 30, 1945, in Manila, and the Shanghai *Stripes* covered them in exhaustive detail. Arraigned on October 8, Yamashita was charged with war crimes leading to the deaths of over 60,000 Filipinos, Americans, Allied nationals and even some Germans by privation, torture and executions. The board was headed by Major General Russell B. Reynolds. Movies of tortures were admitted in evidence and a parade of over 200 witnesses testified over the course of five weeks to such heinous crimes as the Japanese bayoneting or decapitating, by the infamous Samurai swords, more than fifty civilians in Manila, in the so-called Red Cross Orgy, that occurred in the Red Cross Building on February 10, 1945, with many women and children among the victims. Indeed, the prosecution's bill of particulars listed thousands of atrocities. For instance, the people of Batangas province alone described the mistreatment and murder of more than 25,000 unarmed, noncombatant women and children in that area. Someone testified that a Japanese captain revealed that they intended to kill all white people in the Orient. There were lurid accounts of Japanese soldiers' rape pools, the victims of which were young girls and prominent socialites in Manila.

Yamashita was also charged with issuing direct orders to kill all Filipinos and destroy their cities. This culminated in his directives for a final orgy of destruction as American liberation forces stormed into Manila. This included a systematic starvation, torture and burning to death of 6,000 Filipino and Chinese civilians in Manila's ancient Fort Santiago.[22]

In response, Yamashita's defense counsel, headed by Colonel Harry Clarke, prepared a writ of habeas corpus, contending that the tribunal had no authority to act under the American Constitution, and planned to appeal to the Philippine Supreme Court, alleging a mistrial. The possibility was raised that the matter might be heard by the U.S. Supreme Court.[23] The defense also entered pleas that the "Tiger," as he was being referred to in the press, had given no atrocity orders and was not even in overall command in the Philippines but only of half the troops on Luzon. As such, he was only responsible for tactical operations in the battles of Luzon and Leyte. His authority, he insisted, did not include personnel matters, discipline, billeting, punishment or supply. As to the atrocities, Yamashita blamed the Japanese Imperial Headquarters, and his aides charged that subordinate officers and even some naval officers were responsible. More specifically, Lieutenant General Akiro Muto, chief of staff under Yamashita, blamed Lieutenant General Koa, the man in charge of war prisoners, for the atrocities. He admitted that Yamashita had issued orders dealing with armed guerrillas, but these did not include women and children. As to the street fighting in Manila, he had issued orders to avoid this but these were not obeyed. Muto also claimed that Yamashita had ordered the evacuation of Manila, but that Japanese army and navy commanders in Manila, who operated independently and jealously guarded their authority, ignored his orders to cease firing. He also blamed Field Marshal Count Juichi Terauchi, commander in chief of the Japanese Southern Region, which included the Philippines, for ordering him to continue the hopeless fight on Leyte and Luzon.[24]

Beyond this, many of the charges concerning starvation could be laid at the feet of United States submariners whose operations caused the greatly reduced diets in the Philippines, one Japanese officer testified. A Japanese supply officer did admit, however, that Japanese troops could obtain foodstuffs from civilians while those held in prisoner of war camps could not. Other officers denied that ships transporting prisoners to Japan or the prison camps lacked food.[25]

When Yamashita took the stand in his own defense, he maintained that the atrocities were perpetrated by his subordinates and were unknown to him. He denied that he had ever issued orders for killings or other brutal measures against civilians. He also asked the U.S. Supreme Court to halt his trial and bring him to Washington for a full hearing before that body and that he be returned to the status of "war prisoner"—instead of "war criminal"—"in conformity with the provisions of the Geneva convention."[26]

In rapid order, the defense and prosecution summed up and closed the case, the chief defense counsel, Colonel Harry Clarke, finishing his with a resounding request for a not-guilty verdict. The chief prosecutor, Major Robert M. Kerr, argued that there was no doubt of Yamashita's responsibility and that by the nature of the crimes, the sentence imposed should be death by hanging. Kerr explained that a person who violated the laws of war was liable to the death penalty and that Yamashita was more than a military commander, he was also governor and therefore responsible for civilian safety. On December 7, the board, headed by Major General Russell B. Reynolds and four other U.S. generals, convicted Yamashita of condoning the mass atrocities committed by his troops in the Philippines and sentenced him to death by hanging. He was never charged with personally having harmed anyone but he was accused of never having acted to prevent atrocities. The *Stripes*' editor concluded that he had had a fair trial, which he never gave to any of his victims. In his last statement before the board, Yamashita stated that his conscience was clear and thanked the commission for its fair trial.[27]

Some days later, on December 18, the U.S. Supreme Court ordered a formal stay of execution of Yamashita and declared it would decide on the matter of a prospective civil trial for him. In the new year, on January 7 and 9, the Court heard four hours of argument on Yamashita's contention that he was improperly tried by American military commission in Manila. After some weeks of deliberation, on February 5, it refused Yamashita's petition for a retrial, being no doubt persuaded by Solicitor General J. Howard McGrath's arguments that military tribunals were not a court but a branch of the executive arm of the government and that therefore the Supreme Court should not intervene. Furthermore, any enemy belligerent who invaded U.S. territory gained no legal rights thereby, and was not entitled to recourse through the civil courts. Finally, military authorities in the Pacific war crimes trials were carrying out the declared intention of the U.S. President and Congress to bring about the apprehension and prosecution of war criminals. This was therefore the established foreign policy of the United States over which civil courts had no jurisdiction. The matter was then placed into MacArthur's hands. MacArthur upheld Yamashita's sentence, also ordering that he be stripped of his uniform, decorations and all other appurtenances that signified that he was ever a member of the military profession, and hanged as decreed. MacArthur thereupon directed the Commanding General of Western Pacific to execute the judgment. On February 8, President Truman, though he did not review the trial as such, scanned the plea for a possible clemency decision as he might have for any ordinary American citizen, but rejected it.[28]

The end was not long in coming. Lieutenant General Tomoyuki Yamashita, the erstwhile "Tiger of Malaya," was hanged about 3 A.M., at Los Baños, near Manila, on February 24, 1946. He met his death like an ordinary criminal, facing his end sullen and impassive. His last words were that he was praying for the Emperor's long life and perpetual prosperity. He asked his guard if he could bow in the direction of Tokyo, a request that was granted. The guard later admitted, however, that he did not know in which direction he had pointed. Though Japanese newspapers prominently featured his execution, there were no editorial comments, and no demonstrations were reported upon the death of one who was generally considered a hero by Japanese of all walks of life. A final sad note was recorded by Yamashita's widow, who said that she had expected the result, and like many hundreds of thousands of other bereaved relatives, intended to busy herself with her household duties, and also like so many others, pray for the return of more fortunate times.[29] Elsewhere, however, as in Thailand, Singapore, the Philippines, and in China, in ravaged and raped Nanking, and along Siccawei Creek in Shanghai, only the willows would weep.

VI

The China Scene Changes

"After that some more stuff happened."
— History student examination paper

For all of those who longed so fervently to get home from China, the increasing pace of terminating military operations in both the India-Burma and the China Theaters was gratifying. Indeed, by mid–October of 1945, a few weeks after the cessation of hostilities, virtually the whole of west China closed down. On October 23, Kunming shipped out units of the 10th Air Force headquartered there, under the command of Major General Albert F. Hegenbarger, to Shanghai.

At about the same time, the headquarters of General Wedemeyer and those of Lieutenant General George E. Stratemeyer, commanding general of the Army Air Forces in China, were also transported from Chungking to Shanghai which, as of October 16, 1945, became officially the headquarters of the China Theater.[1]

The *Stripes* duly recorded the change. Weeds were then growing in Chungking streets, one article noted. The average GI felt as though he were the little brother left behind to tend the chores while the family packed up and left on a picnic. And picnic seemed to be the appropriate word. Letters from their buddies fortunate to have made the trip to Shanghai were filled with tales of Stateside steaks, cold beer and the White Russian women available on every hand. The remaining garrison consisted of about 200 officers and 400 EM. While there were still some "chickens" (colonels) around, for the most part, the parade of brass had been greatly diminished, having lost its star attractions. These developments corresponded with events in China which involved the transfer of the capital from Chungking back to Nanking.[2]

But conditions in Chungking soon deteriorated for the average GI there. Styling themselves "the orphans of Chungking," they were not sure what their duties — said to be those of winding up Army affairs there — really were. What they were sure of was that an order of the local commander suggested that he apparently perceived that it was his duty to make life for the remaining men as disagreeable as possible. They had to revert to basic training procedures: They even had to make their own beds and get rid of non-issue items, and in general, uniformity was the order of the day. This was a shock, because during the proceeding months when there were two three-star generals present, nothing of this sort had occurred. Now, there were weekly inspections; failures led to no passes, and all special privileges were withheld.[3]

Following their move to Shanghai, the 10th and 14th Air Forces did not long remain operational. It was announced in Shanghai on December 2 that they were now regarded as surplus and were officially inactivated on January 6, 1946. Accordingly, the headquarters of the two were placed on a non-operational basis and began processing their men for return to the States. Each of the headquarters was going home as a unit. The China Air Service Command headquarters was also declared surplus.

The 10th and 14th were both colorful units. What would become the 14th was created under command of Brigadier General Claire Chennault on July 4, 1942, with its headquarters in Kunming. It was first known as the China Air Task Force, and was made up of four fighter squadrons and one bombardment outfit. Its core was the American Volunteer Group — the AVG — better known as the "Flying Tigers." It was upgraded to the 14th Air Force on March 10, 1943, and Chennault was promoted to major general. The 10th Air Force was activated on February 12, 1942, and operated in India, western China and Burma.[4] Air Force outfits then scheduled to continue in China were three squadrons and a troop carrier group headquarters made up of low-point men and volunteers. The squadrons were the 332nd and 330th Troop Carrier Squadrons and the 530th Fighter Squadron. The Shanghai Air Depot and other service detachments, numbering close to 1,600 men, were also to be retained. Organizations such as the Air Transport Command (ATC), Army Airway Communications System, the 10th Weather Squadron, and some groups liaising with the Chinese Air Force would remain with AAF headquarters in Shanghai.[5]

In addition, the Stilwell Road was abandoned as of November 1. It was now worthless as a commercial highway and was not likely to be kept open by the British, who regarded it as an avenue for Chinese entry into North Burma. Just prior to this, in mid–October, a convoy — Convoy No. 500 — consisting of 107 vehicles manned by 160 people, the last official U.S. Army convoy to use the Stilwell Road, completed its rather arduous journey. It had traversed the 820 miles from Myitkyina, Burma, from which it departed on September 28, arriving at the Motor Transport Service Terminal in Kunming, China, on October 7. It was commanded by Captain Clarence A. Todd of Rome, Georgia. The Road was begun December 1, 1942, when an advance party of American engineers arrived in Ledo, and was completed in the first week of February 1945, when the first convoy rolled into Kunming.[6]

Almost simultaneously, on October 30, the India-China pipeline, the so-called Macaroni Line, ceased operations. On that day, the last of the 180-octane aviation fuel completed its 35-day journey from Calcutta's dockside storage tanks at Bhamo. From there, it had proceeded along the land communications route into Assam, paralleling the Stilwell Road, and then over the Hump into Kunming, China. The pipeline was widely regarded as an engineering marvel and saved much fuel because previously a gallon of fuel was needed to fly another gallon into China. It began operations in April 1945, and delivered 146,116,156 gallons of aviation fuel in the seven months of its operations.[7]

Another spectacular operation also wound up about the same time. In Washington on October 19, it was reported that Brigadier General William H. Tunner, commander of the India-China Division of Air Transport Command (the ATC), had announced that the Hump would cease operations by November 15. Beginning flights in June 1942, as the India-China Wing of the Air Transport Command, this remarkable command had delivered over 776,532 tons of cargo to China in the past two years. The ATC's Passenger Service, from September 1, 1944, to August 31, 1945, had carried 1,204,207 persons, and had flown them 350,209,660 miles. It had also airlifted 195,893 Chinese and U.S. troops with their battle equipment and their 4,400 pack animals over the Hump. In addition, 4,720 patients had been evacuated. At its height in August of 1945, its personnel numbered 35,000, but only 9,000 remained by December 1.[8]

These American operations were paralleled by Chinese activities. With the end of hostilities in August, the Chinese decided that their capital would now be relocated to Nanking, the capital before the Japanese advances had dictated the move to Chunking. The move began in December, and by the 10th, more than 1,500 of the government's staff had arrived there. Five days later, China's executive, the Yuan, began to function there as well, though it would only be in May 1946 that the move would be official. Shortages of housing, water and other utilities, however, forced various foreign ministries to put off moving until spring. In the meantime, they remained in Chungking.[9]

With the coming of spring of 1946, things wound down rapidly in the China Theater. It was announced in early April that it was to be deactivated on May 1. Wedemeyer was scheduled to leave for the States on April 4. His replacement as acting China Theater commander was Lieutenant General Alvin O. Gillem.[10]

VII

Two Redoubtable Staffers: Arthur Goodfriend and Franc Shor

"Oh, it is good to go to war in such good company."
— Private Stewart Mackie Emery, in World War I

The man who had most to do with the founding of the Shanghai *Stripes* was Lieutenant Colonel Arthur Goodfriend. A consideration of his life and times is therefore in order.[1]

Described by one source as a writer, journalist, artist, educator "and often contrarian," and by another as a talented self-promoter, Arthur Goodfriend was born in New York City on June 21, 1907, of immigrant parents from Europe. He was educated in the city's public schools, including the DeWitt Clinton High School. His mother, convinced that he had artistic talent — which he did in fact possess — also enrolled him for a time in the National Academy of Design. Lacking the funds to seek a college career elsewhere, he had to be content with the College of the City of New York, where he was enrolled from 1924 to 1928, pursuing a bachelor of science degree. This he received in 1928, together with the gold bars of a second lieutenant in the U.S. Army Reserve, because he had also pursued that service's ROTC program.[2]

In college, he had worked in various jobs, including that of a runner for the New York Stock Exchange. There he made a friend in the Standard Oil Company who helped him obtain a job as an able-bodied seaman aboard a company tanker, the SS *Benjamin Brewster*, which set sail in 1928 from Hoboken, New Jersey, for Hamburg, Germany. Having arrived in Europe, Goodfriend set out on a six-month German-like *Wanderjahr*. As he expressed it, "From Versailles to the Vatican, from the Louvre to the Prado, from fish and chips in London to pizza in Perugia I imbibed more art, architecture, edibles, and alcohol than in all my earlier existence." Buying a bicycle in Belgium, he pedaled down the lines of World War I's Western Front from the channel coast to its terminus near Switzerland. He followed this with an odyssey to Europe's major universities, from Oxford and Cambridge to the Sorbonne, Heidelberg, Ulm and Bologna. He returned home on the SS *Hamburg* in late 1928.

Seeking work, he landed a job with an advertising agency whose clients included major haberdashery establishments. One of these desired to keep abreast of the latest fashions in Europe, which often centered around the circle surrounding the British Prince of Wales. Goodfriend accordingly followed their whims regarding fashion. He explained: "One personage dominated masculine fashion, the Prince of Wales. The width of his collar, the line of his lapels, the drape of his slacks dictated what was in and what was out. On London's Saville Row I scouted his tailors and cobblers. On the Rue du Faubourg Saint-Honoré in Paris [the equivalent of Saville Row] I shopped haberdashers who held the Prince's favor. On Rome's Via Condotti I sought out the creators of his cravats." There were other things that Goodfriend gained while in Europe at this time: a first-hand encounter with the rise and development of Hitler's Germany and Mussolini's Italy and other momentous events of 1930s Europe.

Lieutenant Colonel Arthur Goodfriend (from The Papers of Arthur Goodfriend, Special Collections, University of Hawaii Library, by permission).

His experiences in Europe whetted his appetite for foreign fields. He persuaded the *New York Herald Tribune* to employ him as a correspondent and send him on a trip around the world seeking advertising revenue from the men's apparel industry abroad. In the mid–1930s, therefore, he found himself in Japan, where he snagged an invitation to attend one of the Emperor's annual garden parties. He then proceeded to China, Thailand, and India. In China, an incident occurred which he loved to recount in years to follow. In Peking, a rickshaw boy became ill while transporting Goodfriend from a restaurant where he had sampled "that most succulent of celestial delicacies, Heavenly Duck." Goodfriend responded to the emergency, noting that since he was "at an age when such a crisis didn't daunt me, I placed him in the rickshaw, picked up the shafts and started to run." But he was stopped by a policeman who took him, the rickshaw boy and the rickshaw to a police station and thence to a courtroom. The magistrate, after questioning several witnesses—though declining to listen to Goodfriend—ordered him to pay the court clerk five dollars, for which he was handed a receipt. Meanwhile, the rickshaw boy had recovered and they proceeded to Goodfriend's hotel. There he remonstrated against the "kangaroo court" which had ruled without hearing his side of the case, but the hotel's bartender, closely examining the document that he had been given, announced, "This not receipt for fine. This license to pull rickshaw."[3]

In India, Goodfriend ranged across the country, especially visiting various British regiments. One of the clients underwriting his trip was a textile manufacturer seeking neckware novelties. In the attire of the British soldiers he found regimental clothing sporting the outfits' colors and returned with numerous examples of exotic materials which were "destined to set masculine attire ablaze with the beauty of Indian regimentals." Also in India, Goodfriend met Gandhi for a short session and an exchange of ideas.

From the Subcontinent, Goodfriend went to Moscow, taking in the celebrations of the seventeenth anniversary of the Revolution. He then journeyed to Mussolini's Italy and later heard Hitler speak to the frenzied populace gathered in the *Sportpalast* in Berlin.

In 1939, the year in which World War II began in Europe, he was again on the Continent. A client in the clothing business relied on dyes produced by a Swiss concern in Basel. The British, however, believed that the dyes contained chemicals from a German source and quarantined them. Through various connections and machinations, he was able to get the dyes released. These left Genoa on the last vessel to carry cargo across the Atlantic.

Late in 1941, as war clouds gathered, Goodfriend, a second lieutenant in the Army Reserve, was ordered to Camp Lee, Virginia. The commanding officer there, Brigadier General James Edmonds, shortly after Pearl Harbor, and aware of Goodfriend's global peregrinations, wanted him to devise a program to teach draftees what the war was all about. Goodfriend tapped the pictorial resources of *Life* magazine to assist in the project. A team of experts put together six picture portfolios which addressed such subjects as the German and Japanese soldier as fighting men; Dorothy Thompson, the well-known journalist, did an abstract of Hitler's *Mein Kampf*; others addressed the geopolitical menace to America and the events leading to America's entry into war.

His success in launching this program found him, in early 1942, ordered to the War Department in Washington. There he found himself under the command of General Clarence Ralph Huebner, later to head the famed 1st Infantry Division in Europe, who was then in charge of basic training throughout the Army. He ordered Goodfriend to the Infantry School at Fort Benning, Georgia. There he was to devise manuals to train soldiers in the details of soldiering at the most basic level: how to fire their rifles, how to do scouting and patrolling, defense against chemical warfare, and first aid for the soldier. Completing this task, he was sent to the Engineering School at Fort Belvoir, Virginia, to address the problem of teaching map reading to soldiers, generally recognized as "the toughest subject in basic training." After considerable development, including how to use the pictures of the body of Betty Grable — as well as his own thumb — to teach contours, the result was a major manual, *Map Reading for the Soldier*. These training aids eventually included Frank Capra's film series, *Why We Fight*, which "stirred soldiers' hearts and minds," as Goodfriend once put it. Promoted to captain following the success of his map-reading work, he was assigned to Major General Frederick Osborn's command, which was concerned with, as Goodfriend noted, "what every general from Caesar to Napoleon declared a determinant of defeat or victory — morale." Osborn's chief aide was Francis Keppel, destined to be dean of Harvard's Graduate School of Education and a United States Commissioner of Education. Many other writers, artists and other creative people, such as Munro Leaf, father of the children's classic *Ferdinand the Bull*, and Theodor Geisel, better known as Dr. Seuss, produced pamphlets, films and other training aids. Journalists and others published *Yank*, the Army weekly magazine, and various editions of the *Stars and Stripes*. Social scientists and psychologists tested GIs to establish their IQs, evaluate their gripes, and ascertain their views on subjects relating to information and education.[4]

It was while Goodfriend was at the Pentagon that he embarked on the first of what would be a series of escapades condoned by higher command: that of masquerading as an enlisted man, one "Private Arthur Goodwin." In this instance, he was ostensibly of the 445th Quartermaster Battalion, shipping out of Camp Kilmer, New Jersey, headed for Europe. With official connivance, he was reported as being AWOL. He was picked up in Scollay Square in Boston and "sent to the slammer." This was located at the East Coast Processing Center, a stockade at Camp Edwards, Massachusetts. Over 3,000 men were imprisoned there and for ten days he mingled with them and discovered that there were many salvageable individuals among the incorrigibles. Conditions there subsequently improved and grievances, if justifiable, were corrected. Compassionate leave was given to men with genuine family problems and there was also a "recognition that when troop trains traveled close to homes and lovers, AWOL merited mercy." Those who could be redeemed were released and reassigned. Dishonorable discharges were handed out to the truly degenerate. Over one thousand men were returned to duty and prepared for shipment overseas, where the invasion forces were being assembled in England.[5]

Goodfriend later used this procedure on numerous occasions, as when he joined the 1st Infantry Division in England in training prior to D-day. Here, he found the troops wanted more information as to what they could expect when confronting the Germans. This insight guided him in his approach to formulating the *Army Talks* training pamphlets. He repeatedly became "Private Arthur Goodwin" while serving as editor-in-chief of the *Stars and Stripes*. On another occasion, he joined the First Infantry Division in Germany as a common rifleman to ascertain how infantry replacements were being treated, a problem of some dimensions. In this instance, he made his way from the coast to Aachen in Germany, where the 1st Infantry Division was engaged in action. He described the conditions: The men were jammed into trucks for four or five days while on their way to the front, had little sleep and inadequate food, were often rained on, and in general, were unprotected. In short, they were "treated like dirt," and by the time they got to the front lines, "instead of being ready to fight we were in very, very poor condition." Returning to his office in Paris, he wrote a lengthy editorial describing the situation, much to the chagrin of Major General Clarence Ralph Huebner, the 1st Division's commanding officer, but he received the accolades of Eisenhower for his efforts, and some grudging acknowledgment of his activities from certain detractors among *Stars and Stripes* staffers. One account recorded that the colonel returned from this exploit with a Combat Infantryman's Badge and half a dozen or more stories based on the esprit of combat squads in action.[6]

Goodfriend declared that he resorted to using "Private Arthur Goodwin" to learn how the rank and file were living and what their attitudes were. He was firmly convinced that he should live as the men were living in combat conditions in the field so as to compare their lot with his own usual existence as a colonel. Normally, he "was living in very, very elite circumstances back in Paris—eating well, bathing everyday, [dressing in] immaculate uniforms, [and] being treated with great respect," where there was little danger. When thousands of men were living in horrible conditions, he asked: "How could I be an editor of [an Army] newspaper unless I knew what they were undergoing?"[7]

Goodfriend was then ordered to England as plans that would come to fruition on D-day, 6 June 1944, unfolded. Here Goodfriend assisted in changing the format and content of a series of pocket-sized pamphlets issued to troops under the general title of *The Army Talks*. Some of the titles included "The British Wife in Wartime" and "Jobs After the War." The series, however, was widely regarded as far too esoteric and failed to meet the needs of troops being prepared for imminent battle. General Eisenhower was among the chief critics, and in a letter to Lieutenant General John C.H. Lee, who commanded the forces' Services of Supply, which controlled morale endeavors, ordered that the men be informed about "the stark and elemental facts as to the character of our Nazi enemy." Accordingly, with Goodfriend's assistance, a new series appeared with such titles as "The Enemy and You," which portrayed the German soldier "as a strong, skilled, but vulnerable adversary." The vulnerability aspect was addressed by other *Talks* which included how "These Guys Fought 'Em," i.e., how men of the "Big Red One" Infantry Division, who had played a role in routing Rommel's forces in North Africa, had taken their measure. Another issue addressed "How Russians Kill Germans," highlighting house-to-house combat and taking panzers out of action. These much more useful pamphlets were, as Goodfriend noted, read as the invasion forces sailed for France.[8]

VII. Two Redoubtable Staffers

On August 24, 1944, Goodfriend, by then a major, was ordered to take over as editor-in-chief of all European editions of the *Stars and Stripes*, establishing his headquarters in Paris. He was to continue in this position until he departed in 1945 to found the China edition of the paper.

After his arrival, he made two important changes. In the first instance, he altered the editorial policy, insisting that editors discuss problems that were more relevant to the fighting men's immediate needs and orientation rather than presenting a generalized approach as heretofore was done.[9] He also emphasized the letters column, variously named but often designated as the "B-Bag Column." This invited soldiers to complain about their officers, their food, and their general service conditions. Thus, as Goodfriend noted, by inviting soldiers' complaints, it provided a release, and became "a very, very popular part of the newspaper. I think it was probably ... one of the best ways of dealing with morale, to give the soldiers a chance to let off steam." In addition, Goodfriend noted that the "B-Bag" was the "most beloved, reviled [and] controversial feature in *The Stars and Stripes*." Illustrating the point, one unnamed colonel, in a letter to "B-Bag," strongly attacked the column, noting that "this man's Army isn't run by Eisenhower or Bradley or Patton or anyone else. It is run by B-Bag and in my book that's one hell of a way to run an Army."[10]

Following his discharge from the Army in 1946, Goodfriend embarked upon an extensive career in governmental, social and educational fields. In the course of his involvement in China, he became convinced that Americans had to do something to help the Chinese and perhaps prevent their slide into Communism. President Truman also "sought some way whereby America's ancient ally, on which so much money and missionary effort had been spent, might escape the Bolshevik embrace."[11]

Accordingly, in 1948, a Joint Commission on Rural Reconstruction, a part of the State Department's Bureau of Educational and Cultural Affairs (ECA), was established. Goodfriend joined the commission in Canton and embarked upon attempts to help the Chinese fight a rinderpest epidemic which was killing off vital water buffaloes in great numbers. He drew illustrations for posters indicating the course of the disease and how it must be combated. His first efforts were in vain because they were not in Chinese, a mistake which he soon rectified.[12] But his efforts came too late. In September of 1949, Canton fell to the Communists and Goodfriend had to flee. His experiences, however, resulted in a copiously-illustrated portfolio, *Through Chinese Eyes*. Herein, he summarized where the West had failed to confront the Communists: "Americans worked exclusively with the wealthy, educated elites. They [the Communists] had infiltrated unions, barracks, schools. We had concentrated on the cities. They had gone into the villages. We dispensed charity, they political indoctrination. We had appealed to greed, prestige, power. They had exploited the human craving for work, joy, hope, dignity. We had aimed our message at the classes, they, the masses. We worked from the top down, they from the bottom up. They won. We lost."

The portfolio was published as a book and widely circulated under the title *The Only War We Seek*, which was distributed by Americans for Democratic Action.[13] The publication was well received among many Americans in high places, including Truman and his Secretary of State Dean Acheson. Indeed, Truman was sufficiently impressed to ask Goodfriend to convey the lessons of China to every American embassy in Asia, from Manila to Teheran. He readily agreed, and in this way embarked "on yet another journey through a troubled world." Goodfriend had hoped that the study and his efforts would provide a basis for a new American policy regarding much of the world, such as in Vietnam, but later ruefully concluded that events to come revealed that the lessons remained largely unlearned in the West, and the traditional approaches prevailed as they still more often than not do to the present day in many locales around the globe, to the continuing despair of many knowledgeable observers.[14]

Goodfriend attributed his failures in China to his still considerable ignorance of Asian people. He hoped to carry out Truman's injunctions and, at the same time, fill the void in his understanding of Asians. He learned that John D. Rockefeller III, the founder of the Council on Cultural and Economic Affairs, sought to expand American knowledge of Asia. As the Council's first fellow, he and his family were sent to Indonesia to live among its people, and to lay a foundation for further activities there. After many months there, however, the family was devastated by malaria and had to return to the United States to recover.[15]

When Goodfriend had regained his health, President Truman invited him to join the U.S. Foreign Service. He was first posted as Public Affairs Officer in New Delhi, India, for the United States Information Agency. Here he assisted in administering the massive flows of money, expertise and information to India designed to ensure that it remained resistant to Communism. However, America's policies in the Middle East, especially in Lebanon at that time, were regarded as anathema to Indians, who saw only an oppressive capitalism coupled with the continuation of colonialism, and he found that his efforts were thwarted. He returned to the United States with little accomplished.

With the coming to power of John F. Kennedy in 1960, and the appointment of Edward R. Murrow as the new Director of the United States Information Agency, Goodfriend found new opportunities. Murrow stated to Goodfriend that the West was well acquainted with Africans at the upper levels, but about Africans "who live in the bush, we know nothing." Therefore, he was asked to visit West Africa, and to "mix with the masses, and learn how we and they can connect." His bailiwick included all of West Africa from Senegal to Zaire. Again, though he learned much about Africans in the bush, by the time he returned to Washington, Ed Murrow was dead of cancer. His initiatives regarding Africa fell by the wayside, whereupon Goodfriend resigned from the U.S. Foreign Service.

His new endeavors centered on the East-West Center that had been established at the University of Hawaii in 1960. Goodfriend became assistant to the chancellor of the new enterprise. Out of its activities there sprang an innovation in higher education at the University, the "New College," founded in September 1970 with an emphasis on openness to students' needs and their participation in the school's administration and functions, a de-emphasis on grades and a reformed curriculum that focused on international relations. In 1971, Goodfriend became chairman of a cultural course. The object was to relate American actions overseas to Asian societies, which seemed desirable at the peak of the Vietnam War. But established educational and administrative forces conspired to end the innovative program and New College expired on August 9, 1973.

In 1977, Goodfriend taught a course for a "Semester at Sea" program on board the SS *Universe*, under the aegis of the University of Colorado. He then enrolled in the Graduate School of Education at Harvard for a semester, but ever restless for new experiences and attempts to further multicultural education and his own learning experiences, in 1979, Goodfriend became a Peace Corps volunteer for the Philippines, remaining for two years until 1981.

He then launched a lengthy odyssey as a peripatetic scholar in search of the ideal higher educational experience. He began with a year at Cambridge University in England in 1982; continuing during 1984 and 1985 at the University of Kyoto in Japan; then at the University of Sydney, 1985–1986; and concluding his venture at the University of Canterbury, Christchurch, New Zealand, in 1987. Meanwhile, in 1986, he began course work at the University of Hawaii in pursuit of a doctoral degree in education, having earlier been denied entry into a Ph.D. program there. His dissertation was a controversial, innovative one consisting of his educational autobiography and based on his long experience in investigating education around the world. It was titled "The Education of Arthur Goodfriend: A Case Study of Autobiography in an Educational Metaphor." He was granted his Ed.D. degree in December 1988.

Subsequently, Goodfriend became, at age eighty-five, the oldest Peace Corps volunteer on record, serving in Hungary from 1991 to 1993. He also worked with the People to People Health Fund (Project HOPE), with homeless people, and the Alzheimer's Disease Association. He died in Honolulu, June 1, 1998.

As to how he was regarded personally, at least two *Stars and Stripes* staffers, Bud Hutton and Andy Rooney, once indicated that many of the paper's staff were the friends of Goodfriend. Outside the sphere of the Army newspaper, where there was often much disagreement about editorial policies, he was considered to be "a gutty, friendly individual who never stood on army ceremony or rank." In addition, staffers at the University of Hawaii's Special Collections, who interviewed Goodfriend for an oral history project, were struck by his "charisma and [the] sheer magnetism of his personality." His dynamism, graciousness and old-world charm also made favorable impressions. Others who knew him referred to his ego, perhaps characteristic of a short man — he was five feet, five inches in height — revealing at least a nominal Napoleonic complex, though this was not a dominant trait. Regarding his family circle and relations with the "women of his life," there was evidence of dysfunction and inconsistency. By any standard, he lived a varied, complex, highly creative life at many levels, in the course of which he met many of the world's most influential people. His accomplishments were numerous and his contributions to the military sciences, his actions as chief editor of the *Stars and Stripes*, his voluminous writings in the fields of international relations and communications, his artistic endeavors, and his perennial search for improved education at all levels, were often commendable. He was witness to many major events in the 20th-century world, about which he has left behind numerous artistic and written records. These included, among many others, various military operations, such as the liberation of the concentration camp at Dachau, his attendance at the Nuremberg war crimes trials, and his endeavors in much of the Third World after World War II.[16]

Other glimpses into his character can be obtained from a self-evaluation in a questionnaire that he filled out when he was about 90 years of age. Therein, he listed his favorite books as those by Horatio Alger, but were he to be stranded on an island, he would desire a volume with blank pages that he could fill with his own prose and art sketches. His ultimate vacation destination would be "heavenly Hawaii." The greatest lesson that he had learned was that there was no value in "things." He was a great proponent of lifelong self-education for all, and as to his own personality traits, he rather gloried in his "intractability," but otherwise he was not exceptional, he concluded, seeing himself as "just another human being." This was not altogether the case, however. The record also reveals that he possessed a spirit of derring-do. Nor did he lack physical courage.[17]

Goodfriend was the Shanghai paper's chief editorialist — for a time. One subject that engrossed him was the cost of the war in terms of money and human life. In the October 17, 1945, issue his editorial was devoted to what a dead soldier might think about the atomic bomb. Most importantly, the corpse might argue, was that, though humans had "dug up a potato that they could not handle," the kind of weapon made no difference. It was death, the most personal and final thing on earth, that mattered. A person was neither more nor less dead whether killed with an arrow or a bomb. Neither did having recourse to statistics as to the numbers killed by any type of weapon alter the fact that all dead persons had one thing in common: They were cold. Humans should also learn, he went on, that there's nothing secret or static in science. Already an obscure druggist somewhere in the world might be making atoms in his bathtub out of "turps and turds," surely an early example of the concerns about a "dirty bomb." Yet another fact of history was that behind every weapon, whether arquebus, blunderbuss, bazooka or bomb, was a human being. Though weapons changed, humans did not. Therefore, whether armaments were rocks or rockets, it was Man who needed fixing.

Another editorial, titled "Voice from the Grave," continued the dialogue with the dead soldier, this one elaborating on the costs of the war. The corpse argued that it cost on average one hundred thousand dollars to kill a soldier in World War II. This was $80,000 more than it had cost in World War I. There were more than 14,000,000 soldiers killed in World War II, more than in all of the wars of the world since 1793. The cost of World War II to all of the combatant nations reached $1,250,000,000,000. The United States alone expended 290 billion of the taxpayers' dollars. This amounted to twice the cost of running the federal government for the previous 150 years. The cost of cracking the secret of the atom cost two billion dollars. Suppose this money had gone into schools, books, roads, housing, food and shelter. Perhaps billions could have been expended in exploring the human mind. The dead soldier therefore wished that people would worry less about the atom and more about "Adam." Had this been done earlier, perhaps he would still be alive, he ruefully concluded.[18]

One of the more colorful members of the Shanghai *Stripes*' retinue was surely Franc Shor. The *Stars and Stripes* in both world wars boasted exceptional newsmen. The First World War edition featured such giants as Harold Ross, who went on to found the famous *New Yorker* magazine; the columnist Franklin Pierce Adams; Grantland Rice, the sports writer; the theater critic, raconteur, and bon vivant Alexander Woollcott; and numerous others. In World War II, prominent writers included Andy Rooney, author and later television commentator, Hal Boyle, Bud Hutton and many others. Certain differences between the World War I and World War II editions have been noted. The First World War edition was widely regarded as more literary than that of World War II, which was generally viewed as perhaps more professional. In any case, World War II staffers often tired of such comparisons.[19] Certain it is that Goodfriend saw in Shor another who could match prominent *Stripes* staffers in either of the world wars. But as Goodfriend once noted, "A man of Shor's many-splendor'd parts was obviously not to be bound by ordinary Army discipline." In the event, "his frequent derelictions were overlooked," in part, because "he rarely missed a deadline." Goodfriend wrote that on one occasion, "he disappeared for several weeks, inviting an AWOL charge against him." Returning to Shanghai, "he claimed that a plane on which he was flying had caught fire over Canton. He had had to bail out and bus his way back." While he indeed "had parachute harness marks burned into his hide," Goodfriend admitted, "I refused to believe so outrageous an invention and warned him against stretching my patience too far." Four years later, when Goodfriend returned to China in connection with the Joint Commission on Rural Reconstruction, he met a Czech who ran a restaurant on Shameen Island off Canton. He warmly greeted Good-

Lieutenant Colonel Arthur Goodfriend on the right of the photo. Irene Kuhn is next to him. Staff Sergeant Franc Shor, of the *Stripes*' staff, is at the far left of the photo. Undoubtedly, the pianist is Gino Smart, who played at Shanghai's Senet Restaurant and who set Shor's celebrated poem "Three Little Girls" to music. The other two men are unidentified (from The Papers of Arthur Goodfriend, Special Collections, University of Hawaii Library, by permission).

friend and his party, saying that members of the group were the first Americans he had served since, back in 1945, a "tall GI, tumbling from the sky, had landed outside his door, doffed his parachute, dusted himself off and, entering the restaurant, demanded a wiener schnitzel, medium rare, and a bottle of vin rose." His unexpected customer was Franc Shor.[20]

At the paper, Shor presided over the poetry column, "Barracks Bards," wrote features, and contributed a regular column, "Yank About China." This was based on Shor's lively imagination and sense of humor, on Chinese lore and legends, and often on what he experienced on his rambles about China beyond Shanghai — though that city was not ignored — especially in Peiping, Kunming and Chungking.

His first "Yank" column, which appeared on October 11, 1945, described a long-running poker game which continued through the summer of 1945 in Chungking. Held in the Red Cross Club, it was intended to help the men while away the literally "long, hot summer." Shor explained that in Chungking, they were all long and hot. Indeed, Chungking is one of China's three infamous "furnace cities," the others being Wuhan and Nanking, all located along the Yangtze River. Beginning in May, summertime lasted through September. The heat was all-enveloping and persistent and there was no relief, even at night. The temperature was hotter at seven in the evening than at five, and at ten, hotter still. By midnight one thought that it could get no hotter but it did. If it was not the heat, it was the boredom. Everyone and everything always seemed the same in Chungking, even the dinners, the unvarying menu of which was meat, potatoes, gravy and cake. Behind the Red Cross Club the Chialing River went down its muddy bed in a never-ending stream. The restaurants were all off limits because of the cholera, and the hills were high, the streets were filthy and morale was low. It seemed, furthermore, that neither the summer nor the war would end: They would go on forever. In an attempt to ease matters, therefore, there was a poker game in Chungking that summer. For eight hours a night a thousand dollars went back and forth across the table. Of course, there was no need to be concerned about the cash. Whether one won or lost, it did not matter because there was no place to spend it in Chungking. Its only purpose was to keep score in the poker game. But if these things once seemed interminable, Shor wrote, by autumn the war was over, as was the Chungking summer, and so, too, the poker game. There would never be another poker game like that, Shor concluded, nor another such summer, and he prayed also, "Please God, never another war."

Other subjects discussed by Shor in "Yank About China" included the fate of GIs speculating in Chinese currency, with some men winning and others losing. In Chungking, the "Street of the Fragrant Smoke," where tobacco had earlier been sold, had been converted into simply "Black Market Alley." And if Americans could win and lose in currency matters, so could Chinese dealers. One of Shor's accounts described the rise and fall of a Chinese money changer who went from rags to riches and back again, though even in his time of losses, he remained as cheerful as ever. In another article, Shor described the extensive black market activities and other operations, chaos and difficulties surrounding the withdrawal of the Americans from Kunming.[21]

Shor was always closely attuned to the situation in Shanghai and passed on his impressions and analyses as he deemed them appropriate. By November, he was pleased to report, prices were a little better. One could get a good meal for a dollar and a sumptuous spread for two. The best liquor, such as Scotch, cost twenty dollars a bottle, or a dollar to a dollar-and-a-half per shot. Gin was a bit cheaper, but those "in the know" drank vodka, produced locally. This could be had at ten to fifty cents a shot. It did not taste bad and had the same effect. Girls were still in good supply, though many were going steady with the early arrivals, and a rapid turnover was also in evidence. Souvenirs were plentiful, and a PX–operated gift shop was getting a terrific amount of GI trade and was the best place to buy many things. Everything in the shop had been gone over by expert appraisers and the soldier got genuine bargains. The shop was one case where the Army had really gone out of its way to see that the GI got a good deal. All entertainment at the Red Cross Club in the foreign YMCA put on many shows, held dances, provided places to sit, and featured a restaurant offering burgers, coffee and a large assortment of cakes. There, one could eat oneself sick for a couple of dimes. The weather was glorious, and on the streets one could meet old buddies who had last been seen in India, Burma or in Chengtu. It was, indeed, an excellent site for a reunion. Ships were starting to move out, headed for home. The Post Command was getting organized and those waiting shipment usually could count on being gone within ten days or so. In short, Shanghai was a wonderful place for anything that one might desire and should not be missed at any cost.[22]

Shor often championed those who were abused by the military's caste system or other inequities that he came across. In one article, he focused on WAC Sergeant Henrietta Williams. Shor recounted the events of an evening at a club in which she was involved. A tall, good-looking girl, she was seated at a table with her boyfriend when a certain captain came up to the table and pointed to the decorations that she wore. They consisted of the usual campaign ribbons but were joined by the Legion of Merit and the Air Medal with a few oak leaf clusters attached. Above these was a pair of navigator's wings, all of which were rarely seen on a WAC's uniform. The captain, who had had a few drinks, had an edge to his voice as he loudly objected to what he saw. His strident attitude greatly embarrassed the WAC and others in the vicinity. He warned her to tell her boyfriend, who had no doubt given them to her, that it was against regulations for enlisted personnel to wear any decorations to which they were not entitled. As to the wings, he wore his because he had earned them and he did not like to see soldiers wearing decorations and insignia that they did not deserve, even if they were women. The WAC, blushing, started to reply, but the captain interrupted, insisting that she should take them off immediately or he would call an MP. She responded that they were given to her by the Army. She was entitled to them and did not have to take them off, whereupon the captain demanded to see the orders awarding her the medals. At this juncture, Shor reported, a certain nice thing happened. An Army Air Forces colonel walked over to the table and spoke to the WAC, wishing her a good evening and hoping that she was having a nice time. He then asked to be excused as he and the captain wished to discuss certain matters. Steering the captain to a corner, the colonel informed him that the girl was Sergeant Henrietta Williams. She had joined their unit at Hastings Mills in India some time before as a draftsman. But she developed an interest in navigation and mastered it on her own. She then studied the Loran navigation instrument and mastered it as well and became a Loran expert and instructor, flying all over India and Burma instructing navigators in its use. She had also navigated C-47s over the Hump. The ribbons that she wore were earned the hard way. His outfit was proud of her, the colonel declared, and "she's a good soldier, and a damn good flier." The upshot, Shor concluded, was that the captain then went home — after he had apologized to Sergeant Williams.[23]

More amusing, and perhaps along the lines of an O. Henry tale, was a story that Shor recounted of a friend, Tommy Stone, who had arrived in Shanghai with him. Stone, like so many others, loved the girls, but he was also a bit frightened by them, fearing that he might end up married. He found a lovely lass named Toni who worked at the Foreign YMCA. Toni and Tommy were soon going steady and Shor wondered how Tommy was coping. He assured Shor that he was safe with Toni because, unlike most men who promised their girls that they were single, even though some were married, Tommy informed Toni that he was married and therefore safe from her wiles. Soon, however, Shor found himself at the wedding of the pair and asked Toni to explain how things had developed when she had been told that Tommy was married and hence unavailable. In reply, Toni simply said that she wanted to introduce her sister, who worked in G-1—where all the records were kept.[24]

One of Shor's most celebrated works was a poem which appeared in "Barracks Bards" in the September 29, 1945, issue. Widely admired and often quoted, it was titled "Three Little Girls," a.k.a. Olga, Sonya and Tanya. It was initially attributed, for some reason, to Goodfriend's alias, "Pfc Arthur Goodwin," but Shor soon made haste to claim credit for the poem. He had Gino Smart, a pianist at the Restaurant Senet in Shanghai, set it to music, taking care to copyright both words and song. This version of the poem and musical score appeared in the October 13, 1945, issue, and the rousing ditty soon became popular. It recounted the lot of three White Russian girls who had lived in Shanghai before World War II, as well as during the struggle, and then emerged into Shanghai's postwar era. It began by noting that the three girls, before the war, dated American gobs, GIs and marines, while making all of the joints and seeing all the scenes, with the result that they always seemed to be well cared for. But the war intervened and the girls missed their free-spending Americans, and because they had to eat, they consorted with the new arrivals, the Japs. This entailed much tweaking of moustaches and sitting on Japanese knees instead of American laps, as well as learning to say "Daddy" in fair Japanese, not to mention listening each evening to Tokyo Rose and going with their new escorts to Japanese shows. They could, however, in return keep their apartments and buy new clothes. But the war ended, and the Japanese left, leaving their Russian girls who kissed them goodbye and then hastened to welcome the GIs once more, and proceeded to sell them their ex-lovers' samurai swords, and all was well once more.

In an editorial reviewing the piece, the editor noted that Shanghai's "Petrushkas" were indeed eye-catching, but were the rank and file to go beyond the bars and cabarets and visit a genuine Russian home and taste true Russian hospitality, see Russian kids dance the ballet, and admire how their culture had been sustained throughout years of exile, they would then learn that Olga, Sonya and Tanya were not the whole story. As to their virtue, he surmised that it was perhaps no better nor worse than among other impoverished and underprivileged people anywhere, whether in Peking, Paris or Pittsburgh.[25]

The "B-Bag" column sometimes included letters praising or damning Shor. A good writer, it might have been said about him that "his words like so many nimble and airy servitors, trip about him at command," as John Milton expressed it about someone else in his "Apology for Smectymnuus." A "Fed-up Lieutenant" was singularly unimpressed, however, informing the editor in a letter to "B-Bag" that the paper's "Yank About China," who flitted about the Chinese landscape "like a gilded butterfly," gave him a pain in the accustomed spot. In fact, Shor's "orchidaceous wanderings" round and about the boites and cabarets of such cities as Chungking and Kunming were not especially good reporting. He needed to go home and wait until he got back to El Morocco or 123 where he could dish out his ruminations to his heart's content. First Sergeant Charles L. Parsons came to Shor's rescue, advising the lieutenant not to clutter up the pages of the paper with his juvenile bickerings. After all, he did not have to read the paper. Corporal William Weatherby, reasserting the negative, accused Shor of having two threadbare formulae: One was his frequent attacks on Shanghai's high prices, and the other, timeworn, trick-ending stories similar to those of O. Henry. He was waiting, he said, for a Shor column about a man who sold his watch to buy a comb for his wife who had cut her long hair to buy him a watch chain.[26]

Weatherby's letter, however, appeared in the January 12, 1946, issue and only three days later, Shor published his final "Yank About China" column. This was to be the last one, he wrote, observing that it was about time for him to quit because he had been scraping the bottom of the barrel for quite some time, no doubt trying the patience of his readers, with a nod to Corporal Weatherby and other critics. Shor acknowledged that it all had been fun, but that three and a half years in the Army was a long time. He had always thought that when the time came to go home and get his discharge that he would be the happiest guy in the world, and he would be anxious to leave and look forward to going as quickly as possible. He rather gleefully concluded, when these had all come true, that he had been exactly right![27]

In the following issue, his Shanghai roommate and fellow staffer, John Clift, took over the "Yank About China" column and explained Shor's absence. "Shor is no more," he began, noting that Franc had announced that he knew someone who was flying to the States and was going along. That man, obviously a pilot — probably of a four-engine Douglas C-54 transport — was headed first to Tokyo for a couple of days, and then to Hawaii and San Francisco. Shor, Clift explained, was one of those guys, like so many others, who had been attempting to get home ever since they landed in China. He was always trying to bum a ride to the U.S. and had finally succeeded. Clift confessed that he himself was rather relieved and would no longer have to apologize that he was not Shor when some PX girl, or perhaps a girl at a party or on the street, spotted his *Stars and Stripes* patch. In any event, Shor had departed and must have hugely enjoyed the flight home, no doubt reflecting that some of his detractors were still in China.[28]

VIII
Going Home

"Home is where the heart is."
— Anonymous

No subject filled more space in the Shanghai *Stars and Stripes* than the question, "When do we go home?" This question stood above the rest for the vast majority of American service personnel throughout the world in 1945 and 1946, their families at home, every segment of the populace, and within the military high commands and the American government from the White House to the houses of Congress. If, as one war correspondent noted, war was often best characterized by the word "monotony," such also described the immediate postwar months. The story there was similarly one of a dismal journey from boredom to tedium and back again. As Goodfriend noted, for the average GI "sweating out discharge in China's wasteland, once the first elation [of the war's end] wore off and his thirst for pleasure was slaked, the reaction was dismay and disgust": dismay "that his sacrifices should have proved so useless," and disgust with the Chinese people. To many Americans, "the 'dinks,' 'slopies,' 'gooks,' and 'wogs,' seemed a subspecies, hardly human, venal, filthy, opium-addicted, without an iota of pride in self or country, [and] willing to sell their sisters for the price of a bowl of rice." Beyond this, the "sources of China's distress lay so deep as to defy understanding," and American servicemen were "physically and psychologically lost in an alien culture they could not comprehend, loathing everything they smelled, heard and saw — the stink of the honeybuckets, the cries for cumshaw, the sight of vermin-ridden beggars, the crippled, diseased and dying in the streets, the rats and flies, the indifference to human and animal suffering." Accordingly, "their letters to B-Bag chorused the ever-mounting outcry, 'I want to go home!'"[1]

As might be imagined, poetry addressing these concerns appeared in vast quantities in the paper. The news that one was "going home" was a source of great exhilaration when it touched any individual. This event was perhaps nowhere better captured than in a poem by Lieutenant A.L. Crouch, titled

"Troop Transport." Therein he noted that he eagerly awaited the day when he would be the boy who was suddenly carried away, "in a transport of joy." Another verse, "Song of Home," by Private First Class H.A. Lee, was infused with happy notes and employed an expression common in those days, "The Golden Gate in Forty-Eight." In his case, however, he learned that 1946 was to be his year, and not only that, he would make the journey in January, only a few weeks hence. Less fortunate was the case of Sergeant Arrin Waite, who was not privileged to know when he would sail. Accordingly, his poem, "The Things They Do," bore a note of frustration. He observed that the things that the Chinese were doing in Chengtu and the songs that they were singing in Kunming, while colorful and romantic, could not hide the fact that he, and many others, were getting frantic, and indeed had developed passions positively satanic, "for their mates in the States."[2]

The points system, discussed above, was at the heart of much concern in the China Theater — and in other theaters. Inevitably, it came in for its share of poetic attention also. The first issue's "Barracks Bards" column included a poem about a certain GI who was "big stuff" back in the States. He owned a bank and was loaded with cash, had a grand home and a fancy car, and was a habitué of such establishments as the Stork Club. Nevertheless, he greatly envied one of his buddies because, while the rich man was new to the service and had only recently arrived in China, the veteran, T-5 Harry Kent, was the proud possessor of ninety points, and hence the title of his poem, "My, How He Envies Me!"[3]

It is noteworthy that the Army's Chief of Staff, General Marshall, clearly understood the attitudes of American service personnel and those on the home front regarding demobilization and identified key aspects of the problem. He was well aware that once the fighting ceased in the European Theater the "natural reaction of almost every man will be an overwhelming desire to return home, to get clear of the tragic scenes of destruction and the surroundings of discomfort in which he has labored so long, to rejoin his family and resume his civil occupation. His family will be equally impatient and probably even more articulate. Appeals will be made to our representatives in Congress to bring pressure on the War Department to do this or that, for this person or that person. The papers, the columnists, the broadcasters, will carry the reflection of this great impatience." To assist matters, Marshall was certain that chaplains could "play a large part in solacing [GIs'] outraged feelings and in giving spiritual guidance, bringing [them] down to a philosophical acceptance of where [their] duty lies.... It will be difficult for [them] to accept this situation without turbulent reaction. That will constitute one of the problems you must face."[4]

Shortly after the capitulation of Germany, Marshall gave testimony before the House War Department Subcommittee on May 25, 1945, in which he surveyed the status of the Army. He noted the great progress made since 1941, extending to the time of Germany's defeat. Following this event, he indicated that "there is little of military secrecy as to the general nature of our plans for the coming year. The offensives in the Pacific are to be intensified to the maximum degree." This great momentum must be "sustained until world peace is actually within our grasp. It would be a costly mistake, a hideous injustice to our men in the Pacific to relax now in optimistic estimates of the situation." He was confident of a final victory on the battlefield, but, he warned, "it must not be delayed by optimistic errors of judgment or impatient demands for a return at home to the conditions of peace." The Army would reach its maximum strength of 8,300,000 men on July 1, the beginning of the new fiscal year. In fact, it reached its peak in May 1945, at 8,291,000. He also anticipated that its strength would be reduced to seven million by year's end, as soon as it was possible to "return to civilian life of a large number of men now in uniform who have contributed their share in the armed services of this country." Thus war-weary men who had earned their right to demobilization would be accommodated up to an average of about 167,000 men per month.[5]

Three months hence, on August 10, anticipating the Japanese surrender, and with a clearer picture in view, Marshall acted to initiate demobilization. In a radiogram to Generals Eisenhower and McNarney in Europe he ordered that, on the capitulation of Japan, "we want you immediately to reverse the priorities for movement of organizations and men to the U.S. In general terms first priority must go instanter to men for demobilization."[6] A few days later, on August 15, immediately following the cessation of hostilities, Marshall drafted a more detailed statement for Secretary of War Henry Stimson on the subject. One of the first items of business was to reroute ships that were carrying troops and supplies to the Pacific from Europe and the United States. These were to return to U.S. ports unless they were required for immediate occupation duty or were so close to their Pacific destinations that it would be impractical to turn them around. In these cases, they were to complete their voyages as originally scheduled. Henceforth, all available air and sea transportation "will be utilized to the maximum to return our high score men now overseas to their homes." Separation Centers in the US were to be enlarged to permit the discharge of 500,000 men a month. The goal was then to reduce the Army by 5,000,000 in the next twelve months. Marshall admitted that "more men will have to be moved in less time and over longer distances than ever before. It is a tremendous undertaking." As soon as possible, points would be steadily reduced, the aim being always "to ensure that those who have had the longest and hardest service receive first consideration for discharge." To be sure, some men would experience delays in release "on the grounds of military necessity," but these would be limited to a few highly specialized classifications, perhaps embracing no more than 20,000 men. Though the "eagerness with which the men of the Army and their loved ones await their discharge is evident," some who had not "yet served a full tour of duty overseas will have to sail to foreign shores to relieve others who have been away a long time. They will go to assignments that involve little or no personal danger, but we would all prefer it they did not have to go at all." The conditions of performing occupation duty and otherwise ensuring the peace were such, however, that their use was necessary. Marshall was adamant on this point. Also ever mindful of the devastating effects of the atomic bomb, Marshall concluded that "the next war might destroy the world. It must not come."[7]

Nevertheless, in point of fact, the points system, which worked reasonably well and was accepted by many as being as good as could be expected, contained numerous possibilities for abuse. Accordingly, the *Stars and Stripes* was filled with articles, and especially letters in the "B-Bag" column, charging, for instance, that "armchair officers and typewriter commandoes," that is, those in the rear areas who had seen little combat, were being awarded far too many decorations, which were slaps in the faces of the men who had really earned them. Another evil was the spurious awarding of combat stars for campaign ribbons, a small thing, but each star carried five precious points toward getting home. One of the results was that soldiers who had never cared about decorations all of a sudden began urging officers to recommend them for medals. Others carefully combed their records seeking any advantage which they may have overlooked. It was also obvious that those of a younger age who had not had time to establish a family were at a disadvantage.[8]

Rumors soon circulated that favoritism was often apparent and higher brass and stars in sports and Hollywood were getting quick returns home without much consideration of the points system, while all the ordinary citizen soldier got was a promise that he will be demobilized by July 1946. This was quite a lapse in time, as a writer in the October 8, "B-Bag" column bitterly complained. The *Stripes* indeed routinely reported the demobilization of prominent stars. Many of these were bona fide veterans, however, and had performed loyal, and sometimes even heroic, service—facts sometimes overlooked or downplayed by the complainers. Most readers were unimpressed that Lieutenant Robert Taylor of the Navy had retired after three years on active duty as a flight instructor, and that Lieutenant Tyrone Power, a U.S. Marine Corps transport pilot with active service in the South Pacific, had flown home and into the arms of his wife, all duly photographed for the edification of the viewers. The same was true when Adolf Hitler's nephew, Seaman First Class William Patrick Hitler, was discharged in February of 1946. He had arrived in the United States in 1938, leaving Germany because he detested his uncle's policies, and enlisted in the Navy. He, therefore, had done his "bit" in the good cause of helping to defeat his uncle.[9]

Perhaps more interest than opposition surfaced when the paper reported that Staff Sergeant Joe Louis had been released and planned to resume his boxing career. He had fought over 500 exhibition bouts in the States and overseas since January 1942. In an interview with reporters, Louis noted that he planned first to see every game of the World Series, then underway, and subsequently talk with Uncle Mike Jacobs, his promoter. He would then journey to California for several months of conditioning for his fight scheduled with Billy Conn. He told reporters that at 219, he was fifteen pounds over his fighting weight, but quipped that while he might not move "as fast as I usta," he could hit the same as always.[10]

Similarly, when Jack Dempsey, the former heavyweight boxing champion, became a civilian again and stepped out of his Coast Guard Commander's uniform, there was little dismay expressed by readers. Dempsey became president of a television concern to televise boxing at a salary of $250,000 a year. He would also continue to operate his Broadway Tavern and Great Northern Hotel in New York. He did assist in a major bond drive after his discharge, being temporarily back in uniform for the event.[11]

Red Skelton, the comedian, and his wife, Georgia Davis, were photographed as Skelton returned to civilian life after eighteen months in Army. He claimed to be the only film star who went into the Army a buck private and came out the same, a fact that may well have headed off any charge of favoritism. At least he was no coddled brass hat.[12]

Much later, in February 1946, Mickey Rooney, fresh from staging shows in Europe for armed forces personnel, and who then had fifty-seven points, was being flown to the States. Further accounts revealed that he, a T-4, was awarded the Bronze Star for exceptional courage while performing as an entertainer. Rooney, assigned to the 6817th Special Services Battalion, had traveled with small unarmed groups into the combat zone, taking his show to the front lines. His three-man jeep show was composed of a musician, a singer and a master of ceremonies. He moved with the troops, armed only with battery-powered megaphones and accordions, saxophones, clarinets, and trap drums. Rooney later recalled in his memoirs, "We put on our first show between two Sherman tanks in a Belgian snowstorm, with sixty guys in the audience, three miles from the front, with the sound of howitzers booming in the distance."[13]

Such commendable action was unimpressive to some readers, however. In a letter to "B-Bag," T-3 Daniel T. Holbrook included a poem, "Rhyme and Reason," which questioned Rooney's activities. The poet admitted the star's fame and accomplishments, recounting that he possessed many talents: He could act, dance and sing, and also ride a horse, while simultaneously wooing such heroines of the Silver Screen as Hedy Lamarr. But what was controversial was that he "stunned the world" by earning fifty-seven points in only twenty months. Holbrook complained that his own thirty-five months of service had only netted him thirty-eight. In another letter, three privates first class and two privates explained that they had been in Asia for twenty-two months with combat time and only possessed thirty-six points. Why was it, they also wanted to know, that Rooney rated a plane trip home for discharge and they could only travel by ship and were lucky to do that?[14]

VIII. Going Home

Even dogs of the K-9 Service Corps seemed to be singled out for prompt return, perhaps ahead of qualified service personnel. The *Stars and Stripes* published several articles and photographs of the returning animals, including a picture of "pipe-smoking Bob," apparently the first dog to see action in Italy. His early arrival in the ETO, however, may have provided him with sufficient points to make him fully qualified for return to the United States. Bob sailed home on the SS *James Duncan* with 191 other infantry scout dogs, all no doubt ready for a decent bone and maybe even a new doghouse made possible by the GI Bill of Rights' loan provisions.[15]

But as to the seemingly neglected and abandoned average GI, his fate was highlighted in a letter in "B-Bag" signed simply "Leftenant," and by one soldier, Sergeant William G. Johnson, who noted that he had received a stack of Stateside funnies and to his surprise and amazement found that even his old comic strip friends, including Skeezix and Joe Palooka, had been discharged from the Army. The lone exception was Lieutenant Terry Lee of *Terry and the Pirates*, by Milton Caniff. Surely Lee had sufficient points to get home, but it occurred to Johnson that perhaps the fact that Terry was in China may have had an effect on his redeployment. Then, too, he also may have had to help repatriate the Japs. Things must really be tough when a man could not get out of the Army from China, even in the funny papers.[16]

The issue of going home, in the weeks following the surrender of the Japanese on the decks of the USS *Missouri* on September 2, 1945, steadily gathered momentum. The *Stripes* was filled with information on the progress of getting everyone to the States and discharged from the service, as life for the GI in China took on a harder edge, with impatience growing daily. Certainly, both in the field and in Washington, those in charge revealed an awareness of the depth of feelings among GIs worldwide regarding the desire to get home as early as possible. In the October 4 issue it was reported by the War Department that a total of 1,116,000 service personnel had been released from the service under the points system since demobilization had begun officially on September 12. On average, about 32,000 were being returned to civilian life daily. Also, between May 12 and September 21, 1945, about 1,687,000 personnel had been brought back to the USA from overseas, notably from Europe. As to men in the Far East, Marshall announced in mid–October that all American military personnel would be out of the CBI by July 1, 1946, though it was plainly a long time between October and the following summer.[17]

Perhaps even more gratifying was that in addition to the Navy and War Departments, Congress's interest in the demobilization process intensified, no doubt in response to many complaining constituents and for budgetary reasons. In October, a spate of releases from Washington were calculated to soothe ruffled feathers and perhaps inculcate some patience in the GIs. On October 5, it was stated that the required numbers were to be dropped to sixty points for male Army enlisted men on November 1. As of October 1, for WACS, the necessary thirty-six points would be dropped to thirty-four. WAC officers were to be reduced from forty-four to thirty-nine points. Except for medical department officers, male officers of all grades, including warrant and flight officers, would be dropped to seventy-five.[18]

Brigadier General Robert Berry, the assistant personnel chief in the War Department, went further, asserting that points would probably be reduced to fifty by December 1, as it was the only way the Army could continue discharging 45,000 men a day, a new goal that had been set, partially in response to the swelling tide of complaints and evidence of discontent from every quarter. The House Appropriations Committee, however, proposed an even more rapid demobilization of all the services to drastically reduce government spending. To these ends, the Committee demanded that both the Army and Navy immediately adopt a policy of releasing officers and men as rapidly as they became surplus, no matter what their point count was. The Committee declared that it was unjust to hold an individual beyond the time when his services were required. This was also an imposition upon the taxpayer.

There was, in fact, a challenge to get all military personnel back home and out of uniform. As of October 15, 1945, 1,930,000 personnel remained in the Atlantic area, 2,010,000 in all Pacific areas and still 3,050,000 in the States. Certainly the paper applauded the Committee's views and noted that it was the war of logistics that had won World War II, but wondered why the men could not be gotten home just as expeditiously. Yet progress continued apace, and by October 30, Washington announced that 2,000,000 personnel had been discharged since VE Day. Also of relevance was that some 44,799 peacetime enlistments had been recorded in the same period. In addition, not all service personnel were getting out of the service. Furthermore, 400,000 German and Italian prisoners of war would be sent back to Europe from the United States in lots of 500 by March 1946, making further shipping available for Americans abroad.[19]

To move things along more expeditiously, the Department of the Army decided to free all surplus stateside GIs. Beyond this, discharges in general were being speeded up, and in October, 800,000 soldiers would be separated, up from the 200,000 for September. Yet this development led to numerous complaints, the troops still overseas wondering why these men then Stateside, many with very few points, should not be sent overseas as replacements.[20]

While much of the information had to do with the services in general or pertained largely to the forces in Europe, other articles making for more satisfying reading in the Pacific and the Far East were those similar to a story appearing in the October 8 issue. This stated that the Navy reported in early October that thirty-five transports with a capacity of 50,000 were being loaded with high-pointers in the Far East, that twenty-seven other transports were already en route home with 25,000 men, and that other vessels were on their way to staging areas. Therefore, some 75,000 additional personnel would not be chanting the time-worn refrain, "The Golden Gate in '48," but the much more acceptable ditty, "We're Gonna Arrive in '45."[21]

The Navy also began bringing high-pointers home on board Third Fleet warships returning to the States, scheduling 14,000 for this service in October. The men boarded ships that were sailing directly to separation centers such as Seattle, Portland, San Francisco, San Pedro and San Diego. In addition, the Navy began converting warships, especially carriers, for use as troop transports. This so-called Magic Carpet Fleet included the 35,000-ton aircraft carrier USS *Saratoga* and eighteen escort carriers.[22]

One of the escort carriers was the USS *Makin Island* (CVE-93), which sailed on December 10 with 161 officers and 1,059 enlisted men. Staff Sergeant Ed Hogan, the paper's managing editor, in his account, "GI Thoughts on Boarding That Ship for Uncle Sugar," appearing in the December 11, 1945, issue, described his impressions and emotions as he, having accumulated the necessary points, departed for home. He and his shipmates were about to realize their fondest dreams, he wrote. Joyously, they were on their way back to Main Street, USA, to drugstores' soda fountains, to the juke joints, or maybe to Joe's Bar and Grill, and some, perhaps, to Carnegie Hall. He was amazed at the huge space available and was impressed by the hundreds of bunks filling the void. It was altogether nice to be going back, and one wondered if they would ever again see spring in Italy, summer in Greece, fall in France, or winter God only knew where. He wondered, too, if there would be a next time and whether one would have to return once more in uniform, get shot at again, and have to worry about a shell or a dive-bombing Stuka having one's number at last. While one might not remember the name of a favorite bar in Rome, or would forget a certain telephone number in Athens, or a hundred other things, one could not forget that the war was apparently over. Nevertheless, because hate and suspicion were still rampant, many did not seem to notice, and the killing went on in China, Java, and elsewhere on the globe. Nonetheless, he and the other GIs would no doubt reflect that the war was worth fighting, but prayers would also be sent heavenward that they would never ever have to do it again.[23]

Rather quietly, meanwhile, considerable activity in Kunming logged significant numbers of men being funneled from there over the Hump to India. By October 4, some 10,000 American soldiers had passed through Camp Ting Hao, a China Theater staging area at Kunming. Colonel John E. Walker, commander of the camp, reported that this number had been attained at Kunming in only thirty days since shipping had begun on August 29. A month later the numbers had swelled to 44,000 of the 75,000 GIs in China at war's end who had been flown out over the Hump to Indian ports. Thus, without fanfare, many China Theater GIs were unobtrusively sent on their way back to the States.[24]

Occasionally, personnel in Shanghai awaiting passage home were pleasantly surprised by the turn of events. In early November, while some were sweating out the arrival of their tardy transport, the *Annabelle Lykes*, the sudden, unexpected appearance of the *Hocking* (APA-121), a Navy auxiliary personnel attack transport, instantly brightened the outlook of the people involved. Port officials rapidly reacted, and on November 12 boarded 1,100 GIs, 418 navy enlisted men, fifty army officers and thirty-eight naval officers onto the ship. The *Hocking* was scheduled to dock on the West Coast about December 3, in time for the fortunate passengers to make it home by Christmas.[25]

As Thanksgiving of 1945 rolled around, while many GIs remained abroad, the paper was happy to report that many service personnel who had been overseas were eating the festive meal at home for the first time in many years, cause enough for celebration.[26]

Attitudes and wartime customs on the home front contributed to the ferment of demobilization. The people there had been immersed throughout the war by the pathos of the struggle's countless dangerous situations, stark conditions and the strain of separations. The presence of blue-starred flags in innumerable dwelling windows, denoting people in the service, and those bearing gold stars, signifying the loss of loved ones, were ever-present reminders of the sacrifices involved. Dreaded telegrams from various agencies, informing the recipients that a family member was killed in action (KIA), wounded, or was a prisoner-of-war or missing in action (MIA), kept civilians at home ever on edge.

The cultural scene played its part in focusing on the strains of wartime and on the long-awaited demobilization to follow. Newsreels, documentaries, and feature movies contributed to these ends. One was the movie *Since You Went Away*, released in July 1944, by United Artists. Produced by David O. Selznick, it was a poignant portrayal of family life during the war and highlighted such subjects as the difficulties of raising children in wartime, the question of whether or not women should do war work, and the loneliness that pervaded the household. The absent husband, who was missing in action, is a continual haunting presence in the film. Finally the wife learns, appropriately at Christmas time, that he has been located, is safe, and more importantly, is on his way home, highlighting the innumerable absentees from other family hearths of many in the audience. When, after V-E and V-J Days, it seemed that these absent members were being unduly delayed en route, the intense pressures being exerted on all involved to get them home were reinforced.

Certainly holidays loomed large in the consciousness of many in the war years because of the central role that they played in family life. An Irving Berlin song, "White Christmas," was introduced by Bing Cosby in the 1942 musical *Holiday Inn*, released by Paramount Pictures. Greatly popular at home, it also strongly resonated with armed forces personnel, becoming a perennial, nostalgic holiday theme song of prime importance.[27]

In popular art, Norman Rockwell recorded two homecoming events on covers of the *Saturday Evening Post*, both in 1945. One, called *Homecoming, GI,* appeared on the May 26 cover a few days following the German surrender on May 8. The setting is a tenement neighborhood in any American city. A decidedly redheaded GI arrives home to be greeted by a crowd of exuberant friends and family members—all redheaded—complete with his girlfriend, appropriately waiting "next door." The second appeared on the October 13 issue, after V-J Day. Titled *Homecoming, Marine*, it features a Marine Corps Private First Class. An obvious veteran of the Pacific campaigns, he is seen regaling family members and friends gathered around him in a garage or machine shop with his war tales. He, as so many others certainly did, uses souvenirs, including a captured Japanese flag, for his "show and tell."[28]

As 1945 drew to a close, some began to feel even more intensely a sense of abandonment because Christmas especially was traditionally a family celebration. The war had now been over for several months and many servicemen still lingered on foreign shores. While there had been considerable progress in returning service personnel, clearly there was still much to be accomplished. Certainly some of the complainers were now on their way home and much tension that might have been present was eliminated. Nonetheless, there were a sufficient number still remaining to give those in control headaches aplenty.

By year's end, things took a decided turn for the worse. While the demobilization logistics were proceeding, in many instances quite expeditiously, other factors intruded. One major consideration concerned America's China policy. Many American high officials were determined to assist Chiang in redeploying his troops to prevent China from falling to Communism. Duplicity surfaced as to statements and rationales justifying the use of planes, ships and manpower in the face of demands that these be employed to get U.S. veterans home. This was compounded by the need to repatriate the Japanese, both soldiers and civilians, in a timely manner. The strain of all of this would eventually erupt in GI demonstrations and what amounted to de facto mutinies around the globe.

The reasons for repatriation of the Japanese were made clear by Secretary of State James F. Byrnes. He disclosed in Washington on November 22 that the U.S. government had informed the Japanese government on August 17 that in carrying out the terms of the Potsdam Declaration, the Supreme Commander would oversee the surrender and see that Japanese soldiers were returned to their homeland. The withdrawal of American troops in Asia hinged in part on this understanding. In the meantime, certain Japanese soldiers were keeping their arms by Chiang's instructions because they were holding certain territories for him against Communist forces. Wedemeyer also authorized some Japanese to retain their weapons to guard supply depots and other installations.[29]

Another part of the demobilization picture was the necessity of keeping sufficient armed forces in place to ensure the peace. These matters were addressed by *Stripes* in an editorial in the November 9 issue. What was needed was to retain enough American manpower to present a stern mask toward Japan and Germany. But the sticking point was that American GIs overseas were in the main unwilling to dedicate themselves to long-range occupation duty. They only wanted to remove themselves from the war's bad memories by digging a hole, climbing in, and forgetting as quickly as possible that the rest of the world existed. At the very least, the editor continued, Americans should recognize that the huge investments of the war must be protected. Also, whether they liked it or not, people around the world looked to America for leadership. Accordingly, what had been won by American blood must not be allowed to revert to a wasteland of disorder, distrust and despair.[30]

One soldier, Sergeant B.W. Mooney, was worried that the Japanese Emperor was still in place and thought he must be forced out for the unconditional surrender demands to be realized. If these were not implemented, the next generation would undoubtedly have to go to war again. Mooney feared that by going home too early, Americans would end up paying a heavy price later.[31]

General Marshall had similar concerns. Speaking before the *New York Herald-Tribune* Forum on October 29, he warned that the U.S. demobilization at the present rate amounted to a disintegration of the armed forces, which seemed coupled with an abdication of a sense of world responsibility by Americans. The atomic bomb meant that more and not less attention must be paid to U.S. responsibilities. Marshall charged that the pressures for a rapid demobilization were caused by "a widespread emotional crisis of the American people," and added that if Americans were to nourish the infant United Nations Organization and thereby set up some possibility of world order, "then definite measures must be taken immediately to determine at least the basic principles for our postwar military policy." The world now sees the United States falling back into its familiar peacetime habits, he concluded, a further cause for grave concern.[32]

Despite such warnings, however, the wailing of those wanting to return home grew ever louder. An article in the November 14, 1945, issue of *Stripes* explained that these moans were reaching Washington in increasing volume as criticism of the nation's redeployment program mounted in Congress, among labor unions and in other circles. A spokesman for the War Shipping Administration in Washington, which transported most of the troops, acknowledged that the heat was getting hotter. He indicated, in rebutting the criticism, that his administration only followed orders of the Joint Chiefs of Staff and that the schedules he had been sent were being carried out on time. One Army spokesman admitted that one major difficulty was the scarcity of seamen to move the troops, though he estimated that the Army would be only seven days behind in its schedule on January 1. Various congressmen, however, concluded that matters could be accelerated and insisted upon further action. Representative John Rankin, a Democrat of Mississippi, vociferously contended that all of the brass hats in Christendom could not convince him that it was necessary to keep as many as six million men scattered throughout the globe in "uniformed idleness," while their personal affairs went to whack, their educational opportunities vanished and their families cried for them to come home. He further demanded the discharge of a million men more than anticipated by Christmas. Among the documents pouring into Washington were seven thousand petitions circulated by the newly-established Servicemen's Wives and Children's Association of Pittsburgh urging immediate release of all fathers from military service. In response, Senator Chapman Revercomb, a Democrat from West Virginia, recommended that Congress pass a resolution freeing all dads from the armed services. He met with opposition, but many legislators promised to consider the matter in their January session. In addition, merchant seamen of the National Maritime Union threatened a strike unless more ships were made available for troop shipments.[33]

Yet the news was not unremittingly gloomy. Positive developments surfaced from time to time. The November 30 issue of the *Stripes* reported that four Navy transports and aircraft carriers (CVCs) were to transport to the States about 9,000 officers and men out of Shanghai in the next twelve days. By December 10, all personnel in high-point categories were to be scheduled out on these vessels. In the December 12 issue, a report from Wedemeyer stated that the 16,000 Army personnel now in China, of whom 12,000 were in Shanghai, should dwindle to fewer than 6,000 by month's end. The Marines in Tientsin finally received word that some 5,000 replacements had sailed from Norfolk and would soon relieve the high-point Marines there.

The reasons to celebrate, however, were often tempered by untoward developments in China and in Washington. In Shanghai, rumors surfaced that ships for late December shipping schedules had been canceled, and other disquieting news, which contradicted what many regarded as set policy, was soon forthcoming. Colonel R.C. Wittman, Wedemeyer's G-3, noted that while current shipping schedules would be maintained, he also admitted that some 6,000 army personnel would still be needed after January 1 to administer Theater activities, maintain guard and dispose of approximately 1,200 surplus planes and other stocks still in the possession of the U.S. Army. Also a change in the Theater's mission or other unforeseen conditions might necessitate retaining more men than contemplated when the original shipping schedule for December was established. These hints proved to be forewarnings of more dire things to come.[34]

One of these was a substantial bombshell in the form of Truman's revised China Policy set forth in an article in the *Stripes*' December 17 issue. Speaking in Washington on December 16, Truman, in a watershed address, referred to the earlier Cairo and Potsdam Agreements, according to which the United States was working in close collaboration with the Chinese national government to remove all Japanese influence in China. To these ends, the nation had assumed a definite obligation for the disarmament and evacuation of the Japanese troops from China. The U.S. Marines were in North China for that purpose, and retention of U.S. forces would be continued until after the completion of that mission, that is, until after the Japanese surrender terms had been carried out.[35]

U.S. support of the Nationalists was not for the purpose of attempting to influence the course of China's internal strife, Truman averred, though this was not altogether the case, as events would soon reveal. He emphasized that the removal of Japanese influence in China would ensure that China could take her place in the world as a unified, democratic and peaceful nation. This was the purpose of the maintenance, for the time being, of U.S. military and naval forces in China. There was also criticism of Chiang's stance, and Truman wanted to see the Nationalist Chinese expand their present one-party rule to include representatives from all political factions, but he also urged the end of autonomous armies such as that of the Communists. Nonetheless, Truman also recognized that the steps necessary to achieve political unity would have to be worked out by the Chinese themselves, and that intervention by foreign governments would be inappropriate. Bearing out the president's posture, requests from the Chinese Nationalists that the U.S. Army transport three additional Chinese armies to North China and Manchuria were denied. The American mission that had assisted in the repositioning of Chinese troops used to disarm and repatriate all Japanese nationals had been completed, the Army announced.[36]

Undoubtedly, the President's speech changed things in China to a considerable degree. These were explained on December 20 in a straightforward statement made by Wedemeyer in Shanghai. This noted that the Truman Policy altered the redeployment program as it had been carried out heretofore. As soon as the Japanese had surrendered, it was the natural instinct of every soldier, whether professional or otherwise, to turn his thoughts to home, he continued. He was in keeping with what most GIs had been fighting for: to get the war over as soon as possible so that they could once more resume life and pursue their own welfare and happiness. Also after the war had ceased, the "punch and enthusiasm" displayed in carrying the fight to the enemy had subsided, replaced by a sense of nostalgia for home. Until quite recently, Wedemeyer went on, the policies of the government with reference to China had been to affect the withdrawal of nearly all American forces in China by January 1, 1946, or by the spring at the latest. Plans to do that had been set in motion. But in light of Truman's statements, new policies were to be implemented in China. First, American forces were to further assist the Chinese central government in the repatriation of approximately 3,000,000 [sic] Japanese scattered throughout the China Theater. They would also assist the Chinese in moving forces by air and sea to certain specified liberated areas, moves that were already well underway or accomplished. In addition, they would protect U.S. property remaining in China. Finally, they were to plan for the organization of the U.S. military to create a United States Military Advisory Group in China, about which little

VIII. Going Home

had been said to this point. This was to be composed of volunteers. In view of these considerations, there were three categories of American military personnel that must remain for the present in the China Theater: the 561 professional soldiers; the 260 high-pointers, half of whom were to be released by January 1, 1946; and the 8,672 low-pointers who were not eligible to return. Wedemeyer promised that he would do everything in his power to get these home as soon as they were eligible. In the meantime, however, he had canceled two ships in December as a result of the changes in the evacuation plan.[37]

Further clarification came in the December 27 issue, which noted that only so-called scarce GIs would be held past their discharge-eligibility dates. Also, approximately 900 personnel were to leave on the ship *General Eltinge*, due in Shanghai on December 28. This was the last vessel listed for December departure and would mark the end of mass movement of military forces from China, as one article rather ominously concluded.

To ease the minds of many who were affected by these new developments, Washington announced on December 20 that as of January 1,1946, the Army was to reduce points for enlisted personnel to fifty points and officers to seventy. This would make 600,000 additional men eligible for discharge. Length of service was also slashed to forty-two months for enlisted men and forty-eight for officers.[38]

The Shanghai *Stripes*, in an editorial "The Presidential Answer," further sought to pour oil on the troubled waters of the demobilization problem. Responding to a letter in "B-Bag" which asked "Why Are We in China?" the editor concluded that the presidential statement of December 16 and Wedemeyer's further elaborations laid everything on the line. They firmly believed that GI presence in China was to carry out U.S. policy and that the repatriation of the Japanese was essential to securing the peace. To these ends, the president was carrying out the will of the American people, and if the policy was wrong, appeal should be made to the people and Congress for changes. In the last analysis, the editor concluded that no one wanted to rush home only to have to get ready to wage another war twenty years hence.[39]

These views were similarly advanced by the *New York Times*, which warned in an editorial on December 31 that too rapid demobilization gravely endangered peace. It had been previously stated that a new American world policy was focused on not drifting into isolationism as had happened after World War I. The U.S. was indeed apparently bent on taking whatever measures might deter any new aggression. Unfortunately, the cries to bring the boys home, which made every congressman scurry about seeking to keep his job by strongly supporting these demands, was having untoward consequences. The same was true regarding the ending of the draft and the demobilization of the "citizen" army in favor of a small "volunteer" force and a small navy. It was a fact that the many who had risked their lives deserved to get home at the earliest possible opportunity and also should not be saddled with the task of policing the lands they conquered. Nonetheless, Congress and the president should provide adequate replacements for service abroad from among those who had not had combat duty, the *Times* further asserted, and also to develop an adequate permanent system to meet all eventualities. Therefore, the pell-mell rush out of Europe and out of Asia, being pushed by congressional pressure, amounted to a new retreat into isolationism. Were it not checked, it would endanger the peace that had been won.

On New Year's Eve, the *Stripes* published two major articles calculated to alleviate the anxieties that the Truman Policy was causing. One headline noted that 10,000 Marines were soon to go home, while another trumpeted the news that an additional 3,000 to 4,000 Army personnel would be brought to China to help supervise Japanese repatriation. This would bring total Army personnel in China to between 12,000 and 15,000. Wedemeyer thought that the repatriation program, proceeding at rate of 300,000 per month, would be completed in eight to ten months. If the Chinese Military Advisory Group were to be approved, then a permanent U.S. force would be in China. It, however, was to be staffed only by Regular Army personnel or volunteers.[40]

Other balm came in the issue of January 5, which noted that the CTRS (China Theater Replacement Service) in Shanghai had closed up shop and that remaining men were to be turned over to G-1 for processing. Some 14,844 personnel had been processed since its creation date on October 29. The sailing of the *General Eltinge* on January 4 had ended these operations, because there were only thirty men eligible for shipment home remaining, and these could be handled with no difficulty. A few days later, Wedemeyer stated that all enlisted men and women who met current discharge requirements would not be retained in China against their will, though commissioned officers could be kept an additional sixty days if their services were required.[41]

IX

The Worldwide Collapse of GI Morale

"When badgers fight and everyone's a foe."
— John Clare (1836)

The system of demobilization had seemed to be working more smoothly, though there were numerous fits and starts, and a great deal of pressure was being exerted from many quarters to these ends. Many high-pointers had, to be sure, been returned home and discharge rates were being accelerated. The Truman Policy, however, had caused much concern, especially in China, where more men were required, none of whom was to replace men bound for home. These developments might have been absorbed by the GIs with no more than the usual griping had matters continued along the same course. But at this juncture, Secretary of War Robert P. Patterson unexpectedly announced in Washington on January 6 that worldwide demobilization would be retarded. His reasons were several: In the first place, there were difficulties in getting overseas replacements. Patterson also noted that the rapid discharge of servicemen was resulting in widespread disintegration, causing critical conditions in several locales. He indicated that the points system was still intact, but revealed his notion that points had been counted only up to V-J Day, an idea at variance with the common understanding that points were still accumulating for men overseas. Otherwise, men in the States accrued the same number as those still abroad. Patterson further indicated that discharge criteria would gradually be lowered to reach the minimum overseas requirement established at 797,000 personnel by July 1, 1946, the number deemed necessary to ensure the peace. In the past, Patterson noted, as men could be spared and returned home, the required points had been successively reduced. This would no longer be the case, because in some instances personnel might be detained until they could be replaced, thereby preventing a crippling of the occupation forces. Shipping would no longer be a factor as there was plenty available.[1]

Simultaneously, Lieutenant General Joseph T. McNarney, the occupation commander in the ETO, announced in Frankfurt the end of U.S. Army redeployment from Europe. Release of soldiers subsequently would depend on whether they were essential in their jobs and whether replacements were available. Acting War Secretary Kenneth C. Royall, in the absence of Patterson, who had just departed on an inspection trip around the world, elaborated, asserting that American hysteria to get the boys home was endangering the occupation policy. Therefore, he declared, the ending of the unrest was the responsibility of the American people, the source of much of the pressure to get the men home.[2]

In any event, the pattern of returning armed forces personnel from overseas and the GIs' reaction to these developments abruptly changed throughout the world by January 7. The January 8 issue of the *Stripes* reported that the day before, about 2,500 angry GIs had marched four abreast through Manila to the headquarters of Lieutenant General Wilhelm D. Styer, commander of the Western Pacific. The crowd was wildly enthusiastic but an orderly meeting had preceded the march. The men denied that the demonstrations were riots because no property had been damaged. Their action was also timed to call attention to their plight in advance of the expected arrival of War Secretary Robert Patterson and was in protest against all explanations given by him and other Army heads as to why the men were still in the Philippines. The men furthermore planned to see the congressional Mead Committee, also due to arrive shortly. Finally, it was intended to send a strong message to Congress that either matters were straightened out regarding the GIs' return home or they would not be returning either, i.e., to Capitol Hill.[3]

The lead article in the January 9 issue noted that perhaps as many as 20,000 GIs had again demonstrated in Manila. General Styer, who declined to appear in person, stated in a written response read to the crowd that the changing international situation made it impossible to send all eligible men home immediately. He denied that the War Department had broken promises made as to returns or that it had extended its shipment schedule over a six-month period that had originally been set for three. Underscoring the men's feelings, an assembled band played a funeral dirge at the end of the reading of Styer's explanation, and the rally closed after passing — amid thunderous cheers — a resolution demanding a congressional investigation of the demobilization program, as well as reviewing U.S. foreign policy. The document also stipulated a speedy lowering of critical point scores, full use of all available shipping, the immediate return to the U.S. of all troops except those needed for occupation duties, and a rapid sorting out of surplus property disposition. A five-man GI committee was elected to confer with Secretary Patterson, soon to arrive in Manila.

More light was shed on the Manila situation by Hal Boyle, a roving reporter of the Shanghai *Stripes*. In a story datelined from that city on January 8, he observed that morale was then at its lowest ebb in the Pacific areas. The idea of going home had developed into a clearly defined mental state, he wrote, and efficiency and discipline were seriously undermined. Officers and men alike revealed a growing resentment against high Army and Navy brass, threatening to turn the remnants of what had been the world's most powerful armed force, in only five months after the war, into little more than a mob. Most servicemen now believed that they had done their duty to their country, and because no military danger then threatened it, logically they should immediately be sent home.[4]

Meanwhile, in Paris, about 2,000 soldiers paraded to the headquarters of the Army's redeployment camp at Le Havre complaining that they had been alerted four times for a January 2 departure and then told that they could not sail before January 15. In the United States, at Andrews Field in Maryland, 200 Army Air Force enlisted men protested demobilization inequities.[5]

Elsewhere, 4,000 soldiers stationed at Batangas in the Philippines raised $3,700 to finance a full-page ad in newspapers in the U.S. demanding Patterson's removal. On Saipan, 6,000 20th Air Force men spent $3,600 on cables to the War Department criticizing its failure to reduce point scores.[6]

In Frankfurt, Germany, some 5,000 angry troops were dispersed by fifty armed paratroopers. No bloodshed resulted, but there was a fistfight between a lieutenant commanding the troopers and one of the demonstrators.[7]

On January 10, in another outbreak, 1,500 Honolulu noncoms held a meeting and contributed funds for a long cable to Truman demanding that he renounce the War Department's newest policy. They advocated a ten-point drop per month and the release of all men with two years of service. The meeting was attended by Lieutenant General Robert C. Richardson Jr., the Middle Pacific Commander. He found no objections to the men writing individually to their congressmen, but warned that they must not take matters into their own hands, which would bring the Articles of War into play. He would then have to take disciplinary action, which was the last thing that he wanted to do.[8]

On January 11, 5,000 EM assembled in a Calcutta park to air gripes at the War Department's tardiness in demobilization. Thousands more met in Seoul and issued a formal statement to Lieutenant General John R. Hodge, stating that they did not understand why the War Department insisted on maintaining an oversized peacetime Army overseas under present conditions. In Korea, however, the occupation forces were operating at below strength, weakening the protests.[9]

The widespread protests remind one what the Prussian officer, Major General Friedrich Wilhelm von Steuben, said about American Colonial troops in General George Washington's army: that they had to be told the reasons why when they were given an order. Then, and only then, would they be willing to follow it. The protesting GIs seemed to be true heirs of these forebears. Austin C. Wehrwein, in an article titled "Don't Blame the GIs," wrote that while it was true that American prestige abroad had taken a terrific beating from the GI mass meetings, the GIs should not be blamed. The fault lay elsewhere.[10]

The Shanghai *Stripes* also published an editorial in the January 9, 1946, issue indicating that reports from around the globe were focused on GI unrest, but the best possible news from the China Theater was that nothing similar had occurred there. While the men wanted to go home, they knew exactly what the score was. When they were eligible for discharge, they would be sent home. Until that time, they had a job to do, and would do it. The credit for the high morale in the Theater was given to General Wedemeyer. He had laid out the facts plainly and frankly, including unpalatable information such as when he had to cancel ship sailings. If such frankness had been the order of the day elsewhere, GIs would no doubt have been deterred from demonstrating, he concluded.

Predictably, the editorial produced a sharp reaction, and many readers, who had previously supported the paper, now bitterly castigated it. One letter in "B-Bag" headed "Court Jester's Stool," signed by a "Homesick Corporal," rejected the notion that morale was high and that the men did not want to go home. All except the volunteers "who had never had it so good" wanted to go home.[11]

Other letters emphatically concurred. One from Lew Rhodes, who had earlier praised the staff for editing a good paper, now rejected the *Stripes*' position, which he said no longer reflected GI views. He charged it with evading the issues such as why they were in China in the first place. For months now, the men had been under the yoke of a dictatorship, Rhodes declared. In another letter, Sergeant B.L. Dombrowsky bitterly assailed the paper's "apple polishing casuistry," which had greatly upset his stomach and the assertion that there was high morale present was a piece of self-delusion. While Dombrowsky had high praise for the billets and chow in Shanghai, which were on the whole excellent, these facts did not in any way mitigate the prevalent irritation and discontent. Since V-J Day, most of the troops had been doing little more than killing time and fraying their nerves. Though the paper maintained that they knew exactly where everyone stood and exactly what the score was, just where did matters stand and what was the true score? he sarcastically asked. Signed by an impatient, married sergeant, another letter charged that the recent *Stripes* editorial was a major brown-nose job, and "Fed-up Looey" agreed. Though it was true, he admitted, that the soldiers were enjoying themselves in Shanghai, he would gladly trade 1,000 nights in Shanghai for one quiet evening at home.[12]

Many of the men in Shanghai, however, tended to absolve Wedemeyer of these untoward developments. Austin J. Edmonds admitted that he was homesick and restless but realized that Wedemeyer and Stratemeyer had no control over general policy. He also appreciated the ending in Shanghai of onerous military practices and inspections, such as military courtesy campaigns and roving bands of majors patrolling streets to get "name, rank and serial numbers," and other petty annoyances that the Army had inherited from its European forefathers and which, for a time, had been imposed there. Wedemeyer showed

IX. The Worldwide Collapse of GI Morale

good common sense in not forcing these on the men in the China Theater. They, in turn, should give him credit for treating them like free American citizens and not as troops in the Prussian Army.[13]

Meanwhile, also on January 9, the beleaguered American president responded to the irate GIs at a press conference. He noted that the armed forces were being demobilized as quickly as possible. Certain circumstances had slowed this down, however, Truman admitted. One of the most important was the recognition that the USA had to assume its responsibilities of keeping the peace. This included destroying the war-making potentialities of hostile nations that were bent on keeping the world in a state of war.[14]

The men were no doubt encouraged to learn that Congress generally supported them. Senator John McClellan, a Democrat from Arkansas, for one, agreed that the War Department's slowing down of demobilization was a breach of faith with the servicemen. In fact, demobilization should be speeded up, not slowed down. In addition, in San Francisco, CIO Longshoremen's Union President Harry Bridges cabled dissatisfied GIs in Guam and Manila, encouraging them to keep playing the game and assuring them that the union would continue to support them at home. He acknowledged that the troops had fought to save the nation when things were tough and they would now in turn support them. They had already struck on December 3 demanding more ships for returning troops.[15]

In Yokohama, when Secretary of War Robert Patterson arrived on his world tour, he was met by a group of 8th Army GIs who mounted a "near mutiny"; at least, so it was perceived by Colonel Charles A. Mahoney, the Service Command Provost Marshall. He broke up the demonstration and, according to a pamphlet titled "Discharge," soon circulated by certain GIs purporting to contain the facts as to what had happened, had called the soldiers "goddammed babies," and threatened them with prison sentences. Mahoney charged that the gathering had been stirred up by a coterie of Communists and hotheads. In his version of events, Mahoney stated that he had asked them if they were real soldiers or merely Boy Scouts. He told them that they were not acting like soldiers, that they were insulting a man who was a soldier before they were born, and ordered them to break it up. Patterson, who significantly had been surprised to learn that no discharge points for overseas service had been recorded since V-J Day, claimed to have seen no such demonstration, certainly nothing like that charged by Mahoney, though some shouting GIs had clustered around his auto. Nonetheless, no matter what the facts were, Lieutenant General Charles P. Hall, acting 8th Army Commander in Japan, strongly reprimanded the troops, emphasizing that the eyes of the world—and particularly the Japanese people—were watching with interest the signs of a breakdown of morale and discipline among the occupation troops.[16]

General Eisenhower, the Army's new Chief of Staff, on January 10, also reacted to the turmoil, authorizing overseas commanders to ship all surplus men home regardless of their point scores, and ordering troop requirements cut to a minimum.[17]

In Manila, GIs met Ike's words with cheers and celebrations and the Associated Press reported that General Ike now "owned" the city. Manila soldiers still planned, however, to meet Patterson and the Mead Committee, even though their main concerns had been addressed. In Tokyo, MacArthur went a little further than Ike and ordered that no ship was to return to the U.S. from the Pacific with empty bunks.[18]

Wedemeyer, on January 11, lauded the China Theater men for not staging demonstrations as elsewhere in the world. He knew that orders often caused hardships and dangers, but the men of China Theater had not failed and he thanked them for carrying out his instructions loyally and effectively, and without complaining. The government had recently announced a policy in China indicating clearly that there remained a job to be done and his men had risen to the challenge, he declared. He also promised to continue to keep the men fully informed.

The General, however, had spoken prematurely. In the same issue, another story recounted that more than 400 soldiers assembled, though without rancor, at Shanghai's Foreign YMCA, taking over the main ballroom in an orderly demonstration. The men drafted an open letter to Patterson stating Wedemeyer's indication that the American mission in China was a threefold one: to disarm and repatriate Japanese soldiers and civilians; to guard government-owned property in China pending its disposal; and to set in motion the Military Advisory Group. But the facts were that no GIs in Shanghai were involved in Japanese repatriation. Most of this work was being done by 55,000 Marines in North China and some units of the Navy and the Chinese Army. Thus no Army GIs were needed for this work. In addition, the major part of American war surplus had already been sold to the Chinese government. This sale would permit the withdrawal of U.S. personnel from isolated bandit-infested locations in the interior and elsewhere. The letter also charged that Wedemeyer had not been straightforward in his statements about the U.S. Military Advisory Group (MAG) planned to support the Chinese. In a letter to the paper on January 7, Wedemeyer had written that the MAG had not yet received the approval of the government of China or the U.S. But it was the contention of the soldiers' open letter that the Army had no right to "lend-lease" them to the Chinese government. If there were needs for a strong Chinese Army, which an Advisory Group was to assist in developing, then the government should use civilian technicians and volunteers from the Regular Army. The civilian-soldiers had been drafted to serve the nation in a time of war, not to implement postwar State Department policy. With approximately 10,000 troops currently in China, Wedemeyer had also noted that 5,000 additional troops were to be sent in not as replacements for men now in the theater but as a supplementary force. Why was this reinforcement needed when the 10,000 men still in Shanghai seemed superfluous? they asked. The men also requested that soldier representatives from Shanghai be allowed to meet with the Mead Committee, which, because of the troop unrest, had redirected some of its earlier goals of only looking into surplus disposal. It would now also consider the redeployment issue and irregularities in the points system, and would convey GIs' complaints to the proper channels. Their request was granted.[19]

In addition, on January 14, Wedemeyer met with a fourteen-member committee, which included two WACs. He talked things over with them face-to-face, and manifested a measure of disappointment with even the small levels of meetings in Shanghai. He indicated that he deplored protest meetings, stating that he was available personally to deal with GI problems. He said that if any man who could show that he was being held in Shanghai with no cause for retention, he promised to address the matter immediately. He was informed that 300 men were being held in this way, and others as well for the Military Advisory Group. Wedemeyer promised to investigate but indicated that details of the Advisory Group could not be released because of the need for top secrecy in certain State Department policies. Wedemeyer further indicated that he would not bar demonstrations if they were orderly and did not interfere with military work. Subsequently, the men assembled at the race course for another mass meeting. Four men, a corporal, two PFCs and one T-5, were selected to meet with the Mead Committee. The EM did reiterate their deep respect for Wedemeyer but they were determined to discuss their work conditions, noting that the majority of them were simply inactive and essentially were only taking care of themselves.[20]

In a letter to "B-Bag," an "impatient and married sergeant," in a telling criticism, touched on other matters. He noted that, while the Army contended that its presence in China was intended to prevent another war, many others argued that, in fact, this might provoke one. Perhaps more to the point, whether or not there would be another war in twenty or twenty-five years was up to the leaders of the future, and was not in the hands of contemporaries. Meanwhile, men who had faithfully served in the war just ended were being sacrificed to the false theories of various reformers, opportunists and profiteers.[21]

By mid–January, events had reached a breaking point. To be sure, the brass and many other leaders at several levels had responded to the GI demonstrations. MacArthur, who uncharacteristically seems to have been generally responsive to GI demands, lowered points from fifty to forty-eight, and men with thirty-eight months of service were eligible to return to the States. Officers were dropped from seventy points to sixty-eight and forty-seven months of service. At the same time, the Navy indicated that the repatriation of 4,000,000 Japanese from throughout Asia would hasten withdrawal of Marines from North China. By then, 100 LSTs were engaged in repatriating 100,000 Japanese military and civilians monthly. These were being manned by Japanese personnel, thereby releasing 10,000 Navy men for discharge. An additional 100 Liberty Ships would soon be engaged in the same duty. Eisenhower announced that all commands had been cautioned against giving basic-wearied veterans more basic training simply to keep them busy. The Army Air Forces were to release all men with fifty points and forty-two months, no matter what their specialty was.[22]

On January 13, Ike announced that he would address a joint session of Congress that week to discuss GI unrest. In Frankfurt, "harried" General Joseph P. McNarney admitted that the demonstrations there had served a useful purpose by pointing out some things that needed to be addressed and by siphoning off some steam. He met with a soldier delegation and both agreed that no more demonstrations were necessary. Nonetheless, he reiterated that American forces were still required and could not leave Europe immediately because of occupational responsibilities, disposal of surplus property, and control of Nazis and prisoners of war. In Honolulu, Lieutenant General Roy S. Geiger, commander of Marines in the Pacific, forbade Marines to demonstrate, noting that it was traditional for them to go to their commanders with their troubles.[23]

On January 13, in Shanghai, the Chinese, sensing an opportunity to demonstrate for their own reasons, entered the fray when 20,000 Chinese students, of grade school, high school and college level, in an impressive demonstration, marched six abreast in a half-mile-long column, along a two-and-a-half-mile trek, extending from the Foreign YMCA to the Bund. They demanded, in both English and Chinese, that American troops go home. They also had their own agenda, making demands on their own government for freedom of speech, press and assembly, and attacking Nationalists for firing on a recent student demonstration in Kunming where four students and one teacher had been killed. They further insisted on the removal of corrupt officials and prompt trials of traitors. On the following day, another march proceeded through Shanghai's business district, reiterating pleas that U.S. troops go home.[24]

In Washington, various officials did what they could to inform all concerned as to demobilization progress. On January 14, new plans to these ends for the Army, Navy and Coast Guard were revealed. A two-point drop in Coast Guard scores became effective on February 2. The Army ordered the reduction of basic training to six weeks, thereby getting more replacements in the pipeline. The Navy pointed out that it had already released 1,316,299 officers and men from its peak strength of 3,300,000. Similarly, the War Department recorded that 5,000,000 men had been discharged from the Army, which had numbered 8,300,000 at its peak. Also on January 14, Nimitz and Eisenhower went before a joint session of Congress to report on the worldwide servicemen's unrest.[25]

Meanwhile, also on January 14, Secretary Patterson arrived in Shanghai. He was met by officers, officials, and about 1,000 silent and orderly fatigue-clad EM. He was handed a petition for a public meeting. Wedemeyer had earlier met with soldier representatives and asked them to show order and restraint and reiterated that he was in a hot seat and needed their cooperation. He was not worried about their conduct, and knew that they were simply expressing the common feeling about wanting to go home. There was a further injunction: He reminded them that the eyes of the world were upon them and he expected that they would conduct themselves as the gentlemen that they were. Two soldier representatives, Privates First Class David M. Miller and Charles Trenckmann, reminded the men that they had no fight with the Army but merely wanted to go home on points. They further praised Wedemeyer, observing that they had no quarrel with him either, which resulted in a rousing ovation. Wedemeyer further agreed to an elected committee to meet with him weekly.[26]

The letters in "B-Bag" at that time reveal the continued frustrations. One praised Dick Wilson for his accurate portrayal of Marine morale. A joint letter castigated Marine Major General Lemuel H. Shepherd's statement published in the January 1 issue. This argued that they were not professional Marines, as Shepherd had stated, and indeed in their unit, ninety-five per cent were reservists or selective service men. The men stationed in Tsingtao were still bathing out of helmets, their general living conditions were deplorable, and consequently they were experiencing extremely low morale.

The infamous *Stripes*' editorial of January 9 continued to draw flak. One letter, signed by "A Frank Yank," suggested that despite the praise for him, Wedemeyer was not beyond reproach. He should have been asking GIs how they were filling in their time, and had he done so, would no doubt have discovered that some of their thumbs were "swollen from twiddling." Corporal George B. Patterson and twenty-five others resented being kept "ill-at-ease-in-ODs," reflecting the sentiments of another who had declared that being in China and unable to get home was to live the life of a caged wild animal.[27]

Not agreeing to a mass meeting, Patterson did confer with a twelve-man group in closed-door session and stated that Ike's speech later in the day would no doubt answer their questions. Described as a polite listener, Patterson took careful note of what was said. He was also given a lengthy letter outlining GI concerns and promised to put it in the proper hands, adding that he himself would also investigate.[28]

On his part, Wedemeyer agreed to set up a GI representative council. Similarly, soldiers in Manila elected a nine-man committee, which claimed to represent 139,000 men in the Philippines, to present their demobilization complaints to Patterson, due there following his trip to Shanghai.[29]

Meanwhile, testifying before Congress, Ike promised that every enlisted man with forty-five points or thirty months' service would be out of the Army or en route to separation centers by April 30. Also, every man with forty points or two years' service would be out of uniform or in the process of demobilization by July 1. As to their work, or the idle moments that they complained of, Ike observed that one did not send firemen home if they were simply playing checkers on occasion; they might be needed later. Similarly, some servicemen should be retained on duty at a safe level in case they might be required.

Answering another sore point, Ike indicated that indeed points were to be computed from V-J Day, September 2. Admiral Nimitz, who appeared at the same time before Congress, reported that the Navy had kept to its demobilization schedules and therefore there should be no complaints.[30]

In various ways, further attempts were made to meet the demands of the troops. Even the Marine top brass uncharacteristically responded. Major General Louis E. Woods, who commanded the 1st Marine Air Wing in North China, began sessions in his office to hear the complaints of his men, though he pointedly noted that these discussions would only include those who had not demonstrated. In some cases, he started men home who had been overlooked in the general release procedures. Some with personal family problems were also returned.[31]

But the stick as well as the carrot was employed. Soldiering by representative committees was not a familiar, nor generally accepted, feature on the American military landscape. Accordingly, General Eisenhower also banned all further mass demobilization demonstrations, though he left the "gripe door" open for individual complaints. He further instructed theater commanders to release surplus personnel and told Inspectors General to listen to individual complaints. Wedemeyer obeyed, and indicated that the soldier committee that had been set up would function without impediments, because it remained one of his objectives to keep informed as to the views of those under his command. In Frankfurt, Germany, on January 17, General Joseph McNarney, U.S. occupation commander, also followed Ike's instructions and banned all unauthorized demobilization demonstrations.[32]

The combined carrot and stick approach, and other factors, resulted in a quieter mood among GIs worldwide by the end of January 1946. There was also opposition to the demonstrations by some of the men themselves. Sergeant P. Grano, for one, thought that the mass demonstrations on demobilization were disgraceful, and several "Burned-Up Gyrenes" stated that they would be ashamed to set foot on American soil if their return had resulted from such mutinous demonstrations. From Canton, Lieutenant Franklin J. Wallace wrote an engaging letter on the matter. He was in command of a detachment detailed to search for crash victims in the mountains, i.e., some fine GIs, who gave their lives so that some "half-baked 28-point, long-haired renegade shoe clerk could cry when it was all over 'I wanna go home.'" His men lacked privileges, regular mail service, Russian dancing girls, and other amenities, such as PXs, doctors, movies, nightclubs, bars, and a quartermaster, not to mention time for protest meetings. Another letter, from a "Probable World War III Vet," argued that with the war only six months over, the armed services had been slashed by better than half, which left the remaining occupation forces sorely handicapped by losses of key people. This resulted in the work of peace being done in a slipshod manner, all the consequence of the "cry babies" who wanted to get home at all costs. The consequences were that much of the world was again undefended, he declared, allowing Fascist elements to plot World War III.[33]

More thoughtful was a letter from Lieutenant William R. McKenzie, who indicated that while America had won the war on the battlefield, it was being rapidly lost by a too-rapid demobilization. The Army was on its way to disintegration, and consequently the war might just as well have never been fought. Nations that had been conquered had to be occupied to keep them from falling into the same hands as before. In China, the men were being retained because of the State Department, not the War Department. One of the reasons that the war was fought in the first place was that the American people refused to permit their government to participate in world affairs. Isolationism was the culprit. The government seems to have learned a lesson here; it did not appear, though, that the citizenry had learned the same one.[34]

What is often missed in the debates about this phase of wartime service with its attendant bitterness and widespread impatience about getting home was that the men had deep-seated motivations. Those getting home earlier were in a much better position to find jobs. What about housing? And cashing in on the benefits of the GI Bill, which was improved as time went on, making it even more desirable to get in on its benefits? College enrollment slots also had to be secured. There was, of course, the "girl next door," who could not be expected to wait forever. Those already with established families needed to help see to their nurturing. Furthermore, it had been a long war. Those in the Far East were well aware that for Europeans the struggle had commenced in 1939; in Asia, however, the war had begun in 1937.

Beyond this, Americans in general had not had an easy road. Indeed, American citizens, whether servicemen or civilians, had endured a far longer siege than encompassed solely by the war years. There had been the Depression years before the grueling and anxious period of the war itself. It was time to go home and tend to one's own business and that of the family; time to bring an end to the battle on the home front, as well as an end to a wartime stance in the theaters overseas.

This perspective was well understood by many commentators. FDR, in his Philadelphia speech accepting the Democratic renomination on June 27, 1936, prophetically noted, "There is a mysterious cycle in human events. To some generations much is given. Of other generations much is expected. This generation of Americans has a rendezvous with destiny." It has been said that from those to whom much is given, much will be required. But what of a generation to which little was given yet much was also expected? From one perspective, the Depression years seemed almost necessary as a "conditioner" for the nation's preparation for the far greater exertions and harsher demands of World War II. The historian Eric Bergerud has explained, "The generation of young that fought World War II was extremely well suited to the task. The formative event of their time was the Great Depression. Although a dreary period of history in almost every respect, the Depression helped mold a generation of youth uniquely qualified for war."[35]

Another vexing issue having bearing on the widespread unrest was that despite allegations to the contrary, it was well known among American military personnel in China that some of America's efforts were focused on helping Chiang to counter the Communists. Both in Washington and in the heart of Wedemeyer reposed a deep sense that Chiang needed help if he were to forestall the growing power and influence of Communism. There was, however, little support for or understanding of this use of America's resources and manpower within the ranks of the veterans desiring to go home.

The assistance was considerable. In late October, a report in the *Stripes* recorded that the 10th U.S. Air Force had flown 27,000 troops of the Chinese 92nd Army from Hankow to Peiping. This was accomplished in nine days with one hundred C-46s, veterans of flights over the "Hump," bringing in 3,000 men per day. The 443rd Troop Carrier Group had earlier earned a Distinguished Unit Citation for flying the Chinese 6th Army to Nanking. The Peiping move was completed on October 23. The 513th Troop Carrier Group, based at Shanghai's Kiangwan airfield, was also involved. One of its pilots later recorded that moving the Chinese troops was completed in forty-nine days of operational flying, and the airlift "was believed, at the time, to be the greatest mass movement of troops by air in history."[36]

Shortly thereafter, it was reported in Shanghai on November 2 that after moving Chinese 6th, 92nd and 94th armies to Nanking and Peiping, with the loss of three American air crew, the men of the 10th Air Force, under the command of Major General Albert F. Hegenberger, were redeploying to Kunming and Shanghai bound for home. Such movements, according to Wedemeyer, were ostensibly to assist the Chinese in the repatriation of over 1,000,000 Japanese from the China Theater to be disarmed and sent home. But no U.S. men or equipment were to be used in the fratricidal war, as Wedemeyer, among others, stated erroneously. In his memoirs of this period, *Wedemeyer Reports!*, he confessed, "I could not admit that I was endeavoring to stymie the Chinese Communists and their masters in its endeavor to establish its sovereignty over the liberated territories as my directive permitted." He was often "needled" by "Communist-sympathizing American and other correspondents concerning the help I was giving to the Nationalists, under cover of my directive to arrange for the repatriation of the Japanese." Thus baited, he stated, "I tried to remain calm and keep my wits about me so that I would not be betrayed into any indiscreet remark. I answered [these critics] by telling them that I did not formulate policy but simply carried out operations in consonance with directives from Washington." This he did, he wrote revealingly in his memoir, "by interpreting my vague and contradictory instructions from Washington in the most elastic fashion possible."[37]

The culpability of Wedemeyer and others in this regard was apparent to

IX. The Worldwide Collapse of GI Morale

many. Private First Class L.B. Agate, for instance, writing in "B-Bag," charged that while it was true that U.S. troops were not firing shots, they were transporting Nationalist troops into advantageous positions, and as such, Americans should have the courage and honesty to call a "spade a spade." America was plainly helping the Kuomintang troops to wage war against the Communists. Therefore, the consequences accruing from such actions had to be squarely confronted. The editor informed him that General Wedemeyer, at a Peiping press conference on November 8, had admitted that by placing Chiang's troops in North China, the U.S. was materially strengthening the central government's position. But he made it clear that the United Nations officially backed the central government, and that Chiang's troops were the only ones authorized to disarm the Japanese in China. They must therefore be assisted in these actions.[38]

Typical of the attitude of many GIs toward Chiang was that of Roger Tuttrup, a Marine veteran of Okinawa. He was initially sent to Peiping as a mortarman, and later to Taku, a port city in East China, as an MP. He noted that their ostensible duty was to repatriate the Japanese, but the real purpose, he affirmed, was to keep Chiang Kai-shek in power and hold the Communists at bay. He and his buddies, however, "hated Chiang Kai-shek. 'Cause it was all rich people. I met people there that were classier than anybody I've ever met in the United States. With paintings, tapestries, real wealth." By way of contrast, the Chinese peasants were so poor that they "would throw babies away. Somebody had thrown away a baby and there were some wild dogs. These dogs were eatin' up the baby." Therefore, though their own life was not too dangerous, and "we had cheap girls [and] cheap liquor," they were protecting the very corrupt government of a "lousy son of a bitch," and that was not acceptable. Influential Americans such as Henry Luce, the publisher of *Time* and *Life*, an avid supporter and apologist for Chiang, were also suspect. Tuttrup noted that the Marines once held a parade in Luce's honor. As a result, he declared, after the war he switched to *Newsweek*.[39]

But the inconsistencies and lack of clarity regarding U.S. foreign policy continued to vex many service personnel. A frank editorial in the *Stripes* in the midst of the troop demonstrations argued that the U.S. State Department must decide precisely what America's postwar policy would be. Muddling through, as was the case formerly, had failed and the worldwide troop unrest was a clear indication of this. Key would be a consideration as to just what America's mission was in winning the peace, the number of troops needed and the source of those troops.[40]

Mixed in with the debates regarding getting everyone home was the question of continuing the draft. Here, though, there were reports that 360,000 volunteers had been inducted into the armed forces and that an all-volunteer force was now possible. There was apparently no need for continuing conscription nor for keeping men who were not volunteers in service any longer. This influx took some of the strain off the pressures demanding accelerated demobilization. Among the men were many reenlisting while still overseas. Even some officers, notably those with reserve commissions, exchanged their bars, oak leaves and even eagles for master sergeant stripes in the Regular Army. One of these was former Lieutenant Colonel Raymond C. Griffin of Atlanta, Georgia, who declared, as he was sworn in, that the life of an enlisted man was definitely preferable.[41]

The new men were no doubt in part enticed to enter the armed forces by the aura of glory which hedged the armed forces, notably the Air Forces. Despite the heavy losses sustained by such units as the Eighth Air Force in the European Theater, the glamour of the silver wings had a strong appeal. The U.S. Air Force, which was soon to be established as a separate branch of service, found itself consequently well-launched. Wartime propaganda, including numerous war films, further stimulated the recruitment drives. Interviews with those reenlisting in the armed forces also revealed that many did so because of uncertain labor conditions back home. Others wanted to travel, and some, such as aspiring medical personnel, wanted to obtain free technical and specialized instruction before enrolling in a medical school.[42]

Another substantial boost was the worldwide recruiting drive authorized by the Recruiting Act of 1945, announced on November 18. Intended to enroll a million men into the Regular Army, it provided generous terms, benefits and privileges heretofore unknown. Some provisions, reflecting the various hearings on the brass's privileges, discussed above, were extended to enlisted men. Military personnel could now retire after twenty rather than the previous thirty years of service. An immediate ninety-day enlistment furlough, in addition to a regular annual furlough, was authorized. Travel pay, at the rate of five cents per mile, was also provided for those on leave. The highest temporary grade attained could be held in the new period of enlistment by those then on active duty. Those enlisting for three years could select the arm and theater in which to serve. Benefits of the GI Bill of Rights would also be available to those reenlisting.[43]

Certainly, recruits were needed, as a report released in Oklahoma City on November 20 by Lieutenant General Ira C. Eaker, Deputy Commander of AAF, made clear. He declared that soon the AAF would be reduced to 200,000 men from its peak strength of 2,494,400 and 5,000 planes from 70,000. Yet, this low figure was offset by an announcement in Washington on November 18, that the Convair B-36 *Peacemaker* was ready. Dwarfing the B-29, it possessed great range and could deliver atomic bombs to any target in the world. Nor was this all. Another report, released in Dayton, Ohio, on November 21, revealed that the Army Air Forces were embarking on ambitious high-tech programs. This looked forward to General Arnold's conception of the "push-button war" of the future which could be fought with fewer rank and file airmen, though it would need more highly trained technicians than ever before.[44]

IX. The Worldwide Collapse of GI Morale 109

As the winter unfolded and spring arrived, things calmed down. The actions of the high command in righting some wrongs had contributed to the situation. In addition, the passage of time, during which many men were shipped home in the normal course of events, alleviated much of the stress. Nonetheless, for those remaining, their patience was continually tried. In the circumstances, the ships that would take them to the States remained a focal point and, in one case, became the stuff of legend, if only locally and fleetingly. This concerned the USS *General Hugh L. Scott* (AP-136) which was scheduled to take home 1,650 GIs who had been waiting for some weeks since early February to board her. To these persistently impatient men, she seemed to be a phantom vessel rather like the fabled Flying Dutchman. The agonizing pace of the developing story was captured by the paper's writer-turned-poet John Davies, in his poem "Excelsior" (with apologies to Henry Wadsworth Longfellow). He wanted to know, in no uncertain terms, "wot is wot," and especially, "Where in Hell is the General Scott?"[45]

Yet, on February 20, the paper had published the text of a War Department radio cable which clearly stated that the ship's delayed arrival was not the consequence of any authorized change in its schedule made in China but the results of the Navy's sailing instructions, which called for a modified Great Circle route from Seattle to Jinsen, Korea. This course required seventeen days and eight hours en route. The *Scott*, therefore, was not due in Shanghai until February 28. The paper's readers apparently took little heed, clearly not wanting to hear such news, and persisted in their irritation.

After a painful wait, at last a ray of hope appeared and the exciting news broke that on February 28, the specter—according to a special FLASH! column on the front page of the March 1 issue—had been sighted off the Yangtze. Because of choppy waters, however, she would not arrive for another day, and would then anchor at the estuary's Woosung docks before proceeding into the Whangpoo River to tie up in Hongkew.

On March 2, the paper proudly published a photograph of the Kaiser-built vessel on its front page, taken just after it had docked the day before. The ship disembarked 840 welcomed replacements for the China Theater, retaining on board 1,194 troops from Korea who were also homeward bound. The ship's crew were harassed about their alleged lateness, and were told that the *General Scott* had been demoted and rechristened the *Private Scott* for its tardiness. The ship's first lieutenant, Lieutenant Commander Robert Somes, however, declared that they were in fact on schedule and that they did not know that they were famous until that day. Obviously, the Navy's sailing procedures did not harmonize with the dreams and plans of the waiting GIs. In any event, the passengers were elated that the ship was no phantom. Due to sail to Seattle, it departed Shanghai on March 5—on schedule.[46]

When the paper could, then, it reported good news pertaining to homecoming. For instance, in the March 25, 1946, issue an article appeared about the conditions at Seattle, the last lap home for many coming into the States from Asia. Though the men on the *Scott* would not read the article, undoubtedly many of them had already experienced what it described. Though such articles may well have stimulated the men's impatience, they must have also been read with a sense of high expectations. This stated that some 500,000 troops would be expected in the following months. The arrival would be all that one could ask for and was described in glowing detail. It featured a welcome boat, with an Army band, beautiful girls and various entertainers on board. The band would continue to play as the ship docked, though it was not recommended that any overexuberant GI dive in the water for an early welcome kiss as one soldier had recently done. The Seattle waters were usually quite cold even in the spring. Normally, at port side, at the order to debark, the troops would surge down the gangplank, weighed down no doubt by their souvenirs, often featuring "meatball" pennants and samurai swords. If relatives were waiting, a few minutes were allotted for greetings. They would then board trucks for the seven-mile trip to the staging area at Fort Lawton. One of the first things on the agenda was their first Stateside meal, loaded with fresh vegetables, potatoes, hot biscuits, lettuce and tomato salad. There was also fresh butter surrounding a thick, juicy steak. Then, if there was room, there was also ice cream, pie, and of course, all the cold milk that one could wish for, a not inconsequential boon. A brief orientation session followed, where papers were distributed, and the troops then proceeded to a 260-foot-long supply counter where they were fully re-equipped with a complete class "A" uniform. Another formation brought the men to a place to check baggage for the special train which carried them to the reception center nearest to their homes. The entire process had been greatly accelerated and some men only spent six hours on base before finding themselves on the train headed home, though more time was required for others. The account proudly reported, however, that it was a rare instance when more than twenty-four hours were required to complete the process. Though rail was the usual means of transport, some fortunate New Englanders and East Coast personnel flew home on one of the four flights that departed daily. Obviously, the congestion at the West Coast ports, which had fouled up the arrival of thousands of troops during Christmas in 1945, had been solved.[47]

At long last, the inactivation of the China Theater was announced, effective on May 1, bringing an end to the tumultuous preceding months. On April 1, Wedemeyer had stated that the China Theater would cease to exist. Secretary of State Byrnes admitted that this was a move to counter Soviet and Chinese Communist propaganda about the presence of American troops in China. Hopefully, this would make the Communists more amenable to the efforts of General Marshall to negotiate an end to the Chinese civil war. The differences of opinion between Marshall and Wedemeyer as to the extent that America should support Chiang was no doubt an additional factor in making the decision. Naval and Marine operational control reverted to Admiral Cooke of CIN-

IX. The Worldwide Collapse of GI Morale

PAC and Army operations were placed under the direction of the U.S. Army Forces in China (USAFC). Wedemeyer had assumed command of the Theater in October 24, 1944. At its peak it had 65,000 Army personnel, reduced to 6,000 by the end of April. Discharges of the remaining men were to proceed as rapidly as possible. The men in Chungking were also to be withdrawn when the Chinese formally moved all governmental activities to Nanking, also about May 1. Wedemeyer and his staff departed Shanghai on April 4. Also on April 1, in Tsingtao, it was announced that by the end of the month, the famed 6th Division of U.S. Marines, which had been organized on Guadalcanal in September 1944, and which had won distinction on Guam and Okinawa, was to be deactivated. This was accomplished by disbanding the 15th, 22nd and 29th Regiments, while the famed 4th was kept intact and sent to the newly-formed 3rd Brigade in Tokyo, which was formed at the same time as the deactivation. This action reduced the Marine forces in China from 53,000 to about 34,000. These numbers would be steadily reduced in the coming months.[48]

X

The Effects of Soldier Unrest on the Soldier Press

"The power of the press is great, but not so great as
the power of suppress."
—Lord Northcliffe (1918)

The furor surrounding the troop demonstrations had untoward consequences for soldier newspapers, contributing to and accelerating their substantial diminution in the months following World War II. In particular, this involved various editions of the *Stars and Stripes*. Throughout the history of soldier newspapers in the United States the issue of censorship was a perennial concern. There were also frequent disagreements about the degree to which readers could express themselves and, in addition, the extent to which enlisted men could exercise real power in making decisions about the content in and the management of their press. There were always a certain number of brass who despised the very notion of a soldier press, certainly one with EM control or significant involvement. Then, too, there was the question regarding freedom of the press issues in a military setting.[1] The soldier demonstrations brought several of these factors into focus. Coupled with them was not only concern with the management of the points system and the relatively slow pace of redeployment to the States, but the controversial caste system in the services. Accordingly, how these issues were reported in the press became a matter of great moment.

A short time before these matters fully emerged, the China *Stripes* had warmly praised the Honolulu edition of the *Stars and Stripes* as a "Bible of Free Expression." Don Whitehead, who wrote the article, lauded the paper as a model of openness which rapped brass hats, rebuked Congress and spoke its mind about official double talk on demobilization, which it charged was confusing Pacific soldiers and sailors, causing them great unhappiness. The Honolulu paper, which was born in May 1945, consistently supported enlisted men on all occasions, and it had upheld freedom of the press despite attempts by heavy brass to muzzle its GI editorial staff. The paper boasted a circulation of over 90,000, forty percent of which were sailors, though it was officially an Army paper. Its liberal policy was ascribed to Lieutenant General Robert C. Richardson, Jr., commander of the Army forces in the mid–Pacific Theater, who consistently supported the paper's board of editors when high-ranking officers suggested editorial control. For example, when in September a certain brigadier general ordered supervision and control of all editorial matter in the paper, Richardson refused. Similarly, when a colonel posted an order stating that information, news items or gripes to any source for publication must be forwarded through the public relations officer, Richardson had it promptly rescinded. This positive pattern soon deteriorated, however, when the Honolulu edition advanced a strong stance against the military caste system. This led to difficulties with General Richardson, who ordered the Honolulu edition to cease publishing soldier letters and to refrain from criticizing the high command. The paper complied, though it continued to charge that it functioned under duress. Only a few weeks later, however, on January 30, 1946, without explanation, the Honolulu paper ceased publishing and its staff was sent home.[2]

The Shanghai *Stripes* likewise did not fail to deal with the subject of a free soldier press. It took strong exception to a statement made by Brigadier General Charles T. Lantham, director of the War Department's I and E section, in which he defined his version of freedom of the press. In his view, soldier papers were entitled to the same freedoms as the Hearst or Scripps-Howard chains. But, he went on, reporters for these papers would not normally attack either Mr. Hearst or his policies. Were they to do so, they would be fired. Why then, he asked, should the staffs of soldier publications feel entitled to attack War Department policies and high officers who are responsible for their formulation? To this position, the *Supplement* editor of the *Stripes* responded that, nonetheless, even the Hearst papers printed letters which attacked the owner and his policies. So did "B-Bag" columns in the *Stars and Stripes*, even when they do not necessarily reflect the staff's opinions. The source of ninety-five percent of criticisms leveled at the Army were in the "B-Bag." A major criticism of Lantham lay, however, in his comparing the War Department to a regular publisher. The real publisher of the *Stripes* was in effect the citizens of the United States. Lantham also failed to realize that in a democracy, men of the Army could get their stories presented in Congress and in the press at home. Finally, General Wedemeyer made it clear that he wanted his troops to be free to express their gripes and he had a commendable record of trying to right any wrongs detected. If the general had to wait for the usual channels to get information as to what his men were thinking, he would not be able to respond as quickly as he often did. This was reason enough, if others did not exist, for a free soldier press.[3]

These concerns also surfaced in the Marine camp. The Shanghai *Stripes*' editor charged the Marines with blatant censorship when the December 27 issue of the paper, which contained an article written by Dick Wilson about low morale and deplorable conditions in North China, had been banned by Marine commanders. Nonetheless, smuggled copies found their way into Marine hands. The editor protested to Wedemeyer that all readers must have free access to news. An unnamed Marine private first class, in a letter to the paper, confirmed that a copy had been spirited out of Shanghai. Needless to say, he reported, the local newspaper, the *North China Marine*, firmly under the heel of the brass and widely regarded as simply a "house organ," had nothing to say about the conditions that Wilson reported in the *Stripes*. The private demanded freedom of the press even for Marines.[4]

Further examples of news censorship arose. For one, the Army ordered its radio station XUSF in Chungking to soft-pedal reports of GI demonstrations and assigned an officer to carry out the order. Staff members of the *Daily Pacifican* paper, published in Manila, further reported that instructions from the top had denied their right to print news which reflected criticism or dissatisfaction with official policies of the War Department or theater commanders. A similar censorship descended upon the Honolulu and Tokyo editions of the *Stripes*, which even proscribed dispatches from the United Press and Associated Press agencies. Colonel W.E. Waters, in charge of the Education and Information Section of the Armed Forces in the Western Pacific, stated that supervision of subject matter in letters in the mailbag columns had also been found necessary. General Richardson, however, reopened the columns after a one-day blackout, at least for a time.[5]

But in February, the issue of a free soldier press surfaced in a major way at the Tokyo edition of the *Stripes*. This was not surprising because it was generally known that MacArthur was never comfortable with a free soldier paper. The news broke from Tokyo that the managing editor of the *Pacific Stars and Stripes*, published in Tokyo, T-3 L. Pettuis, and Tech. Sgt. Barnard Rubin, a feature columnist who authored the paper's "Japan Today" column, were notified on February 11 that they were relieved from duty and sent to a replacement depot on Okinawa for reassignment. The action was taken on the orders of Colonel John F. Davis, commanding the Information and Education Detachment of MacArthur's headquarters in Tokyo, under whose supervision the *Stripes* appeared. He said that the transfers were necessary because the pair did not fulfill the qualifications for their job. In response to this action, eleven members of the fifteen-member staff asked for a full investigation by General MacArthur. The staff charged that the orders stemmed in fact from the censorship issue, which was an outgrowth of the uprisings among GIs. Specifically, they noted that in their opinion these transfers were linked with the statement signed by members of this staff on January 9 which charged that open and implied pressure had been brought to bear to delete, distort and otherwise dilute news items in a way calculated to serve the personal and professional interests of the Army hierarchy rather than presenting the unvarnished facts. Davis denied this, noting that the men were not qualified and this determination was his alone and did not come from anyone in higher authority.[6]

Immediately, MacArthur's Chief of Staff, Major General R.R. Hall, ordered a stay of the transfers so that the case could be investigated. The letter by the staffers had proceeded through channels to MacArthur via Davis, who, however, rejected it as an irregular procedure and in his rejection also held that the signers were plainly not familiar with the articles of war. Nonetheless, Davis acknowledged that the matter had been brought to MacArthur's attention and an investigation was already underway.[7]

The issue that Davis was really acting on, or used as an excuse, was that the two Tokyo *Stripes* men had failed a loyalty check. This check was in accordance with a War Department radiogram of January 20, 1946, which arrived in the midst of the GI uprisings, and which ordered the immediate screening of Information and Educational personnel to establish their complete loyalty to the United States. This prompted eighteen of the paper's staffers in Tokyo to send a telegram to the Chairman of the House and Senate military affairs committees asking an investigation of the Army policy and the procedure that permitted branding men as disloyal to their country without giving them an opportunity to defend themselves. In response, three congressmen asked the Army for a full investigation of the Tokyo incident. Sergeant Rubin also requested that Colonel H.P. Dittmore of the Inspector General's office in Tokyo provide evidence of his disloyalty, and demanded that if none was found then he would ask for a public retraction, an apology and his reinstatement to the staff of the Tokyo *Stripes*.[8]

Meanwhile, in the Shanghai *Stripes*' February 18 issue's "B-Bag," Sergeant A.P. Levine, of the USMCR, attacked the "cantankerous, vitriolic" syndicated columnist Westbrook Pegler, whose column dated January 23 had directed all the bile and spleen he possessed at GI journalism, especially smearing the *Stars and Stripes*. Pegler's charges were far-reaching. Such journalism, he averred, should be banned. Singling out the *Stars and Stripes*, he wrote that when this publication came along, Communists and "Pinks" first promoted a great expansion of such journalism and then contrived to plant themselves on the staffs of these publications or elsewhere in press relations offices. As data in Army intelligence had positively determined, he concluded, their purpose was to sit out the war without being killed or hurt, all the while acquiring information and attaining influence for use in the future. Levine charged that Pegler, "a vicious, underhanded inksniper," was once again waving the red herring, a stunt that he had often performed since becoming a brown-nosed literary hack at the disposal of any bigot who had the money bags to keep his rice bowl full. In fact, Levine continued, the rapid expansion of GI journalism was a natural attempt by Yankee initiative to keep pace with the phenomenal growth of the armed forces. It was neither novel nor cowardly for men who did not have direct contact with the enemy to be in the Army. In fact, the great majority of soldiers were in this category. Pegler had deplored the rights of service newspapers to employ the most vicious of these "guttersnipe gossips" as correspondents and columnists, who possessed the right to publish the most disruptive rumors about superior officers. Levine charged that Pegler was perturbed because "enlisted men all over the world [now had] a device whereby they too can castigate." He concluded that the Army must be praised for correcting many wrongs brought to light because it gave the "opportunity for the beacon of criticism to glow continuously."[9]

But Pegler had allies. One was Ernie Anderson, counsel for the House Un-American Activities Committee, who had stated in Washington on January 23 that there was evidence that Communists had agitated among some of the U.S. soldiers who had demonstrated. He alleged that this was especially true in Frankfurt, Germany. A New York City organization — unnamed but clearly a Communist one — had circulated handouts which indicated that U.S. foreign policy was all wrong and implied that the soldiers were being kept overseas solely for political reasons. Anderson's and Pegler's attitudes were among the first rumbles which would peak in the Joseph McCarthy era in the 1950s, when the noxious weeds of distrust and suspicion would sorely plague the nation.[10]

In the meantime, MacArthur acted on a report of the Inspector General's office in Tokyo. This recommended that Rubin and Pettuis be transferred, their release based on the grounds of questionable discretion and integrity, though their loyalty to the U.S. remained unsullied. The two men were to be sent to the replacement depot at Yokohama for normal reassignment, instead of to Okinawa as originally ordered, on February 7. There was also a recommendation by MacArthur's counterintelligence section on January 29 that they not be assigned to any sensitive duty. Their questionable discretion and integrity stemmed from the fact that each held membership in the American branch of the Communist Party and had at times infused their writings with Communist thought. This action prompted the editor of the Shanghai *Stripes* to note that the word "sensitive" had taken on new meaning in Tokyo and that anyone on the staff of the *Stripes* there could not have the most innocuous original idea. Thus, all staffers had to agree with the current chief or they were not regarded as qualified to hold down a "sensitive" job there. He questioned why this might be, concluding that this development at the Tokyo *Stripes* was happening in Japan, where the emperor still sat serenely on his throne. He asked whether it could be that it was more of a crime for one to have lived in the United States and been listed as a member of the Communist Party, than to have lived in Japan and openly and defiantly stabbed America in the back. Some readers, such as an Air Forces major writing to "B-Bag," asserted that the answer was an emphatic yes. At least the Japanese were loyal to their established government, he argued, while it was impossible for a member of the Communist Party to be loyal to the Constitution and to America. Thus, he concluded, even an open attack against another nation, no matter how barbarously executed, was certainly more honorable than an insidious undermining of one's own government.[11]

Upon further reflection about the Tokyo case, the editor of the Shanghai *Stripes* in another editorial asserted that an ominous threat — which he hoped was unintentional — to America's traditional press freedoms had appeared in Japan when General MacArthur upheld the removal of two staff members of the Tokyo *Stripes*. He noted that the terms "questionable integrity and discretion" were arbitrary, and could be twisted into a justification to oust anyone who did not agree completely with his higher-ups' views. Nonetheless, he recognized something of the complexity of the case, and changed tack concerning his judgment of the Tokyo *Stripes*' writers. He asserted that the Inspector General's report alluded to a far sounder basis for arriving at a decision. This was Rubin's and Pettuis's apparent intention to misrepresent the news. This was not acceptable, and when an editor or writer presented the news in a biased manner to advance his own personal beliefs, he thereby separated himself from the fraternity of *Stars and Stripes* newsmen. Such bias betrayed the multitude of GI readers who looked to their papers for a factual presentation of the news, and was the yardstick to be used in measuring all newsmen, he concluded.[12]

The Tokyo *Stars and Stripes* did not lose altogether in its confrontation with the high brass, but nevertheless, what it forfeited demonstrated the importance of the attitudes of the commander-in-chief in the specific area of operations as to the admissibility of a free soldier paper. This was borne out in another case, this one involving the Mediterranean *Stripes*. In Rome, on March 18, the paper announced it would discontinue its popular "Mail Call" feature rather than submit it to the commanding general's supervision. The entire staff of fifty-five threatened to resign unless censorship was lifted, and Major Hal Kestler, the publications officer, sent protests to the nation's highest leaders, including President Truman, Secretary of War Patterson, and Chief of the Army's General Staff, General Eisenhower. Kestler charged that as per orders of Lieutenant General John Clifford Hodges Lee, his staff was to supervise letters written to the "Mail Call" column. On March 20, the War Department upheld Lee's right to act as he had, but offered no explanation of its position.[13] Finding no relief, Kestler reported on March 28 that he had been removed as publications officer and that the paper's entire staff of fifty-one men and three junior officers had asked to be assigned to other duties. Kestler had also requested that Lee court-martial him to get at the true facts of his administration.[14]

Whatever transpired, which is not altogether clear, in Rome on April 1, Lieutenant Colonel A.D. Clark, the new officer in charge of the Mediterranean paper, announced that General Lee had rescinded the order of March 13, requiring the paper's GI letter column be approved before publication. Kestler, however, was not reinstated, but he withdrew his request for a court of inquiry and the remainder of the staff of three officers and fifty-one enlisted men also agreed to drop their request for reassignment. Kestler stated that in fighting and winning the battle, he had been a casualty but was perfectly willing to make the sacrifice.[15]

These developments in the midst of the GI demonstrations resulted in the soldier press's being put on the defensive, though it won some of what proved to be short-term victories. It was still recognized, however, that in theory, at least, and for the moment, a free soldier press remained a useful and desirable institution. These conclusions were advanced in an editorial in the April 2, 1946, issue of the China *Stripes*. The editor noted that Bill Mauldin had recently told a board probing the Army caste system that in areas where the troops had their own papers, got straight news and were allowed to blow off steam, as in letters to the editor columns, there was less tension. Mauldin had further declared that if soldiers everywhere had their own free press, there would be no need for the gripe board then investigating the Army's caste system. He stated that while both the Tokyo and Rome editions had been muzzled, when he worked as a cartoonist in Europe under Eisenhower he enjoyed complete freedom of expression, but that other soldier journalists had not been so fortunate. As the Shanghai edition's editor explained, there was a certain amount of pride in both officers and enlisted men alike when they could pick up their own military newspaper and find, not handouts, blue-penciled news or communiqués fit only for simpletons, but the same kind of news they demanded and generally got from their newspapers back home. He further argued that a free press for military personnel and civilians alike was one of the reasons the war had been fought. To be sure, the editor concluded, the Shanghai paper did not have a censorship beef and never had one. Of that they were proud, but not particularly grateful. Being among those who advocated a free GI press, the Shanghai staffers considered that the absence of a brass knuckle in their mouths was simply the norm to be expected.[16]

As time passed, however, conservative Regular Army attitudes eventually prevailed and as many of the protesters and other critics of the Army system were discharged, the proponents of the free soldier press and their views became far fewer. The soldier press, lacking the leavening influences of the citizen soldiers and their democratic principles as pertaining to the free press, waned, and was altered almost beyond recognition. Undoubtedly, the strife of the redeployment crisis contributed to this development. Beyond this, some GI papers lacked the moxie to take on the military establishment, making the stands of such stalwarts as the Rome *Stars and Stripes* all the more noteworthy. One paper, for example, which weakened its stance from that of its origins as a bona fide GI newspaper was the *CBI Roundup*. Late in its career, it was widely regarded as simply a tool of the high command, making its soldier-journalists appear as so many "Mr. Milquetoasts." As Bud Hutton and Andy Rooney explained in their book, "for a long time *The Stars and Stripes* was part of the free press."

Eventually, however, "the soldiers who published it lost their fight against martial law and the paper became pretty much of a military house organ. But that happened only long after S&S had spun its pin-wheeled way into the hearts of the doughboys...."[17]

XI

The Marines

Semper Fi

As always when considering United States military affairs, the distinctions among the several branches of service have to be taken into account. This was as true in the China Theater as in any other. This had an impact on the content and operations of the Shanghai *Stripes*. Because the paper had been created as a paper for all the armed services in the Theater, their differences and unique requirements had to be considered. J.K. Perloff, though of the U.S. Naval Reserve, thought that he knew something about that distinct arm, the Marine Corps, as manifested in a poem he addressed to them. Labeling them a most austere outfit, with their dignity and strength, he said that they, like the fabled Cabots and Lodges of Boston, answered only to God. They were unmistakable with their glittering gold braid and their uniforms' sheen, so they must therefore be of the species that were known as Marines. Perhaps even Mars, the mighty war god, should not unleash his sword, nor even stir, until the Leathernecks gave him the word, Perloff alleged. Not only that, the sun never set nor the moon beamed unless authorized by the Marines.[1]

To the Marines in China in 1945 and 1946, however, there seemed little that they could authorize or command. They hardly appeared in charge at all; in fact, they seemed to be at the whim of numerous forces many of which they could not comprehend. They had marched into China fresh from hard service on Okinawa and elsewhere, and may have well expected some respite from what they had endured. Instead, they found a kaleidoscopic, tumultuous, topsy-turvy world. Numbering about 53,000 men, they were located in North China, principally in Peiping, Tientsin, Taku, Chinwangtao and Tsingtao. Some also patrolled the railroads and guarded rail cars from the Tungshan coal fields to Chinwangtao and along the Chinwangtao-Tientsin line.[2]

Undoubtedly, the situation in China at the time contributed to sending mixed signals to the Marines. They were well aware of the traditions and exploits of the Old China Hands of the Marine Corps in the 1920s and 1930s. The famed

4th Marine Regiment, for example, had been stationed in Shanghai from 1927 until 1941. Other Marines served as the guards at the U.S. Legation in Peking. From March 1938, still others had been in Tientsin, where they had relieved the U.S. Army's 15th Infantry Regiment stationed there since 1912. This duty had been coveted by men in the prewar Marine Corps, and for the men lately arrived from bitter battles in the Pacific, a China assignment still had much appeal. But the Marines found their situation difficult to assess. While many of them had been welcomed with open arms, as in Tientsin, for example, they also found themselves in the midst of the intensifying civil war in China between Chiang's Nationalists and the Communists. Officially, they were to maintain a strict neutrality, but the American commanders in the China Theater were not of one mind in this regard. There was also ambivalence in Washington, and no clear-cut policy was in place. In the event, on occasion, Marines were used to assist Chiang's troop movements into North China, which, however, provoked armed clashes with the Communists, as well as resulting in blown tracks, train derailments and ambushes. Inevitably, the Marines sustained casualties. Though these amounted to a mere handful compared to the toll from the island campaigns so lately concluded, they were particularly hateful because the war was supposed to be over, and the rising casualty list loomed large to the men who then manned the isolated guard posts and rode the dusty coal trains of China.[3]

The Japanese presence was another disruptive factor with no clear-cut solutions. There were over a million Japanese soldiers and civilians present in North China. Many of the soldiers were still armed, and their surrender and disarming needed to be formally accepted. They also, together with the civilians, had to be repatriated. In some instances the Japanese were allowed to keep their weapons and to assist in guarding railroads, coal supplies and military stores, as well as to help keep the Communists and Chiang's Nationalists apart. On occasion, Marines and armed Japanese troops stood shoulder-to-shoulder, no doubt, creating awkward situations for both. In addition, the disciplined strength and tactical and technical know-how of the Japanese appealed to both sides in the Chinese civil war, and local Communist and Nationalist commanders, sometimes hard pressed for man power, attempted to recruit their former enemies as allies. Fortunately, the Japanese caused little difficulty because most of them were more than eager to quit China and return to Japan. One official Marine document also noted that the Japanese respected and even feared the Communists, and that they were quite willing to free themselves from the incessant forays, ambushes, and sabotage.[4]

Certainly, the conditions in Peiping were surprising. Some 3,060 Marines had entered the city in October directly from the battlefields of Okinawa, going from the worst to the best of conditions. They took up their quarters in the old Marine Barracks of the Legation Guard, which had ceased to exist on December 8, 1941, when the Japanese imprisoned the guards. The Marines were captivated by the charm of the old Manchu capital that had not been harmed during the war, particularly its soothing, tree-lined, quiet streets, and its palaces. Indeed, one sometimes forgot that even in the midst of savage war, life simply went on relatively undisturbed at several levels as it did in wartime Peiping. After the war had ended in September, the Japanese were still in the city in large numbers, many fully armed, and relations between them and the Marines were governed by strict military courtesy and discipline. As they traveled through the streets of Peiping on their business, the Japanese threw prompt salutes, though these were usually met by blank stares from the Marines. There had been some alarms but in general, unlike Tientsin and Shanghai, Peiping was a slow-paced town. There was some night life, but shopping and sight-seeing were also popular, as was the regular showing of movies in the barracks. The Red Cross had opened a club in the former Italian Embassy and many activities were conducted there. The Marines in Peiping also turned some attention to entertaining their buddies coming up from Tientsin for visits.[5]

In North China, the shores of the Gulf of Pechili and the Shantung Peninsula were under Communist control except for the major cities. The decision to order Japanese troops to surrender only to Kuomintang or U.S. troops had the effect of aligning Japanese and puppet groups against the Communists. As representatives of Chiang's forces, the Marines therefore came under suspicion by the Communists as serving as a Kuomintang spearhead. Marines in Peiping had come under some sniper fire from Communist forces as well. Indeed, by mid–November, both Peiping and Tientsin were virtually besieged, and the Communists controlled the waterways and railroads in these areas. The Nationalist troops flown into Peiping the previous few weeks were in short order overwhelmingly outnumbered.[6]

In this situation, certainly the dangers to the Marines were real enough, and in early November, Wedemeyer admitted that there had been some clashes between the Marines and the Communists. But he stated that the Marines were not the aggressors and that every effort would be made to avoid confrontations in the future.[7]

Even routine patrols were dangerous. Goodfriend, as was his custom, decided to get out of the office and into the field to survey the situation firsthand. He joined a Marine patrol near Peking and described what they encountered. On this occasion, there were twenty Marines led by a major and a lieutenant. They carried carbines, BARs (Browning automatic rifles), .30 caliber machine guns and a defective radio. They suddenly came upon a Communist force numbering about 4,000 heavily-armed men equipped with Japanese rifles, machine guns and mortars. Immediately after contact was made, the Marines "tumbled into a ditch beside the road, deployed as quickly and as well as they could, and prepared to fight if they had to." Of course, tactically, they were in a hopeless situation. Their fate hinged on the intentions of the Communist force, and on blind chance. One shot from either side could have started a fire fight, a massacre and an "incident" leading to who-knew-what end. What happened, instead, "was an example of what ordinary men can do, in serious emergencies, if their intentions are good, their heads cool and their lives at stake." The Marine lieutenant and a Communist captain met by the roadside, a quarter of a mile farther along the road within the Communist lines. They swapped cigarettes, smiles and ding haos. Through an interpreter, arrangements were quickly made for the passage of the Marine party through the lines. Meanwhile, all kept their heads and demonstrated patience, self-control and sensible behavior. Therefore, no one got hurt. Goodfriend admitted that it was not wise nor fair to generalize about such a small incident. Nonetheless, his being on the spot made certain things clear. First, it seemed obvious that the United States, China, and the entire world were sitting on a powerful keg of dynamite. Second, men, on their own, did not want to kill or be killed. Third, ordinary people could smile, smoke, chat and find a peaceful solution to tough problems. Thus, he observed, if this could be done on an open road with simple armed people, and if reason, restraint, friendliness and common sense could prevent a local incident, was there not hope that military chiefs and diplomats could solve matters without triggering another bloody war? Unfortunately, he concluded, the good example that occurred on that country road fell on deaf ears.[8]

Meanwhile, in Tientsin, when the Marines entered on September 30, 1945, the Japanese surrendered and the Marines moved into the former American compound there, though it required much "GI'ing" to shape up the barracks and the area. The city greeted the men with great acclaim, one account noting that the streets were packed with Chinese of all classes and European expatriates, and the trucks and marching troops had to force their way through the happy, flag-waving throngs as they marched to their billets in the former International Concessions. To many of the men, it seemed that the warmth of their welcome must have exceeded that of any other during the war.[9]

The units which arrived in Tientsin were from the Third Amphibious Corps and its 1st Marine Division, arriving from Guam and Okinawa. Business had been continued under Japanese occupation but Japanese currency was occupation money and soon lost its value. Americans, paying in sound currency, produced an immediate business boom because they previously could not buy stuff for their home folks on the islands in the Pacific.[10]

Also in the Tientsin area, the Marines encountered examples of Communist propaganda — paper bullets instead of rifle rounds. Already adept at this form of warfare, the Communists bombarded the Marines with billboard admonitions. The blandishments — in English — had a ring of truth about them, and they also sought to take advantage of the men's desire to return home. They bragged that it was the Communists who had successfully fought the Japanese while the Kuomintang was absent, having left the Communists in the lurch. The Communist 8th Route Army had courageously fought the enemy for the past eight years, during which they had killed, wounded and captured 6,000 of the Japanese and "traitor puppet forces." The signs asked the Marines to inform their officers about this true state of affairs, and encouraged their immediate return to the United States. They did not attack them, but rather extolled their battle records in the Pacific, adding that in the era of peace, it was appropriate that they reap the rewards of their arduous service. Their wives and children were anxiously looking forward to their early return to enjoy a pleasant life at home. While ostensibly the Marines were in North China to disarm the Japanese troops, in reality they were conspiring with those invaders to help the Kuomintang, thereby provoking a terrible civil war. The Marines therefore should carefully consider who they were actually assisting.[11]

There were hazards too, beyond the armed clashes, and a report circulated that two Marines in Tientsin had died after drinking bad booze. Another Marine was shot by a "smiling" Chinese who stole his horse, and an unarmed American Marine sergeant was shot from his mount by three Chinese civilians. This resulted in an order that Marines were not to take horseback rides or excursions in city areas including Peiping, except as parts of large groups on conducted tours.[12]

Another locale where the Marines served was the city and environs of Tsingtao, on the eastern shore of the Shantung Peninsula. This was a former German city held when Germany possessed concessions in China. Here the Marines helped guard and support the shipping in of thousands of Nationalist troops, men of the 8th Central Government Army which poured off U.S. warships into Tsingtao, all provided with American arms and equipment. The streets of that city were then patrolled by 12,000 Marines, though many of the guards were Japanese who were permitted to retain their arms for this purpose. Thus, the Communist complaints that Japanese and American troops were arrayed against them had a sound basis. The Marines also presided over one of the last surrenders of Japanese forces in the Tsingtao area. Major General Lemuel C. Shepherd Jr., commanding the 6th Marine Division, accepted their capitulation on behalf of Chinese government.[13]

But such work hardly elevated Marine morale, as Hal Boyle, a *Stripes* staffer, pointed out in an article in the December 29 issue. In the article, titled "Tsingtao OK — But Not for Marines," Boyle wrote that none of them thought anything positive about the city, and simply wanted to know why they were there. The only American property that they had to guard — alleged to be a major reason for their deployment there — was their own equipment, as one disgruntled Marine put it.[14]

Boyle's remarks were rebutted by General Shepherd, just relieved as the commander of the 6th Marine Division in Tsingtao. Speaking in San Francisco on December 31, on his way to Washington, he stated that the Marines had a job to do in China. A great number of Japanese were left there and they had to be disarmed and repatriated, and the Marines wanted to do their duty because they were professionals.[15]

Shepherd was answered, as one might expect, in the "B-Bag." One letter, signed by "My Morale Is Low," sent verbal roses to Dick Wilson, who plainly understood the feelings of the men he wrote for and about. But General Shepherd was wrong to "snow" the Marines in China with his professional soldier and high morale talk. He advised the General to apprise himself of their true attitudes before speaking for Marines in China. The 53,000 there, he noted, wanted the truth about their lot and their morale to be placed before the public eye, and he praised the *Stripes* for accomplishing that. More pointed was another letter, signed by "25 High Morale? Marines," which observed that there were numerous draftees in the Corps who did not see themselves as professional soldiers. In fact, the letter went on, some ninety-five percent of the Marines in their outfit — not identified — were either reservists or selective service men, all enrolled for the prescribed formula of the duration plus six months. There was a job to be done in China, they recognized, but this was for professional soldiers, which they decidedly were not. They had been stationed in Tsingtao for three months, and were still bathing and washing out of helmets. Others, signing themselves "Disgusted Marines," wanted to know why the Chinese could not disarm the Japs and allow the men who fought the war go home. None of the Marines could be convinced that they were in China for any reason other than serving as a barrier between the warring Chinese armies. As to their guarding China's railroads, Sergeant C. Houchin, in a letter to "B-Bag," concluded that if the Chinese government could fight a civil war, they could surely spare a few of their soldiers to guard their own rail lines.[16]

There were also dangers in the Chinwangtao area threatening the 7th Regiment of the First Marine Division and the 29th Battalion of the 6th Marine Division. There the Marines were engaged in helping to unload the Chinese government's 13th and 52nd Armies from U.S. 7th Fleet vessels. But these activities resulted in Communist reaction, and on November 16, General Wedemeyer threatened to order U.S. aircraft to strafe a Communist-held village near Chinwangtao, unless the small-arms fire endangering U.S. did not cease immediately. While nothing came of this, a later report noted that one Marine had been killed and another seriously wounded at Anshan, about forty miles southwest of Chinwangtao. This was one of the better-publicized armed conflicts that the Marines fought with the Communists.[17]

There was another side to American and Communist relations. Six Marine aircraft crashed on the Tatze Mountain in a snowstorm on the Shantung Peninsula — which was in Communist hands — in December, killing ten men. One bailed out and another was seriously injured; both were found and cared for by the Communists. They were later returned to the Marines.[18]

Despite some positive aspects of the Marines' situation, the sluggish pace of getting the Marine combat veterans home, the slow rate of the repatriation of the Japanese, and the use of American ships, aircraft and manpower to transport Chiang's troops to North China and elsewhere, had resulted in their morale's hitting the skids by the end of the year. Dick Wilson, a *Stripes* correspondent writing from Tientsin in late December, charged that the China Marines were, in fact, cracking up, and that the morale of trigger-happy, battle-weary Marines in North China was at a low ebb. From Tientsin to Chinwangtao, more and more Leathernecks were daily succumbing to deep depression, he asserted. The consequent nightly drunkenness of men still mourning buddies who fell in Pacific campaigns resulted in the wrecking of bars and cabarets, brawls with civilians and other Marines, with occasional shootings. These incidents indicated that nothing else mattered to many of America's fighting men who had had too much fighting, and who only desperately wanted to go home. They had been part of the 10th Army, but it was split up; the high-point Army men were sent home, while the Marines found themselves still in China. They had landed there in full battle gear and expected more fighting from the powerful, well-armed and undefeated Jap army still in place. Things had improved of late, he admitted, but in September and October, officers of many outfits wondered if the Marines' rigid training and discipline would be sufficient to check the tide of resentment that rose when the men became convinced that they were only pawns in a political chess game. Wilson visited with numerous Marines in all conditions and situations and found that all — officers and enlisted men alike — were generally Peter Oboed. Thus, so it seemed, not until the combat-worn, homesick veterans were back home, to be replaced by low-pointers and regular Marines, would the morale of America's Leathernecks in China recover.[19]

With the coming of 1946, the negative attitudes of the Marines were also in evidence in the midst of the worldwide troop disturbances. Accordingly, the Marine high command turned some attention to implementing damage control procedures. They recognized that at the heart of their discontent was that many high-point Marines were still in China. Accordingly, some Marines who had demanded to be shipped home got their wish when it was reported that 5,000 officers and men of the Marines, including 3,600 enlisted men and 100 officers of the Marine First Division and the Third Amphibious Corps, would leave Taku, Tientsin's port. They would sail on the fast Army transport *Wakefield* on January 10. The transport had just brought in replacements for the veterans. Other Marines of the Sixth Division were to depart from Tsingtao when the *Wakefield* made its way there en route to the States.[20]

Also, General Keller E. Rockey, commander of the Third Amphibious Corps, announced in Tientsin that since the Marines had arrived in North China in October, some 16,300 high-point men had already gone home. This reduced Marine strength in North China from a high of 62,000 to 45,000 by about mid–January. He also promised that all U.S. Marines who were eligible under the point rules would leave China, by March 1.[21]

His remarks were reinforced by Brigadier General Louis R. Jones, commanding the Marines in Peiping, who confirmed in early February that Fifth

Regiment Marines who saw action on Okinawa would be started home when replacements arrived later that month. To be sure, it had been a long time since the battle for Okinawa had been fought, but at last something seemed to be working for them.[22]

Thus, though the Marines felt themselves discriminated against, at length there were some decisions made to get them homeward bound. The February 5 issue, for instance, noted that U.S. Marines with forty-five points would go home on March 1, affecting about 5,200 EM and 209 officers. This move was made possible by the impending arrival of 6,300 replacements en route. Also in mid–February, a Marine Corps spokesman indicated that there were then 45,000 Marines in North China patrolling the railroads. Nonetheless, Marine demobilization was said to be ahead of schedule and the Marines in China were in fact then officially regarded as under strength. Not only that, but experienced troops were in short supply. By mid–April 1946, except for a small number of regular offices and NCOs with combat experience, the majority of the Marine contingent consisted of troops fresh from boot camp who accordingly lacked even basic military skills. Though schools were set up in China, because of the press of duties, instruction was accomplished mainly by on-the-job-training.[23]

Marine official records cannot be depended upon to convey the entire story of how the rank and file felt about their involvement in China. For this, the Shanghai *Stripes* helps to fill the void and round out the picture. Two issues in particular involving the Marines were closely followed. One was that of assisting the transporting and repositioning of Nationalist Chinese troops, which continually rankled. These efforts were considerable, involving about 100 LSTs, manned by about 7,000 seamen. These vessels transported more than 100,000 troops of three Chinese armies and their horses to Chinwangtao for rail movement into Manchuria. By mid–December, after five weeks' work, the three divisions of the New Chinese Sixth Army had been unloaded. By year's end, the horses were yet to be shipped. In addition, 42,000 men of the New First Army from Hong Kong and two divisions of 25,000 men of the 71st Army were shipped from Shanghai. Eventually eight armies would be sent into Manchuria.[24]

Another ongoing operation, that of Japanese repatriation, was also a source of Marine discontent. Both sailors and Marines, numbering almost 100,000 men overall, were crewing the LSTs and supporting operations, a most unwelcome duty for the Yanks. They worked under virtual combat conditions. The seas were stormy, the vessels in poor condition, some even having been in collisions, and disease was rampant, especially among the Japanese civilians. Quarantine was not possible. Only a few Chinese could handle the ships, so that most of the burden was borne by American service personnel. Some Japanese ships and crews were also involved but these were under American command.[25]

Nonetheless, some progress was reported. By late January, about 80,000 Japanese military and 86,000 civilians had been transported to Japan. This was at a rate of about 50,000 per month. There remained about 144,000 military and 233,000 civilians to be returned. Soon, however, that problem no longer concerned Americans. A large headline in the *Stripes*, which must have been read with pleasure by all hands, told the story: "US Repatriation Mission Finished; Nips Taking Over." Staffer Dick Wilson proclaimed that the largest part of the China Theater's mission, that of repatriating the Japanese, had been concluded as far as American involvement was concerned. In late January, he wrote that the last American-manned LST had departed China for Japan, marking the end of the three-month-long program which had committed the U.S. to carry out the terms of the Potsdam Agreement. The 100 LSTs had sailed their last trips, having been replaced by Japanese-manned vessels. Some Marines and Army personnel would still be involved in the repatriations, but only in an advisory capacity. The Japanese were using a few LSTs and six Liberty Ships with other ships scheduled for the duty from the fleet of captured Japanese vessels. These would be manned by Japanese crews but under Chinese command. The U.S. Army was then mainly involved with getting Chinese troops to Manchuria, and were treating them medically and equipping them. The LSTs engaged in the repatriation of Japanese were reassigned to this duty. The controversial program was not provided for in the Japanese surrender agreement, as was Japanese repatriation, but had been decided on later as part of U.S. foreign policy instituted by the State Department.[26]

Further evidence of the concern of the Marine high command with the well-being and morale of their troops was manifested when Lieutenant John D. Trawick, a psychiatrist in the 3rd Amphibious Corps, was ordered to analyze the situation. His study demonstrated that the morale among China Marines was greatly improved by early February. While generally rebutting the assertions by Wilson and Boyle in the pages of the *Stripes*, he acknowledged that a few months back, a large percentage of high-point men from combat units had still been in China. These men had come out of the Pacific islands, and their presence in China ushered in an intense period characterized by loud, incessant demands that they be sent home at all costs. But with their departure, Trawick asserted that things were much improved, and very few Marines then in China were so insecure emotionally that they could not function as civilized people.[27]

Yet as Trawick had admitted, there were problems of some magnitude, and ongoing attempts were made to defuse them. For one, the commander of the North China 1st Marine Air Wing, Major General Louis E. Woods in Peiping, on January 17 agreed to hear complaints of his men who had not demonstrated. This was one of a series of "gripe sessions" the general conducted. He heard the airing of the usual mess, clothing, housing and recreational facilities shortcomings. One man had a girl in trouble in the States and Woods sent him home on an emergency leave to sort things out. The most serious complaints he heard had to do with pronounced homesickness, and there were some high-pointers who had been inadvertently left off the homeward-bound complement through clerical errors. A number of these were promptly sent home. At Tsingtao, he had previously heard complaints from two married men whose wives revealed that in the States it was reported that all Marines in China were volunteers for their jobs. They threatened divorces if it were true that their men had chosen China instead of coming home. He sent them to the States on emergency furloughs to convince their wives that they were in fact in China under orders. One private complained that he had tried unsuccessfully for three months to get glasses for his rapidly failing eyesight. The General was incensed and indicated that the man was to be flown to his Tientsin headquarters at once and the doctor there was to be ordered to fix him up, and if necessary the General would pay for the glasses himself. (It was probably not necessary!) Beyond such complaints, the General thought that things were generally in good shape. Thus, though only a few men were assisted, the General's willingness to listen, and to take some action, had no doubt boosted morale.[28]

In another instance, at the height of the turmoil, a constructive step for keeping Marines of the Sixth Marine Division well-informed and dealing with their individual problems was taken in Tsingtao. *The Straight Scoop*, a program aired every Friday night by radio station XABU, was devoted to informing the men of many details that concerned them and fielded questions from the listeners. It had been organized by Major General A.F. Howard, commanding the Division. Reflecting the General's apparent genuine concern regarding the personal affairs of his men, the *Stripes*' editor hoped that further efforts would be made to deal adequately with legitimate problems. If implemented honestly and wholeheartedly, the General's initiatives should succeed, the report concluded.[29]

There were other innovations calculated to raise Marine morale. For one, on November 17, radio station XBOR was launched for the benefit of men of the Marine First Division in Tientsin. In January 1946, Marine commanders negotiated a tax exemption by the city of Tientsin for the twenty percent luxury tax normally charged against all restaurant checks.[30]

Another was the establishment of an Enlisted Men's Club for sailors and Marines. Study courses were also set up for the Marines in Tientsin, and Sergeant William Camp, formerly of the *San Francisco Chronicle* and the journalism faculty of California University, launched a forum for the discussion of world problems. Simultaneously, the Marines launched a touring show, *Stand By for Music*, featuring musical and variety acts, the talent coming from their own ranks. After performing for the Marines in North China, it appeared, to great acclaim, at the Capitol Theater in Shanghai.[31]

Slowly, but more to the point, was that many of the Marines' concerns with demobilization were being met. In the February 7 issue, a note indicated that the Peiping Marines—those of the Fifth Regiment Marines who fought on Okinawa — would be starting home that month when replacements arrived. Also, the *Marine Phoenix* steamed into Shanghai on March 17 bringing in replacements, and departed with more homeward-bound troops. A bit later, Washington announced on March 11 that the Corps would soon slash points so that nearly all Marines with combat service would be released by midsummer 1946. After July 1, length of service would the main factor for discharge. By that date, all women Marine reservists would be eligible for discharge, and by September, nearly all selective service and reserve personnel would be separated. The points required for shipment home were steadily reduced until, on July 1, they were set at twenty-five points for men and zero for women. Also, after July 1, thirty months' service would make a Marine eligible for separation. Beyond that date, the points system would be retained only in consideration of parenthood and for the few remaining personnel who had combat credit.[32]

Things improved for the Marines after this. Under the dateline of Tientsin, April 10, 1946, Major General Keller E. Rockey, commander of the Marine Third Amphibious Corps, announced that all forty-point officers and men would be out of China by April 15.[33]

On May 1,1946, the China Theater was deactivated, and by the end of June 1946, the number of Marines in North China had been cut to less than half of the original strength committed in September 1945, with only 24,252 men remaining. Fortunately, the mission of the Corps was also correspondingly reduced, though clashes with the Communists continued.[34]

The deactivation also resulted in a new designation of Army units there as the U.S. Army Forces in China were placed in the charge of a new commanding general, Lieutenant General Alvin C. Gillem, Jr. Operational control of the Marines reverted to the Commander, Seventh Fleet, and the III Amphibious Corps was directed to contribute to the fleet's mission to support the foreign policy of the United States in China. Though it was not formally stated, this included assisting the United Nations Relief and Rehabilitation Administration (UNRRA), which mounted a major effort to supply China with food, clothing and other materials. China was allotted more of this aid than supplied to any other country, greatly adding to the Marines' security burdens.[35]

The failure of Marshall's mission to China (see account below), which he acknowledged in early 1947, and the growing success of the Communists in the civil war, dictated a steady reduction in U.S. forces committed there. On January 6, 1947, Truman ordered Marshall, acting upon his own recommendation, to return to Washington permanently. This had considerable impact on the Marines, who then steadily reduced their presence in China. By June 21, 1947, they had terminated their activities in Peiping, Tangku and Chinwangtao. This essentially ended twenty-one months of quasi-war with the Chinese Communists. When the last of the Marines cleared Tientsin on September 1, 1947, Tsingtao became the only significant Marine duty station in China. From this base, they were prepared to support American interests in Shanghai,

Nanking or Tientsin, where most American nationals were still living, by infantry assistance and airlifts if required.

The Marines would remain in Tsingtao for some months to come. They were occupied mainly with training and guard duty. The troops enjoyed respites from their routine with extensive liberty privileges, recreation facilities and off-duty educational activities. A considerable number of dependents were permitted to come out from the States, in keeping with a postwar policy of reuniting service families wherever possible. This rather serene state of affairs was marred by the fact that the fighting between the Nationalists and Communists grew steadily more violent and bitter, always raising the possibility of Marine involvement. This continued until late in 1948, when it was apparent that the Communists would soon bring an end to the civil war, emerging as the victors, which had long been foreseen by Wedemeyer, Marshall and numerous other American observers on the ground in China. As the Communist tide rolled toward Tsingtao, the U.S. State Department, in November 1948, ordered American nationals to evacuate China. To protect them, the Secretary of the Navy ordered the 9th Marines, a reinforced battalion then in Guam, to embark for China to Shanghai to assist them. Simultaneously, Marine units in Tsingtao began to withdraw. When the 9th Marine's mission was completed by February of 1949, and they boarded ship in Shanghai, the Marines at Tsingtao also boarded ship and remained afloat in Tsingtao harbor while the Communist drive continued in their direction. In early May, only shipboard Marines were in the area, and the American presence in China ended altogether by June of 1949.[36]

Those Marines who perhaps thought that the service parameters, the attractive conditions of service and salubrious existence of the Old China Marines who had been in China in the 1920s and 1930s would be resumed, were no doubt bitterly disappointed. The war-torn country, riven by a menacing and growing civil war, was a far cry from that which the Marines had served in earlier. From 1945, the Marines, as an instrument of American policy, were first committed to assisting in the disarming and repatriation of Japanese soldiers and civilians. They were also involved in helping the Chinese national government to reestablish its sovereignty over occupied territory. Ordered to avoid involvement in the civil strife — though they appeared to the Communists to be actively involved, which they in fact were — they walked a narrow line. The Marines also supported General Marshall's attempt to secure peace in China, a forlorn hope which failed. The Marines then reverted to their traditional role as protectors of American lives, interests, and property in China. In ever-restricted parameters, the Marines had little scope for action and when the defeat of Chiang's armies forced the final American withdrawal, they provided a security force that ensured the escape of hundreds of Western foreign nationals and many Chinese as well.[37]

XII

The Conduct of Servicemen in Shanghai

"Damned from here to Eternity."
— Rudyard Kipling, "Gentlemen-Rankers" (1892)

From time immemorial, it has been acknowledged that military personnel are often synonymous with bad behavior. As the British poet Rudyard Kipling put it in his poem "Tommy," soldiers do not ordinarily "grow into plaster saints." The Chinese themselves, drawing upon a long experience, intoned in a proverb: "Good men do not become soldiers; good iron is not wrought into nails."[1] Shanghai at war's end seemed an especially likely venue for soldierly disturbances. Nonetheless, for many observers, it was not, for all of that, acceptable or excusable. Bad conduct was simply "bad" in itself, but to the Shanghai *Stripes*' editors it seemed especially deplorable because American military personnel seemed bent upon undermining the hard-earned peace. The resulting morass reflected the nation's loss of the moral high ground, which had been earned by those who had spilled their blood in the battles leading up to the peace.

Rowdyism was mixed with high spirits and high jinks as American soldiers and Marines in from months of rugged duty in China's interior or from the island campaigns, and sailors off ships after long stretches of duty, poured into Shanghai. Their presence transformed the city. They often cheerfully dispensed chocolate and gum to street urchins and, cavorting through the thoroughfares, sometimes took over rickshaws, putting their bewildered drivers into the passenger seats for wild rides through the streets. Their uncouth vivacity, however, horrified the populace and much of their horseplay greatly offended them. Cases of U.S. MPs and Shore Patrol sailors abusing coolies were especially deplored.[2]

An unnamed flight officer also detested this conduct, especially the abuse of Chinese citizens such as the stealing of pedicabs and rickshaws by drunks, the throwing of torpedoes—a form of fireworks—at civilians, and the general use of cursing and bad language. The *Stripes'* prolific writer, Franc Shor, often turned his pen to the subject of American rowdyism. He wrote in one article that four sailors had walked into a honky-tonk, grabbed seven bottles of vodka, and walked out without paying. A few minutes later, a GI slugged a pedicab driver, knocking him into the traffic-jammed street because the coolie rang his bell behind him. Down the street, a bar owner watched helplessly as an Army vehicle smashed into his front window because the occupants did not like the size of the bill they had paid. As to those high prices, a much more effective strategy would simply be not to patronize places charging excessively. In short, he concluded, many Americans were acting like Nazis and Japs, and generally wearing out their welcome in China. The men were urged to police themselves, and try to leave behind friends rather than enemies when they departed.[3]

Carelessness and accidents further blackened the name of the American military forces in Shanghai, keeping the U.S. Army Criminal Investigation Division busy. On one occasion — there were numerous others— a rampaging Army truck, in a hit-and-run accident, left a trail of wrecked rickshaws, pedicabs, autos and trees, together with two dead and three others seriously injured.[4]

The men themselves were not unaware of the difficulties that their conduct caused, which often defeated the efforts of the traditional Shanghai police, mainly huge, red-turbaned, bearded Sikhs from India, a vestige of the former British Imperial presence. One soldier, who attributed much of the problem to alcohol, was Private First Class Arthur F. Ziegfield. In a naive letter to "B-Bag," he complained that he was upset to learn that American soldiers had been carousing around Shanghai until all hours, and also probably drinking, which could lead only to one thing: women. He was pleased to learn of the midnight curfew then put into effect, and hoped that the officer who was responsible was awarded the Legion of Merit. He himself had spent twenty-one months in the interior of China, he declared, and was honored to have been selected to come to Shanghai. Because these men were part of the Army of the United States, the greatest in the world, they should note that there were plenty of things to see and do there without behaving in an uncivilized manner.[5]

Naturally Ziegfeld's letter was a prime one to answer, as it was by PFC E.M. Stegor. In the first place, Stegor began, getting drunk was not anything new to any serviceman. The boys got drunk anywhere they were. Also, no one had to get drunk to end up with a woman whether in Shanghai or in the States. As to the girls, most of the men there had not seen a white woman for some time and enjoyed entertaining those then available by taking them to clubs. The men were only there temporarily, so why should they not enjoy themselves?[6]

Nonetheless, there were causes that went well beyond the abuse of alcohol. The degrading, brutalizing effects of involvement in intense combat — as ancient as Homer's *Iliad*—played their part. Many combat veterans then present in the China Theater sought release from the age-old horrors of war in the traditional solaces of wine, women and song. These actions, on occasion, resulted in misdemeanors, crimes, mayhem and even murder.

Some Americans maintained that the Chinese were often to blame for the tensions, strife and rowdyism. For instance, though the facts were not clear, a Chinese policeman, after an argument with an American sergeant, was charged with shooting and wounding three American soldiers at the city's racetrack. There were also numerous examples of menacing and threatening behavior toward Allied troops by Chinese civilians. Some aircrews were advised to carry their Colt .45s while in Shanghai to guard against roving Chinese gangs that were prone to prey on American service personnel. While the MPs (Military Police) and SPs (Shore Patrol) were ever-present, to some it seemed that American officers with their "modern Peacemakers" were an effective "deputy force without portfolio." Corporal E.E. Hopfield, in a letter to "B-Bag," asserted that many of the men, who had been issued orientation booklets listing customs and behavior of the Chinese, had ventured forth expecting a favorable response from them. Instead of the expected smiles, they were laughed at and had fingers pointed at them when they walked down the street. Prices automatically skyrocketed when Americans came on the scene and "normal" prices were only for the benefit of local citizens. In theaters, local patrons in the balconies showered Americans with orange peelings—or worse—which led to local theaters' being placed off limits. As a final insult, the identification flags—the so-called Blood Chits—that were worn on the backs of flight jackets, sprang up for sale in stores and stalls and in many cases the wording, which they could not read, made the unsuspecting wearer a laughingstock. Nonetheless, the paper's editor strongly advised that these examples of Chinese bad behavior were no excuse for the Americans to retaliate.[7]

One answer to rowdyism was to set up clubs catering to military personnel. In early November 1945, the Navy opened a large enlisted men's club at 722 Bubbling Well Road for sailors of the Seventh Fleet, the Yangtze Patrol Force and the South China Patrol Force. The usual amenities included food and beer, lounges for reading and writing, game rooms and a barber shop. It also featured a separate lounge for chief petty officers. This was grander than the Army's club, and a second Navy establishment was later opened in the Sun Building in the heart of the city.[8]

The commodious Bubbling Well club, however, did not seem enough for many sailors. They also desired to be admitted to the Army's enlisted men's club, which was established in early December, engendering additional strife. The admission of the sailors to the club promptly caused difficulties and the Army closed it to the Navy. The bitterness which resulted was considerable. It became necessary for First Sergeant George A. Kilroy, President of the Board of Governors of the EM Club No. 1, as it was called, to explain matters in a "B-Bag" letter. Kilroy—in no way connected with the cartoon icon, "Kilroy Was Here"—asserted that the sole purpose of the Army's club was to provide a place where the GI could go, with his buddies or his date, and be assured of a pleasant evening without paying exorbitant prices. As to the Navy's being admitted, however, one problem was that sailors outnumbered the soldiers in Shanghai by at least four to one. If an open-house policy were in place, it would soon be simply another Navy club. It had been decided at first that GIs could invite sailors in as guests, but soon the entrance was crowded by Navy men demanding that a GI invite them in. These then promptly abandoned their new friends and bribed the waiters to bring them separate drinks for cash and the club was soon losing money. The sailors were also responsible for numerous unpleasant scenes, such as throwing fireworks at GIs and their dates while they were dancing, throwing dishes off the tables, and being abusive to the point of vulgarity to GIs' dates, which had necessitated calling the MPs. The Board of Governors thereupon stipulated that the club was to be operated for U.S. Army personnel only. The Navy had its own clubs, in any case, and the Board refused to permit theirs to be just another "brawl joint."[9]

Kilroy was answered by sailor Bill Goephlen and "12 Others," who noted that many of the sailors concerned had been at sea for a long time, and one needed to know how a sailor felt when getting seven hours of liberty after months of continuous sea duty to fully understand their needs. Furthermore, even a belligerent man should be treated like a fellow American. The Navy Club had not reported any trouble to speak of. Maybe the men such as Kilroy did not know how to handle men, he charged.[10]

Several staff sergeants answered for Kilroy, explaining that the sailors were simply troublemakers, and though they had been at sea for some time, the Army's club was hardly the place to raise hell. The Navy was therefore to blame for their exclusion. The answer seemed clear: Both services should run their own clubs as they saw fit, which, with a few exceptions, was what subsequently occurred.[11]

Nevertheless, stronger measures were taken to deal with sailors who were a continuing problem. Repeatedly, Admiral Cooke, the Seventh Fleet commander, was compelled to confine his men to their ships because they persisted in acts of rowdyism ashore, including serious attacks on Chinese citizens. In addition, Chinese and U.S. Navy Shore Patrol officials curtailed indiscriminate sales of blackjacks and fireworks to sailors on liberty because the seamen were beating up rickshaw men and throwing torpedoes into the midst of coolies. Such flagrant misconduct was also punished by courts-martial. It further produced an editorial in *Stripes*, the editor writing that as a consequence of their behavior, America's friends, as well as its enemies, had decided it was composed mainly of bums, bullies and ruffians. One GI, Norman Rubington, agreed, declaring that Americans certainly had to win wars because they seemed always to lose the peace.[12]

XIII

The Marshall Mission

A Bridge Too Far (1977 Movie)

The great debates having to do with demobilization, the need to keep men overseas, and other related matters were inextricably bound up with American foreign policy in the immediate postwar period. This was nowhere more apparent than in the China Theater. Though the Shanghai *Stars and Stripes* was only published until April 1946, its pages frequently contained articles and editorials closely following these matters. These reflected the awareness of the more astute and knowledgeable service personnel that what happened at the highest levels of American policy had direct bearing on the rate of demobilizing America's vast, far-flung military forces. Men in positions of high authority found themselves pulled in various directions by those strongly motivated to get the GIs home and the counterforce of administering the many facets and ramifications of the hard-won peace. It was soon apparent that a Cold War, especially involving the Soviet Union and the West, had emerged with myriad challenges undreamed of only a short time earlier.

As to China, Truman had inherited many thorny problems and had to deal with a bevy of prickly persons equipped with princely egos. There was, in the first place, the Nationalist government headed by Chiang Kai-shek. In the midst of World War II, it was Europe that received first priority of the Allies and was regarded as the primary theater. The same held true for the subsequent Cold War. Yet FDR, especially, championed China and her role in the world, and sought her acceptance as a member of the Big Four. But the Chinese "question" was a complicated one. This was particularly true because Chiang had strong, powerful foes within his Nationalist government. The main opposition elsewhere came from the Chinese Communist Party, which was not only a party with its own agenda, propaganda apparatus and theoretical foundation, but also possessed a formidable army and its own capital at Yenan. In addition, its leadership, led by Mao Tse-tung and Chou En-Lai, successfully captured the adherence of millions of Chinese, in particular among the lower classes, the workers and the peasantry. Chiang's government, for many reasons, was widely regarded as corrupt, and was in truth a veneer glossing over massive corruption and a sea of incompetency. Though on occasion these two major centers of power could cooperate in carrying the war to the Japanese occupiers of much of China, more often they embarked upon actions both overt and covert, seeking military or political advantage over each other. To these ends, Chiang hoarded American lend-lease supplies and his better troops, some of whom had been trained by Americans, against the time when a final, full-scale attack against the Communists might be possible.[1]

Within China, American leaders were generally polarized. On the one hand, some supported General Joseph W. Stilwell, Chiang's Chief of Staff, who favored training a large number of Chinese troops who could be depended upon to carry the fight to the Japanese. Chiang, however, primarily wanted to keep them in reserve to help him against the Maoists. Accordingly, Stilwell regarded Chiang with a large measure of contempt, an attitude well-known to Chiang. Their relationship was therefore often stormy. On the other hand, certain American leaders favored General Claire Chennault, who had gained fame as the commander of the "Flying Tigers" in the early months after Pearl Harbor. Chennault, who went on to command the Fourteenth Air Force in China, was a firm advocate of air power and wanted to use China's growing number of airfields to carry the war to Japan by air. He was also much more personally acceptable to Chiang, and this duality of American influence and power in China caused endless friction.

Chiang at length was able, on October 24, 1945, to force the recall of Stilwell to the United States.[2] He was replaced as the commander of the newly created China Theater of Operations — as distinct from the Chinese-Burma-India Theater (the CBI) — by General Albert Coady Wedemeyer, who proceeded to use some of Chiang's troops to some advantage in the late months of World War II. In the meantime, the main course of the War in Asia largely bypassed China, which, while tying down a considerable number of Japanese troops, was not in on the final kill of the Japanese dragon. The vacuum created in China after the Japanese surrender was filled by several developments: the liberation of major cities in eastern China which the Japanese had overrun beginning in 1937, and the arrival of American armed forces in those same centers. The stage was also now set for Chiang and the Communists to resume full-scale operations against each other. The picture was complicated by the presence of over a million Japanese troops in China who had to be disarmed and repatriated. The considerable number of Japanese civilians, who had arrived in China in the baggage trains of the conquering troops and who helped implement and administer the Co-Prosperity Sphere that was created in the newly conquered Asian territories, also had to be returned home. These were major tasks for the Allies and the Chinese to sort out.

Manchuria, which the Japanese had overrun in the early 1930s, was another cockpit. The Russians were scheduled to move into this area according to a recent alliance treaty signed with the Kuomintang. It was based on the Yalta Agreement signed by the United States, Great Britain and the USSR on February 11, 1945. This stipulated the political conditions under which the Soviet Union would enter the war against Japan, which, before the successful detonating of the A-bomb, was considered vital to securing Japan's final surrender. These treaties included provisions for the Soviets to enjoy "preeminent interests" in the Chinese-Eastern and South-Manchurian Railroads, entailing Soviet occupation of portions of Manchuria. China's "full sovereignty" over Manchuria was recognized, however, and Moscow agreed to conclude a pact of friendship and alliance with the Nationalist government of China. The Soviets acknowledged that the Nationalist government was the sole government in China, much to Chiang's satisfaction. The Soviets also agreed to withdraw their troops, which in the meantime had entered Manchuria. This was subsequently realized on February 1, 1946. This "Treaty of Friendship and Alliance Between the Republic of China and the U.S.S.R." was signed on August 14, 1945, in Moscow just as the Japanese surrendered.[3]

Untoward events, however, marred the agreement. Bent upon recompensing themselves for the huge losses that they had sustained in World War II, the Soviets were soon engaged in stripping Manchuria of all moveable property, including, in many instances, entire factories. With the Cold War beginning to move front and center, their presence and actions in Manchuria were a matter of growing concern in the West. Though Moscow recognized Chiang's primacy in China, in some respects they favored the Chinese Communists. They allowed them, among other things, to collect captured Japanese armaments and stores for their own use. This resulted when the Soviets disarmed Japanese troops in Manchuria, though it had been understood that only Chinese Nationalist forces would perform this duty. On the Soviet side, there were concerns about the U.S. troops in North China and the obvious assistance that they were giving to Chiang to improve the Nationalists' position vis-à-vis the Communists.[4]

Many of the uncertainties of American policy toward China at this time revolved around the colorful, controversial American ambassador to China, General Patrick J. Hurley. He had been sent to China by FDR as his personal representative in August of 1944, and then made U.S. Ambassador to China on January 8, 1945. He replaced Clarence E. Gauss, who resigned as Ambassador to China on November 1, 1944. In the early months of his service in China, Hurley obtained a favorable impression of the Communists, admiring their discipline and their willingness to fight the Japanese. This stance, however, did not endear him to Chiang, and he subsequently turned strongly against the Communists and became a fervent proponent of Chiang and the need for the U.S. to do what they could to keep him in the war. Subsequently acceptable at Chungking, Hurley was widely regarded as a key person in obtaining the recall of Stilwell. But Hurley was far from pleased with the developing situation immediately following the surrender of Japan. Official American policy in China recognized Chiang as the sole legitimate sovereign in all Chinese territory, including Manchuria and Taiwan, just liberated from Japan. The problems facing Chiang were considerable, however. The Japanese had ruled Manchuria, Taiwan, and much of eastern China, and had forced Chiang to the far southwest of China, which he ruled from his wartime capital of Chungking. He then had to reoccupy his country once more, and this meant contesting it with the Russians in Manchuria and the Communists elsewhere, as well as repatriating all Japanese military and civilian personnel. One move was to reestablish his government in Nanking, his former capital. In order to accomplish these goals, he needed to retain the support of the Allies, notably the United States. The Truman administration desired a unified China under Chiang's rule and therefore continued lend-lease shipments. It also provided transport by air and sea to return many Chinese troops to eastern and northern China and prepared them for further movement into Manchuria. These activities, however, caused opposition from the Russians and especially from the Chinese Communists. Chiang's authoritarian and corrupt regime, however, gave Truman and other high officials pause and American policy reflected some caution as it proceeded.[5]

This stance and other factors aroused Hurley's ire and he charged that the Truman administration's policies in Asia in general manifested a wide discrepancy from those announced, such as supporting democracy and anti-imperialism. The actual policy, in fact, seemed bent upon bolstering a new imperialism as well as Communism. He further alleged that many State Department officials in Asia were undermining his and America's policies there. In these circumstances, he returned to Washington in late September 1946, at his own request. Back in the States, Hurley, in several public appearances, presented details of what he was concerned about. Speaking at Santa Fe, New Mexico, on November 15, he asserted that the Chinese Communists were being armed with weapons from surrendering Japanese, were setting up a separate government, and were seeking to destroy the Republic of China. The United Nations must not permit Japanese arms to be so used, he charged. U.S. Secretary of State James F. Byrnes in reply stated that the official American attitude toward the undeclared Chinese civil war was one of "deep regret," for which an amicable settlement was sought. The Communists had charged that Chinese Nationalist troops were being transferred by American planes. Byrnes noted, not altogether truthfully, that certain planes, provided by lend-lease, and "manned by Chinese," were so involved. These troops were on their way to Manchuria, Byrnes explained, to carry out their obligations of accepting the Japanese surrender. The *New China Daily News*, a Communist newspaper, stated that Americans were indeed intervening in the Chinese civil war. Byrnes indicated in Washington that Truman had specifically ordered further lend-lease aid to

China but only to help her secure the surrender of Japanese troops in China and Manchuria.[6]

After weeks of indecision as to his future, during which he indicated that he would return to China, Hurley abruptly resigned on November 26, 1945. His resignation letter consisted of a 1,500-word scathing statement in which he accused professional diplomats of sabotage of U.S. Far Eastern policy and failure to carry out administration policy. Hurley indicated that Roosevelt had charged him with preventing the collapse of Chiang's government, but that American diplomats on the ground in Asia had been advising that Hurley's efforts in preventing the collapse of the central government were not representative of U.S. policy. The next day, at a press conference, he explained his reasons for his departure, points which he elaborated upon in the days following.[7]

At this juncture, Truman and Secretary of State James F. Byrnes, taken by surprise, brought the matter before a Cabinet meeting on November 27. Hurley's resignation was the sole topic of discussion, and the decision was made to appoint General George C. Marshall as his successor. Marshall, who only the week before — on November 18 — had stepped down after his six-year stint as Army Chief of Staff, was preparing for a well-earned vacation. Truman, after the meeting, asked him to "go to China for me." Truman desired above all to attempt to end the civil strife by a negotiated settlement and allow China to emerge as a unified nation that could set out on a peaceful course. Marshall did not feel that he could refuse and was soon in harness again, as the American ambassador to China specifically charged to mediate between the warring factions.[8]

Marshall was given the rank of ambassador, but only for the specific purpose of seeking a negotiated settlement between Chiang and the Communists. The day-to-day diplomatic business was conducted by the American embassy. General Wedemeyer had been offered the post of U.S. Ambassador to China, but after announcing his selection, it was decided that his strong pro–Chiang bias would obviously be a handicap and the offer was withdrawn. It was not until July 11, 1946, when the Senate confirmed Dr. J. Leighton Stuart as the U.S. Ambassador to China, that the post was filled. He was president of Yenching University at Peiping, and a missionary who had lived for many years in China. He was widely acknowledged as a man of "unquestioned character and integrity," with long experience in China and a fine command of Mandarin Chinese.[9]

For the next few weeks, an investigation of Hurley and his mission ensued, during which time Hurley went on the offensive. On December 6, as the Shanghai *Stripes* reported, at the Senate Foreign Relations Committee, Hurley "hurled" bare-knuckle accusations of sabotage against two career diplomats, charging that they hoped that Chiang's government might crash. These were George Atcheson, Jr., and John S. Service, by then political advisors to MacArthur in Tokyo. In addition, he went on, Under Secretary of State Dean Acheson favored giving lend-lease equipment to the Chinese Communists, and Service suggested in October 1944 that Chiang's government be allowed to collapse. Hurley complained that he could not control John Service. He resigned because he expected to be protected and supported by the State Department; instead, he found that the department was determined to force him out of office. Hurley further charged that the government's policies were being sabotaged by State Department officials. Hurley also stated that America had no ulterior designs in China and said that the Chinese could choose their own leaders and decide their own destiny, agreeing with Byrnes that China should be a unified, free and democratic nation. Hurley recounted that he had told Washington on April 2, 1945, that there could be no unification as long as there was a strong force able to fight Chiang's regime and hence lend-lease materials should not be sent to Communists. Hurley, testifying the following day, did feel that concessions might be given to the Communists, but only as a political party and not as a military force opposing Chiang. He also added the name of Acheson to the list of other saboteurs of his policies in China, accusations which led to a direct confrontation between the two men.[10]

Secretary of State Byrnes thereupon justified his department's stances and actions. Hurley's allegations were unfounded, he began. He acknowledged that America's official policy, that the government of Chiang was the only solid foundation upon which to construct a Chinese democracy, was correct. The Chinese central government, however, must be broadened to include representatives of those large, well-organized groups which did not have any voice in the present set-up. Concessions on both sides would be encouraged, Byrnes stated. Service and Acheson were only expressing their own carefully considered opinions, and since neither was under Hurley's orders, they were not being insubordinate.[11]

These appearances before the Senate's Foreign Relations Committee brought an end to the short-lived but explosive Hurley investigation. The committee saw no reason to prolong the matter, a decision that amounted to a rejection of Hurley's charges. With Marshall's appointment, the way seemed clear for some new thinking regarding America's policy toward China.[12]

In Shanghai, the *Stripes* took due note of the proceedings. Two days after his appointment, the paper's editor hailed the "New Team" under Marshall. He thereupon embarked upon a Clausewitzian path seeking to demonstrate that a soldier could also function effectively as a diplomat. He was undoubtedly aware that Clausewitz's view that diplomacy was war by other means might be demonstrated with the same success for him as diplomat as he had clearly gained as a soldier. He was to be cruelly disappointed. Yet initially, as the Shanghai *Stripes* declared, his appointment was very good news indeed. America's No. 1 soldier had already proved that he had plenty of old-fashioned horse sense. America needed such a man in China at that critical moment, though obviously he was sticking his neck out. Another editorial in the December 1 issue took great pride in the appointment, coupled with sincere sympathy. He could hardly add anything to his stature. On the other hand, the risks were considerable. Still, he might be able to bring Chungking and Yenan together and maybe cut the Chinese Gordian knot, and thereby stop the widening of the chasm that had opened up under General Hurley's feet. All of this would require a miracle and if he succeeded, one might even see Marshall as possessing presidential timber. He would be impossible to defeat, were he to choose to run. To be sure, this amounted to his being exiled for a year in the wilderness of China, as a misbegotten emissary of a clueless and confused Uncle Sam regarding the question of "whither China?"

In any event, his appointment signaled a new course for American China policy. In general terms, this meant the abandonment of the American "blank check" toward the Chungking government and a general stiffening of U.S. attitude. Three factors spawned this new approach. First was the resignation of Hurley, who had authored the "blank check" and engineered the removal of Stilwell, who had advocated firmness and demanded that China set her house in order in return for U.S. aid. Secondly, Marshall was expected to use hard-headed realism in place of sentiment. Finally, Byrnes, as brought out in his testimony before the Foreign Relations Committee, stated that in order to achieve the long-range goal of a strong, united and democratic China, it was essential that the central government, and the various dissident elements present in China, approach a settlement of their differences with a genuine willingness to compromise. The new U.S. role, therefore, was to encourage concessions by all sides.[13]

The new line caused the Communists to perceive a weakened position for Chiang's government and it moved to postpone the scheduled meeting of the Political Consultative Council to bring all sides together in Chungking, planned for December 10 to 15. This was to discuss, among other things, the convening of a National Assembly and the drafting of a constitution. Yenan saw a better bargaining position if this was now postponed. Chungking now sought to ascertain just what the U.S. intended to do and what means it might employ in getting concessions to aid them in combating the Communists. Clearly, wartime pressures were off and America enjoyed more flexibility, while the underdog Communists were also in a better position.[14]

Matters were more explicitly set forth by Truman in a 1,200-word statement issued on December 15, on the eve of Marshall's departure for China, discussed earlier. He bluntly told all Chinese factions to cease fighting if they desired further U.S. aid. The U.S. was staking its hopes for world peace and prosperity upon the ability of nations to combine for collective security in the new United Nations Organization (UNO). China's role was to cease internal hostilities immediately and arrange a national conference of all major political elements to unify the country. Indeed, a strong, united and democratic China was of the utmost importance to the success of the UNO and world peace. Breaches of peace anywhere in the world were now a major threat, and events in internal China were no exception. Marshall's role was to seek to bring all elements together. Though the U.S. and other nations in the UN recognized the Nationalist government as the "only legal" government in China, yet modifications were needed. Specifically, Truman recognized that Chiang's government was a one-party institution and that other elements must have entrée. Therefore, an assembly with all present with fair and effective representation was called for. Truman also noted that the diplomatic precedents upon which American policy was based included the Cairo Declaration of 1943, the Potsdam Declaration of July 1945, and the Sino-Soviet treaty and agreements of August 15, 1945. These documents had in common that all were committed to the liberation of China and return of Manchuria to her control. Also, there was the necessity of removing all remaining Japanese influence in China. These goals required the disarmament and evacuation of Japanese troops, and hence were the reasons that U.S. GIs, Marines, and naval forces were in China. The prompt cessation of internal strife was essential. The U.S. had already paid a huge price for these goals. China's one-party government would have to go, but details must be worked out by the Chinese themselves. Intervention by "any foreign government in these matters would be inappropriate." Yet, "autonomous" armies, such as the Communist forces, were inconsistent with these ends. When agreements for the Chinese were worked out, then all armed forces could be consolidated into the Chinese National Army.[15]

Officially, both sides in China hailed Truman's policy statement, though the Communists also registered some skepticism. They did say that they would also welcome a coalition Chinese government and participate in a nationalist army, but they also hoped that U.S. support would not seek to influence the course of China's internal strife. One Yenan spokesman hoped that when General Marshall arrived, this point would be effectively implemented. Nonetheless, Chiang was not happy with Truman's decision to send Marshall to China. He would have preferred Patrick Hurley's return, since he was certain Hurley would have had "complete U.S. sanction and assistance for Nationalist efforts to crush the Communists and consolidate power — but he acquiesced rather than cause trouble for himself in Washington."[16]

As to Marshall, from the outset, he was aware of the difficulties in China which in large measure revolved around the weaknesses of Chiang's regime. The former Secretary of War, Henry L. Stimson, advised him that he must "remember that the Generalissimo has never honestly backed a thorough union with the Chinese Communists. He could not, for his administration is a mere surface veneer (more or less rotten) over a mass of the Chinese people beneath him." Furthermore, Stimson thought that the Communists' "hold on the people underneath them is sounder than [Chiang's] hold over his people," a key consideration.[17]

The Communists were "guardedly optimistic" regarding Marshall's appointment, noting a shift in wind direction now blowing more favorably in their direction. Specifically, they felt that Marshall's mission would inhibit the outbreak of a full-scale civil war, for which they were not yet prepared. On the other hand, they did recognize that the United States' policy was still one of basically supporting Chiang, and that they must neutralize this to the extent possible. Mao had also been ordered by Stalin to negotiate a treaty of peace with Chiang.[18]

Marshall, who characteristically prepared for the mission with thoroughness and as much study as he could squeeze in before his departure, therefore had some warning of the difficulties that he confronted. Upon his arrival in China, Marshall's advisers agreed that the mission's chances of success were slim; one of his key people gave the figure at two percent. Yet Wedemeyer, who favored all-out aid to Chiang, recorded that at their first meeting in Shanghai on December 20, when he had stated that Marshall would never be able to accomplish his mission, Marshall angrily retorted that he could succeed and "that he expected Wedemeyer to help."[19]

Marshall clearly entertained doubts as well, however, and at a meeting on December 26 in Chungking with representatives of the Democratic League — a small liberal Chinese political party seeking some representation in Chiang's government — he identified a key aspect of the difficulties facing the nation: "Implementation, not principles, was the problem in China," he said, further noting that "half the difficulty is lack of understanding and lack of confidence" in opponents.[20]

Marshall never found any reason to alter these views. In a letter to Bernard M. Baruch midway through his mission, dated August 21, he stated that he often had to listen to the outpourings of suspicions by both sides, and found that

> in most instances neither side properly, or even casually, evaluates the fears or suspicions of the other and their effect on the action taken or the attitude in negotiations. When I emphasize this state of affairs neither side treats it as of much importance, but as a matter of fact from my middle position it has appeared to me of the most vital importance because misunderstandings are a fruitful cause of unhappy situations or events.

This view was similar to those made in his final report to Truman early in January 1947, when it was clear that his mission had failed. Now armed with observations and his involvement in numerous substantive negotiations over the year past, Marshall concluded that "the greatest obstacle to peace has been the complete, almost overwhelming suspicion with which the Chinese Communist Party and the Kuomintang regard each other."[21]

The Marshall mission did record some temporary successes, but it was mainly a dismal record of major goals that were almost attained only to fail in the end. U.S.–Chinese relations proceeded along other paths that had to do with the Cold War and the course that the Chinese subsequently followed. The key to Marshall's failure and that of American policy in China in general was identified by a member of the U.S. Embassy staff while Marshall was in China, John F. Melby. He concluded that an essential factor often overlooked in China concerned "the people of China, who might just have a few ideas of their own as to what they would like to see happen in their country. In the long run it is they who will decide." China, he concluded, would not be able to solve its problems "until someone manages to attract the real sources of Chinese power and put them together." That "someone" proved to be the Communists.[22]

America's foreign policy failures, not only in China but elsewhere in the world in the last half of the twentieth century and the first decade of the twenty-first, have also been incisively analyzed by Lyman P. Van Slyke in his introduction to the reissued edition of the U.S. State Department's *China White Paper*. Herein he wrote that these shortcomings were explained, in part, by an omnipresent "purblind anti–Communism." To this could be added "the illusion[s] of American omnipotence, and ... American self-righteousness," coupled with "the cultural gap across the Pacific," reinforced by American underestimation of the difficulties that these imposed. In addition, Van Slyke wrote that there was a significant "split between our attitudes and our actions. Having no great political or economic stake in China, we were inclined to frame our China policy in moral terms; but for the same reason, we were unwilling to back our policies, however just, against the conflicting policies of nations with higher stakes in the game." There was, though, "no conscious duplicity on our part. Our China policy reflected our feelings as a nation; if we were reluctant to back these feelings, it was because our vital interests were not really involved in China." Adding to Van Slyke's assessment, it should be stated that despite his misgivings about Chiang's government, Truman emphasized the need unconditionally to continue to support him. At the same time, the Communists would be excluded from American aid. This stance encouraged Chiang to continue his preparations for decisive military action against the Communists. Mao, however, steadily enhanced his power bases and military strength. The end in China was then inevitable, barring any massive Western intervention on Chiang's side — a most unlikely scenario — culminating in the Communist victory in 1949. American policy therefore negated Marshall's efforts, dashing any hopes of preventing the Chinese civil war. In the last analysis, as was the case throughout World War II, it was Europe that mattered most as the Cold War intensified.[23]

Other reasons for the failure of American policy at this time might include the persistency of a moral sense of America's special status and global mission to right the wrongs of the world in general and to bring the blessings of democracy to all humankind, views at variance with those entertained in many quarters. As to China in particular, these stances had long been conditioned in part by the extensive American missionary and educational activities there in the 19th and 20th centuries.[24]

Though the Shanghai *Stripes* had ceased publication before the end of Marshall's mission, nonetheless, Goodfriend, in one of his last editorials in *Stripes* before departing China, revealed some insight into the Chinese dilemma. In an open letter to the Chinese people, he wrote that he believed that the world's future would be settled in China because this was where Russia, Britain, France, Japan and the United States all met. Accordingly, if China could work out its salvation peacefully then so might everyone else. If Chinese persisted in killing other Chinese, however, the example would be set and the world would no doubt follow their example. While it was not the purpose of the West to meddle in or settle the internal problems of China, he went on, because they were simply too complicated, too diffuse, and too numerous for anyone but the Chinese to settle, all could hope for the best. The Chinese should recognize, then, that the war just ended had been fought to fix things so that free men would have a chance to settle their differences by negotiation and not on the battlefield. Fifty-five million people [or was it more than this?] were dead as a result of the late conflict and now the world was looking to Chiang Kai-shek and Mao Tse-tung to seek peace within China as proof that it had not been fought in vain.[25]

Such was not to be. Perhaps Marshall's mission was a case of "too little, too late"—had it been possible for it to have succeeded in any case is the key debatable point. Marshall's mission was swallowed up by the rapidly developing Cold War, with its European focus, and the Chinese likewise had many roads yet to travel. With the success of the Chinese Communist Party in capturing the country in 1949, there then lay ahead massive internal upheavals and tyranny on a grand scale including the "Great Leap Forward" and the "Cultural Revolution." Only after the death of Chairman Mao and other developments could China again obtain a more congenial playing field, though on occasion it would witness further examples of tyranny, such as at Tiananmen Square. Only since then, with the passage of more time, and the earth-shaking consequences of the opening up of China to the world, has it been possible for Chinese thinkers to emerge in their droves—if not legions—to rethink, yet once more, China's course as it proceeded into the twenty-first century.

XIV

The Shanghai Stripes: Later Developments and "30"

"It was just a joy to run the newspaper [in Shanghai]."
— Lieutenant Colonel Arthur Goodfriend

As the paper matured in the months following its inception, on one occasion, at least, the editor felt it was prudent, because of certain events—not otherwise identified—to state what it stood for and, more importantly, what it would not stand for. Readers were reminded that *Stripes* was written for all men in the U.S. armed forces in the China Theater. Furthermore, it had no more use for the smart-aleck GI than for a pompous officer. It neither looked down on privates nor fawned on the brass. Throughout, it enjoyed excellent relations with Generals Wedemeyer and Stratemeyer, the Army Air Forces commander in the theater, only hoping that its relations with privates and sergeants were as good. It played the news as its editors saw fit, calling a spade a spade without fear or partiality, and sought to present the world in proper perspective. Finally, it hoped to brighten things up with a bit of humor. The "B-Bag" was open to anyone "who wants to stick his head in it and holler," but the paper worked hard to keep out the crank, the professional griper and anyone with an ax to grind. The staff was made up almost entirely of men who were in the newspaper game before they were in the military. All were conscientious, capable and deeply interested in their assignment. They all knew that freedom of the press was not license, and they remembered, whenever appropriate, that they were, after all, still in the Army. To have freedom of the press the newspaper must allow nothing but common decency and military security to influence publication of the news or expression of editorial opinion. While all newspapermen knew this, certain other persons apparently did not. Accordingly, the *Stripes* stated once and for all that it would not take orders from anyone to publish or not to publish any story, though they were aware of the needs to guard military security. Nor would the paper consider requests to submit any of their stories for outside editing. Finally, neither would the paper submit to abusive or nonsensical interrogation.[1]

Frequently, the rank and file wrote in what they thought the paper should be about and how the readership rated it, ever the watchdogs of the hallowed concept of a free soldier press. A letter in the December 13 issue by T-5 Jerry Brois, for instance, indicated that while editorials were desired, not so many should be devoted to larger political themes. Instead, they should address such subjects as where the men's discharges were, why they were in China in the first place, why some of the men were not going home like other guys, and on other subjects more in tune with what the GIs locally were thinking. Instead of political issues, the first item of business was to get the boys home. To these ends, he advised the editor, in a chiding tone, that he might write an open letter to Congress on the subject — if he had the guts.

The negative comments were well balanced with positive remarks, no doubt to be expected when the editorial policy was that of an open paper with the provocative "B-Bag" as regular fare. Among the most appreciative of the paper's readers were the Marines. Typically, one sergeant wrote that at least *Stripes* did not truckle to brass. This was more than could be said about Marine publications. In fact, he asserted, Bill Mauldin would have been shot for insubordination if he had been in the Marine Corps. Indeed, he went on, the doggies (soldiers) were lucky because Army officers showed at least a vestige of being human, and when the brass rankled, they could at least sound off in "B-Bag." But in the Corps, no officer ever suffered any human frailties — not even constipation. The Marines therefore appreciated the paper's splendid work even if rank-and-file soldiers did not. His views were seconded by "Two PO'd Marines," who affirmed that the paper was by far the best publication put out anywhere in the military services. The editorials were frank and to the point, and the publishing of gripes was unheard of in the Corps.[2]

Another Marine from Tsingtao stated that aside from a few high-ranking officers, ninety-eight percent of the Marines, "Seabees," sailors, troops and others looked to the *Stripes* for news, views and discussions of such questions as to why service personnel were in China in the first place. This included the sometimes maligned Franc Shor and the esteemed Lieutenant Crouch.[3]

Some Marines did register complaints, however, asserting that they wanted more news about events in North China where the Marines were engaged. They tired of reading about doggies barking over high PX prices, the conduct of PX women employees, and other such mundane matters when they themselves endured poor living conditions, with no PX girls, and confronted astronomical prices. The editor admitted that they had to rely on press services for news of North China, but to ease matters, the paper requested — and obtained — the assignment of two Marines for the paper's staff.[4]

Also true to form, though, another reader, signing himself "B.K.," exhibited a strong negative stance. He wanted to know what occasioned the recent startling deviation from the paper's previous policies. At one time, he declared, the paper was a newspaper appealing to mature readers, a paper interested in the establishment of a just peace and a world no longer given to factional rivalries. But in the past few weeks, the paper had degenerated into a sensationalist tabloid reminiscent of a typical Hearst scandal sheet. It had also failed miserably to maintain the morale of disgruntled troops in the China Theater, and mainly had recourse to focusing on scandal stories in the States. Referring to the deplorable disintegration of a decent Army newspaper, its only redeeming features were the Mauldin cartoons, the comic strips, and the weekly magazine supplements. The remainder of the newspaper was merely a hodgepodge of fourth-rate O. Henry—a veiled blast leveled at Franc Shor—irresponsible Hearst editorials and stories, and a decidedly unfunny Baron Munchausen.[5]

Similarly, Staff Sergeant John James Moore, who identified himself as a former Pittsburgh newspaperman, laid on his criticism even thicker, charging the staff with operating like high schoolers printing their school paper. The paper also relied too heavily on the wire services: "Could not the staff dig up its own news?" he asked sarcastically. Also the paper should cease its attacks on the high prices charged by Shanghai merchants. This problem could be speedily resolved if the entire city of Shanghai were placed off limits for a week. In short, the paper's staff should act like real newsmen and seek to make the paper a big-time sheet emulating metropolitan papers in the States.[6]

As usual, praise alternated with attacks, and a letter in "B-Bag" in the November 3 issue thanked the paper for Shor's article on the rampant black market activities in Kunming, and his descriptions of the escapades of Chinese civilians riding about in American Army vehicles, all wearing American uniforms when the average GI could not obtain new clothing. This may well have been because supply sergeants—no doubt involved in the black market sale of Army "surplus clothing"—were "on the take." Indeed, that entire issue, the writer concluded, carried a nostalgic whiff of the traditional courageous editorial policy of *Stars and Stripes* editions in other war theaters.

In the January 19 issue, in response to a rather stern letter, the editor attached a note indicating that argued that, while the paper was sometimes criticized for not giving its readers "the straight dope," in fact it attempted always to do just that. At the same time, the paper did not claim that everything was rosy in China and reminded its readers that the presence of the "B-Bag" was to help keep the record straight. Accordingly, as long as *Stripes* was published, it would continue to welcome criticisms or endorsements from everyone.

On several occasions, Wedemeyer reaffirmed his support. When asked his views of GIs' negative criticisms of the paper, he replied that he liked them because he was a believer in a free expression of views, and they reflected the fact that readers had opportunities to express themselves freely. He welcomed criticism as long as it was constructive. He did not agree, however, that all of the comments that he got were unfavorable. He had personally received many letters of appreciation of the *Stripes* in addition to those in the paper that he closely read.[7]

One characteristic that seemed to be most prominent among the staff of the Shanghai *Stripes* was a sense of pride in what they were doing. Goodfriend himself was well aware of the main strengths and key attributes of the paper. He once observed that the Shanghai edition "was a great newspaper because we started it from scratch and I had a wonderful staff and there were no problems or jealousy or anything of that sort." In Europe, he recalled, "I always had problems with staff who resented being there." Furthermore, his European staff did not want a military man over them, so there was always a certain tension. But nothing like that occurred in China. Indeed, he concluded, "it was just a joy to run the newspaper there."[8]

The writer, Dick Wilson, had further comments on the life of the paper. China Edition's "sweet-and-sour-pork-fed junior geniuses" had to learn that publishing a newspaper in China was an experience like no other, especially when compared with one supplying the public's news appetite in any large Stateside city. Where else but in China would linotype operators set copy in a language they did not understand, following copy letter by letter and pulling proofs as on Gutenberg's original presses? Also, where but in Shanghai, where prices were skyrocketing, would virgin-white newsprint be many times more valuable than printed newspapers, lowering staff morale by making them understand that every time they spent time and effort into putting words on paper, they lost an extra eighteen dollars per 700 copies they could have made by not spoiling the pages with ink? Furthermore, what paper but an unmuzzled soldier newspaper could be accused of having both reactionary and Communistic inclinations? In addition, uniquely, the city desk had two telephones, one for English and the other for Chinese. The staff also needed gloves for the cold days when stove contractors were trying to install their stoves.[9]

At least three women maintained the office. As one staffer wrote, one was a very efficient WAC who had been in the Army for three years. She was Tech Sergeant Mary "Sunny" Graham. She thought that the *Stripes* was just another Army section and tried to treat it as such. Accordingly, she promptly GI'd the floors and attempted to make the staff "GI" as well. She later had to admit that she had failed, though as things turned out, she lost some of her own GI polish in the process. Two other women involved were Maria ("The Swiss Fireball") Hanggi, a stenographer, and Eddy ("Sunshine") Dongworth, the telephone switchboard operator.[10]

Among the more useful staffers, if not the best known, was Alexander P. Nikitin. A native of Shanghai and a White Russian, he was the print shop foreman. Lieutenant Pernod's right-hand man, to be sure, the big, balding, friendly Russian did everything from pulling galley proofs to tearing down and rebuilding linotype machines and rotary presses and running the press gang. The main artists of the paper were, early on, Johnnie Blew and Merv Shaw, and later, "vodka-abstaining" Siegfried Reinhardt.[11]

Among those in charge of the paper's always well-filled sports pages, normally two in number, were Lou Miller, former sports writer for the *New York World Telegraph*; a late addition from the Tientsin Marines, Al Levinson; and the sports editor, Bob Shea.

Other significant staff members in the later months were people of the feature department, including Larry Harris, the "B-Bag" editor; Jack Moynihan, feature editor; and "ditty composer" Lieutenant A.L. Crouch, the personification of the "Barracks Bard." Circulation was in the hands of Peter "Tiny" Schulz — all six-foot and seven inches of him — who concentrated on supplying the Shanghai Navy. Among those working with the Marines, though they were in the Army, were Hugh O'Neil and Tom Radtke. O'Neil was often called on the carpet by the Marine Chief of Staff when Dick Wilson or Franc Shor wrote about the Marines. Only two Marines were authorized to wear the *Stripes*' official patch. They were Sergeant Charles "Chuck" Jensen, who was engaged in rewrite, and Staff Sergeant John O. Davies, Jr., of the *Newark* (N.J.) *Evening News*, who was a news editor. Bob O'Hara, of Syracuse, New York, served as the Navy's main correspondent.

The hard-working editors included Dolph Chaney, Charlie Leong, Jim Becker, Crawford Jones, Dick Wilson, Jack Anderson, Abe Rosen and John Davis. The paper also usually had a full collection of "characters." One of those, who fit the "silken adjective" perfectly, was Franc Shor, nicknamed "Rabbit." The "Russian," John Clift, the paper's managing editor, became known as "Bombhead," apparently from his days on the Rome edition of the *Stripes*, when the appellation was lifted from *Li'l Abner*. The staff photographer, Goode, became "Hamfat" after "Hamfat McGooch," also from *Li'l Abner*. This seemed proper when it was learned that his real name was Ham Goode, or, more accurately, Hamilton Philip Goode. The moniker "Egghead" was attached to Abe Rosen, but this became "Shithead," when he once, as makeup editor, allowed the "F" to be left out of the word, "Shifthead."[12]

The personnel used a fleet of nine "press cars," a jalopy brigade of jeeps, to scurry about in Shanghai's traffic. These startled Chinese pedestrians whose fifth-century reflexes could only respond awkwardly to twentieth-century traffic. This resulted in numerous street melodramas along the way.

One measure of the paper's success was the traditional one of circulation. In October of 1945, the paper printed just under 20,000 copies, but the figures jumped to almost 25,000 the following month. Then, in December, with the theater scheduled to close, the figure fell again to 20,075. In January 1946, the all-time low of 19,651 was hit. In February and March, increased circulation among the Marines again elevated the figures to new highs, with an overall average for March of 39,100. There was also a measure of pride that the paper completed its career with the cost to the consumer being the same as at the beginning: two cents in U.S. currency, though in Chinese money the figure had increased from $30 to $40.[13]

As to drinking among the *Stripes* newsmen, the traditions of the craft suggested that many were inveterate consumers of alcohol in copious quantities. There were some exceptions at the Shanghai paper, notably the teetotaler Siegfried Reinhardt, one of the artists. Many others followed the more familiar course, but as one observed in this regard, none would ever forget Franc M.L. Shor, who came to China bearing a large and spacious thirst. To slake it, he was famous for ordering various sorts of alcohol by the case. Then there was the far more common consumption of beer. Larry Harris, in an article in the last issue of the paper, noted that an important scientific discovery made during the life of the China edition was that beer could add something to a newsroom: It was kind to the palate, kept the proper amount of moisture in the atmosphere, eliminated "type lice," washed the floor and encouraged a sort of blasé freedom of the press.[14]

The organizer of the daily trek for beer was one Dolph Chaney, whose cheerful chant that he had a dollar to put on a case of beer was followed by requests that others volunteer additional funding. The money in hand, their boy, Chow, was dispatched to the Szechuen Road PX with a note listing their orders. There Hilda Hauser, the counter-girl, would read these missives, often cast in the style of Finley Peter Dunne's "Mr. Dooley" of 19th-century fame. A typical one explained that the staff had been requested to launch twenty-four boats on the Whangpoo River that afternoon and would require at least that number of filled bottles with which to christen the vessels. In any event, as Harris concluded, this supply of golden liquids eventually flowed down Shanghai's sewers.[15]

One thing that the Shanghai *Stripes* took pride in was its participation in several campaigns with focused aims. For one, the paper was often concerned with the lot of the average Chinese citizens, especially the children, and in the October 8, 1945, issue launched a venture called "Books for the Kids of China," or as it was often presented in the paper, "BF-KOC." This was based on the premise that only through education could China overcome the illiteracy, ignorance and apathy that held her back. Goodfriend noted that among the serviceman's most enthusiastic fans were the kids of China. They grinned and waved at them and *ding howed* them wherever they went. Though they were incredibly dirty, scabrous and poor, nonetheless they were friends who would never forget the GIs, surely the best augur for future happy Chinese-American relations. Backing up the appeal, the staff of the paper kicked in the first fifty dollars. Goodfriend later acknowledged that the program was perhaps a bit naïve; nonetheless, it proceeded with a great deal of publicity, and the campaign eventually brought in US $3,000, though how it was spent and to what specific ends remains unclear.[16]

Another long-running venture was the battle against Shanghai's merchants, restaurants and hotels in attempts to keep excessively high prices in check. This took two forms: one consisted of strong editorials and articles seeking to influence military authorities to deal with price gougers by declaring certain establishments off-limits for military personnel. Another form of attack was launched against the Shanghai municipal government's restaurant and amusement tax, which the paper argued should not apply to service personnel. The paper was encouraged by the fact that the Marine Corps Chief of Staff, General Worton, had earlier gotten his men exempted from the Tientsin municipal government city taxes. Accordingly, in editorials and articles in late February, issues urged the mayor to rescind municipal taxes imposed on U.S. servicemen in Shanghai. He did respond, and after conferences with Army brass, conceded. The paper's editorial on March 1 was consequently a short one, consisting only of the words: "Thanks, Mr. Mayor."[17]

More informal, though no less intense, was a campaign — not confined to Shanghai — to force the dismissal of Japan's emperor, who had been retained by General MacArthur. To many observers in China, and elsewhere in the world, there were fears that a façade was being erected behind which the old trappings would be maintained. The *Stripes* editor once argued that while everything else in Japan — from the Zaibatsu to sykiyaki — was feeling the touch of defeat, the emperor, his home, and his properties were spared by the bombs that had burned and blasted the rest of Japan. Furthermore, American soldiers now stood at attention before the palace. Thus, out of the conflagration of war which had swept over Japan, there emerged miraculously one figure, none other than an unharmed, serene figure, attired in the splendor, dignity and superstition of centuries. He was a god who had grown in stature, now loftier and more resplendent. His unassailable position was apparently so strong that not even an army of millions, supported by the greatest navy in the world, and the most formidable assembly of powers in history, seemed willing to dare to disturb the sanctity of his throne. In addition, the war crimes trials of Japanese then in progress revealed that soldiers committing atrocities were said to have been acting on behalf of the Japanese emperor. This being the case, the editor noted, the seemingly deeply humble little man named Hirohito, otherwise known as the son of heaven, and in reality the propped-up emperor of defeated Japan, had emerged as one of the world's most infamous war criminals.[18]

Another strong editorial further explained. When all had joined the Army, they were told that the mission was to utterly destroy Japan and its institutions. Under General MacArthur's brilliant leadership, millions of American soldiers had fought across 7,000 miles of ocean to get to Japan. Today, however, the victors were stopped by a 100-foot moat at which the people of Japan came to bow, hiss and pray to the man who symbolized the institution of imperial rule which Americans had been told was to be completely destroyed. To be sure, the present occupation was peaceful and orderly, and the American soldier was today wooed as ardently as only yesterday he was being murdered. But if a tranquil occupation of Japan in which the emperor and imperial institution remained — though in a weakened form — was now the Army's mission, then something was snafu and the troops had been sold a bill of goods. Therefore, unless the imperial institution was ousted, he concluded, the peace and tranquility of Japan might someday be interrupted by earthquakes. These would not be because Mt. Fuji was erupting, but rather because a few hundred thousand dead Americans were revolving in their graves.[19]

Indeed, no doubt fearing that he might be unseated, Hirohito, on January 2, 1946, issued a rescript stating that the emperors had never claimed divinity; this formulation was made only in their names by officials in order to bind their people and the throne together. The document further insisted that ties between the emperor and the people did not imply that the Japanese people are superior to other races and therefore fated to rule the world. Nonetheless, the paper argued, no ruler had heretofore denied the mythology.[20]

Another source of pride was a development late in the paper's life. The best postwar story found the paper's own correspondent, Staff Sergeant Dick Wilson, with other intrepid newsmen, first informing the public what the Russians were doing in Manchuria. Another success was the paper's continued publication during a compositors' and pressmen's strike that occurred briefly in late January and early February of 1946. Their strike was aimed at the civilian firm employing them rather than the *Stripes*, however. This resulted in the paper's printing only four pages instead of the usual eight. The shortened versions lasted for only a few days, the January 30 issue being the last of the four-pagers. At the same time, because of the Chinese New Year, the Chinese composing room workers took a Sunday off and consequently there was no Monday, February 4 issue; the Tuesday, February 5 paper appeared on schedule.[21]

The paper boasted three supplements. One was a special illustrated, four-page *U.S. Navy Supplement* appearing on Navy Day as part of the October 27, 1945, issue to celebrate the Navy's 170th anniversary. Much more substantial was an eight-page well-illustrated *Magazine Supplement* appearing on Saturdays, which was introduced on November 3. It was designed to provide articles on specific issues both in China and back home. The editor also promised a weekly crossword puzzle, notes on radio, stage and screen, as well as book reviews, and "a little cheesecake, if you think you can take it." As was the case with the parent paper, the editor hoped that its life would be a short and happy one, and hopefully even shorter than happier. The *Supplement* followed its mandate and developed several topics at some length. The reduction of the paper's operations in 1946, however, led to the notice that the ten editors and writers of the *Supplement* had been reduced to four and it was accordingly necessary to cease publication. The last one appeared on March 9, 1946, after nineteen issues. The last edition of the *Stripes*, on April 13, 1946, also included a four-page Special with features on the paper's history and operations.[22]

There was one extravaganza in the Shanghai *Stripes'* history: an elaborate Rickshaw Derby and Army-Navy football game. Originally scheduled for Thanksgiving Day, for various reasons it was postponed to December 1. First announced in the November 16, 1945, issue, it was billed as a gigantic $7,000,000 (CRB) Rickshaw Derby. Sponsored by the *Stars and Stripes* Sports Department, the derby was run in connection with the Army-Navy football classic. Twenty rickshaws were to be entered, each with one driver and one passenger, a girl chosen as entrant by any branch or office of the U.S. armed services in China. The winning driver was to receive a cash prize and the girl winner named "Queen of the Game" and "Miss Rickshaw of 1945." The race was to begin at 1:00 at the Navy Jetty in Shanghai and from there was to proceed to Nanking Road, on out Bubbling Well to Seymour Road, finally arriving at 439 Avenue du Roi Albert, the address of the Canidrome, the stadium where the game was to be played. The ceremony crowning the winner was scheduled during the game's halftime. The race would be about three and one-half miles, with tight traffic control being assured. The prizes were to be split by the drivers.

Subsequently, the paper was filled with numerous articles, features and photographs of the contestants and other participants. Naturally, General Wedemeyer appeared in accounts and photographs, as in the November 28 issue, depicting him checking the ferryboat-size feet of Cunningham Wong, the rickshaw boy scheduled to pull the China Theater Headquarters entry with his passenger, Mrs. Francis Tong, a Portland-born secretary in the G-5 office. The conclusion was that if the day of the race produced a muddy track, Wong should have no trouble in winning.[23]

Another article focused on Milly Pavlovsky, the entry for the American Red Cross office at Kiangwan airfield. GIs there were concerned about her weight, but she was shooting for 115 pounds despite her fondness for doughnuts and pastry. As to vital statistics, she was 5 feet 6 inches and age 19. Other dimensions had been classified SECRET under provisions of AR 380-5, the paper primly declared.[24]

Other articles highlighted some of the rickshaw pullers, including one discussing the 10th Air Force rickshaw boy, called in English "Dubble Trouble," who had conquered polio as a child and was now poised to pull Margaret Baptiste to victory. Several spoof features recorded the fantastic speeds purportedly reached by some of the entries in speed trials before the event as well as instances of trash talk.[25]

Meanwhile, considerable attention was given to the scheduled football game, sponsored by the China Theater's Special Services. A review of the prospective lineups made it soon apparent that the Navy squad had a greater share of talent as well as a weight advantage and seemed certain to win. Also, two men had professional experience, and in addition, Rear Admiral C.T. Joy, commander of the Navy's Yangtze River Patrol, had "ordered" the team to win that game — "or else."[26]

On Derby Day, the streets were packed with thousands of onlookers, some estimates of the crowd size reaching as high as 1,500,000. The armed forces had also trucked in 10,000 GIs, sailors and Marines, adding to the throng. The entire course was closely packed and the excitement ran high. Flower-bedecked rickshaws — there were nineteen instead of the twenty originally scheduled — with labels of their sponsors blazoned across them, were hauled the entire distance. With the money going to the coolies, the applause to the lovely ladies, and the fun to the tremendous crowd, as one enthusiastic commentator reported it, a grand time was had by all. June Nergaard, a petite brunette, and the coolie Paavo Nurmi-Wong, won the race for the Port Quartermaster outfit. His time was 18:03 over the 3-and-one-half mile course, to take the CRB $2,000,000 first prize — worth about $20 in current American money. June Nergaard was duly crowned "Miss Rickshaw of 1945." Admiral Joy draped the traditional floral Derby Horseshoe over the winning coolie, and he and Wedemeyer presented each of the eighteen losing rickshaw jockeys with a loving cup and other prize money. Initially, the 10th Air Force entry, You-Sa-Houmuchi with Miss Margaret Blanchard as his passenger, took the lead, but after the half, Nurmi-Wong made his bid. Once he was in front, the throng surged around him so that not even Houdini, let alone Houmuchi, could have gotten through the mob.

As to the game, even an Army mule and Navy goat were present, and some 20,000 hot dogs were passed out by the Red Cross. As expected, the Navy won by a score of 12–0. Earlier, on Thanksgiving Day in the States, the situation had been reversed. In several issues in November, there had been running accounts of preparations of Army and Navy squads in the U.S. for the traditional game. Though the Army lost in Shanghai, at home, the Army's powerful gridiron machine beat Navy by a score of 32–13. The difference was two all-America backs: Felix (Doc) Blanchard and Glenn Davis.[27]

Undoubtedly, the staff of the Shanghai *Stripes* lived and worked in interesting surroundings. This extended to the living quarters, which earlier in the paper's life were second to none. The staff were initially billeted in a mansion of a former Chinese high official, which they called their "Grand Hotel." It was located at 769 Yu Yuan Lee Road in the French Quarter of the former International Settlement. This idyllic situation continued until, as staffer Bill Jessup recorded it, in late December, "One *Striper* made a mistake, inviting the lieutenant from headquarters billeting office to a holiday party; another made a bigger mistake, making a successful play for the lieutenant's date." The results were that the staff lost their plush accommodations and had to move into barracks with other soldiers of the China Theater.[28]

Abe Rosen further explained. In an article titled "No Momma, No Poppa, No Billet," he recorded that January 1, 1946, marked the end of not only their plush quarters, but also their freedom, and they were then, as he facetiously put it, at last truly inducted into the Army. They had to move to the eighth floor of the Foreign YMCA, though guests were permitted only as far as the

Bird's-eye view of Nanking Road, Shanghai. The imposing building in the left background is the Park Hotel, the most elegant in Shanghai, and for many years its tallest building. Just to the right is the Foreign YMCA, where the staff of the *Stars and Stripes* lived from January to April 1945 (courtesy The Virtual Shanghai Project (*http://virtualshanghai.net*), Image ID 1632).

third floor. The Foreign "Y," opposite the race course on Bubbling Well Road, was near the elegant Park Hotel, the most luxurious hostelry in the city and for many years the tallest building in Asia. Earlier, they had per diem and their own billet complete with the best cook and bar in town, and a fireplace. They lost their per diem as of December 10, 1945, but remained for a bit longer in the billet until forced to move. Still, at the "Y" they had private rooms, hot showers and Red Cross girls to hold their hands— at bridge, of course. Yet they remained unhousebroken. Beer bottles seemed to be everywhere, and much else, despite the first sergeant's attempts to reform them. They were begged, cajoled and even threatened, but they were adamant. They, at least, won this battle.[29]

The end of the paper's life came rather quickly. The last editorial repeated what was said in the first edition about the hopes that its life would be short and sweet, and rarely had a newspaper so earnestly aimed at going out of business as soon as possible, the editor had then intoned. The editor's last words were simply that that time had finally arrived. After six months, two weeks and two days, the paper was put to bed. The readers were not taken by surprise. The March 23 issue had announced that the paper's managing editor, Sergeant

John Clift, had submitted a written memorandum to General Wedemeyer on March 12 recommending that the paper cease publication following the appearance of the April 13 issue. His reasons were understandable. He asserted that the accelerated redeployment and possible early closing of the China Theater would force a suspension of publication. The April demobilization quota would take the bulk of the remaining staff members home and the paper found it imperative, therefore, to cease operations. Wedemeyer approved the decision, noting that while he would regret the paper's close, there was apparently no alternative. He went on, in a piece of official boilerplate, that he had been proud of the service the *Stars and Stripes* had given in accomplishing the task for which it was founded: the morale boosting of personnel in the China Theater. In fact, as Wedemeyer once confided to members of the staff, the *Stripes* "was the only important morale weapon he had."[30]

The final issue — Volume 1, No. 167, April 13, 1946 — consisted of the usual eight pages and a special section of four pages. In these, the staff produced numerous articles and features highlighting much of the paper's life with some zany features and photographs of staffers, cartoons, and other items of note. This included one last poem by the ubiquitous A.L. Crouch, a parody of "The Night Before Christmas," though its theme was, appropriately, "the night before closing."

There were several summaries of the paper's career in the last issue. One account by John Clift described at some length what had been accomplished. Something out of the ordinary had happened in Shanghai, he began. For one thing, the *Stripes* had begun as a four-page paper, but was soon an eight-pager. This was remarkable when one considered that the Mediterranean *Stars and Stripes* had stayed at four pages for over a year and then reverted to two pages, before finally becoming an eight-page paper. The paper's most extraordinary asset, however, may well have been Arthur (Little Man) Goodfriend, Clift asserted. Indeed, he was as short of statue as he usually was of cash, and just about everybody owned an IOU from the colonel. He had to be put at the top of the list of what had happened in Shanghai. Second was Edmund Hogan, who talked everyone's ears off relating his life's history in Italy, but he made major contributions. There were other extraordinary colleagues as well, but these were now gone and the wire holding everything together had broken. For 167 issues it had stretched and strained, but in the night of April 12, with "Stubby" Pernod, the production chief, last seen going at full speed in the direction of Indiana, it had snapped at last. It was about time, Clift concluded.

Staff Sergeant John O. Davies, Jr., of the Marine Corps, late of the *Newark* (N.J.) *Evening News* and the *Stripes*' news editor, had further comment. He called the China edition a symbol of the democratic ideals for which history's bloodiest war had just been fought. By airplane, ship and sometimes even rickshaw, this edition reached GIs throughout the of Land of Han six days weekly. The China edition was the last of the *Stars and Stripes* sheets and the only one in the newspaper's old annals, which dated to the U.S. Civil War, to boast a freedom of the press charter signed by the theater commander himself. It won the respect of EM and officers alike from Hong Kong to Chinwangtao and from Chungking to Shanghai. The paper could also boast that its gripes column was never called into question, unlike the Tokyo edition, where rightfully or not, there were staff dismissals after policy disagreements with theater officers. It also differed from the situation at the Mediterranean *Stars and Stripes*, where an officer in charge fell by the wayside in a successful battle to lift a "B-Bag" gag order. The China edition had traveled a seldom-obstructed middle road and its letters-to-the-editor column had never been scissored by the censor.

The last "Yank About China" published in the paper was by William Martin Camp, a Marine correspondent. He noted that the Shanghai sheet was the only *Stars and Stripes* edition that had all branches of the services represented on its staff. It also served more Marines and Navy than Army personnel. He noted that he would be returning to Tientsin after the final issue was put to bed to rejoin his outfit, the Marine Third Amphibious Corps. Back in November 1945, the Marines had begun to republish the *North China Marine*, a weekly that had appeared earlier in prewar Tientsin and Peiping. It was suspended in December 1941, when the Japanese took the Marines prisoner after Pearl Harbor. He admitted, though, that the paper always operated under severe handicaps, a reference to what amounted to a strict censorship by Marine commanders. He and Davies hoped to take surplus newsprint, type, ink and other printing equipment back with them to Tientsin to benefit the *North China Marine*, and maybe see it become a daily. As to the Shanghai *Stripes*, he concluded that in particular the Marines in North China would sorely miss the paper. For months, every morning at 10 o'clock, when the Tientsin Red Cross Liberty Lounge opened with coffee and doughnuts, hundreds of Leathernecks sat around dunking doughnuts and reading the paper. It also found its way by air express to Tangshan and Chinwangtao, where Marines were keeping lines of communications open. It appeared, too, at Peitaiho Beach, where Marines occasionally came under fire, and at all other command posts and outposts wherever Marines and sailors served. Indeed, the paper was the only way by which the Marines kept in touch with the daily developments in the puzzling postwar world.

The paper continued publishing interesting articles to the end. One, which appeared in the "Yank About China" column by John Clift, was on the topic of women in the Soviet Navy and how far-fetched the idea would be in the American fleet, though he was unaware that his description forecast developments in the not-too-distant future. He reported that a Russian ship had tied up in the Whangpoo, hardly a newsworthy item in itself. But there were huge differences about that vessel. There was a female radio technician as well as women cooks, and various other specialists whose jobs were only performed by male yeomen, seamen and radiomen in the American Navy. They came complete with long pants and pea jackets, and what would be obvious, the morale aboard was first-rate. Just imagine, he went on, eating a steaming plate of beef stroganoff cooked and delivered as though one were back in Moscow. Then a message would be delivered by a cute, slender girl who would pirouette in to deliver it, something Uncle Sam was not about to authorize. Therefore, he predicted American sailors would continue for years to come to eat the chow that their own "cute little hairy-chested Horace Hamhock tosses out."[31]

Though Goodfriend had departed long before the paper ceased publication, in a way he had the last word, writing in his memoirs:

> Compared with the woes of the European Theater, producing the China edition of *The Stars and Stripes* was heaven.... Blessed with a blithe and gifted staff, utterly free of outside interdiction, untouched by the tensions that in Paris had riven enlisted men and officers, and servicing news-starved soldiers, sailors and marines to whom each day's issue was a benediction, its short life was shadowed only by the clouds of civil strife that, gathering over China, signaled the storm few Americans could, in the ecstasy of victory, foresee.[32]

XV

Conclusions

"Where there is no vision the people perish."
— Proverbs 29:18

"Take not from the past its ashes—but its fire."
— Anonymous

Troop newspapers, as is often the case, flesh out official accounts and records, providing additional insights and information about troop employment at several levels. Compared to other editions of the *Stripes*, the China edition uniquely differentiated among the various branches of the military presence, their conduct, their distinct employment situations and status—their daily rounds in an Asian setting. Its pages also delineated developments and attitudes regarding the vast problems of demobilization and their impact both overseas and in the States. The home front was not neglected because home was never far from the innermost thoughts of overseas service personnel. Yet, the Shanghai paper did not discuss, to the degree that might have been expected, such topics as the development of technology, rocket advances, atomic energy, and the end of colonialism which resulted from many attempts by former colonial powers to regain control in such places as Indonesia, Southeast Asia and elsewhere on the globe. These subjects did not apparently have a wide appeal for GIs preoccupied with more immediate concerns.[1]

The depth and vitality of the Shanghai *Stripes*, however, reflected much more than its response to the daily record of events concerning the servicemen of the China Theater in the immediate postwar era. More important in the China edition were treatments of such topics as the Japanese presence; the burgeoning Chinese civil war; the characteristics of East and West in contact, conflict and contention; and aspects of America's emerging foreign policy seeking rapidly to readjust in the already apparent "Cold War" era.

Also what cannot be avoided in any discussion regarding these years in Chinese history concerns the bigger picture as to what was happening there and its continuing significance. Its course proceeded according to its own logic and along its own path, essentially undeterred by what the rest of the world might do or think. Accordingly, any study involving contacts between Westerners and Easterners — in this case specifically the Chinese — must consider various dimensions of those involvements. These, too, can be profitably examined in the pages of the paper and some conclusions advanced about matters well beyond 1945–1946, extending to the present. This would include the significant question: whither China and the West? Though the Shanghai Stripes could not altogether foretell what was to transpire, the delimitation and discussions of the metes and bounds of China's condition, which was the stage upon which Western forces were sited, provide details about its contemporary status. In addition, some insight into the inherent limitations of what the West could accomplish are presented, even though many Westerners failed to read and interpret the tea leaves with any understanding — a persisting condition. While the war resulted in Japan's defeat, Dick Wilson, in his study about "when tigers fought," states that "as for the outsiders, the war did indeed, as Japan had intended, end European domination of the Asian mainland, and cut the Gordian knot of what to do with Europe's unequal treaties with China." Yet "both China and Japan were bled white by their fighting and had to receive massive post-war injections of American aid. In China's case this was contested by the two sides in her civil war, and the winning Communist Party in 1949 had to do without it." Little else was resolved, and as Wilson concluded, "The Sino-Japanese war is thus a one-off phenomenon, a tragic and wasteful episode which did no good to anyone, a negative example of the unwise use of military power.... But it achieved nothing." America's intervention as well, though it had emerged victorious over the Japanese, and was able to assist China in the short run, was at last voided by significant events that transpired.[2]

Another scholar who drew incisive conclusions regarding the China and the West is Barbara Tuchman. In her fine study of Stilwell and the American experience in China, she notes that China, in the face of monumental, massive sufferings over the past century, with its interminable conflicts with the West, and its internal struggles and strife, and especially in the years from 1932 to 1945 — if not before — "was a problem for which there was no American [or Western] solution." They could "not supply an outworn government [that of Chiang Kai-shek] with strength and stability or popular support. It could not hold up a husk nor long delay the cyclical passing of the mandate of heaven. In the end China went her own way as if the Americans had never come."[3]

The inadequacy of American power to act decisively in the circumstances of 1945–1946 was also clearly understood by the director of the American Military Advisory Group to China in Nanking, Major General David Barr of the U.S. Army. He advised Washington in a hard-headed, clear-eyed statement that "only a policy of unlimited United States aid including the immediate employment of the United States forces to block the southern advance of the Communists, which I emphatically do not recommend, would enable the Nationalist Government to maintain a foothold in southern China against a determined Communist advance.... The complete defeat of the Nationalist Army ... is inevitable." And so it came to pass. To the Western Allies after World War II, China was yet another "bridge too far." Short of the initiation of World War III — a real possibility if other policies had been followed — it would remain "a bridge uncrossed."[4]

A more optimistic view appeared in an unsigned article in the last issue of the *Magazine Supplement*. Titled "L'Envoi," it asserted that Kipling's famous line about East and West should now be rephrased as East is East and West is West, and never the twain shall part. The writer confidently predicted that Americans would be in both Japan and China for a very long time, though he was correct only regarding Japan. He felt that the Chinese would welcome this development because Americans had gained a new, sophisticated wisdom about the world in general and about China in particular. To be sure, he continued, Americans had worn out their welcome in China as GIs perhaps had done elsewhere in the world. Yet despite manifestations of childish and rowdy behavior, and even examples of violent and criminal acts, the Chinese, with a tolerance born of centuries, judged Americans as individuals instead of condemning every uniformed man as a drunken bum, as some of them were. Subsequently, China would, as a matter of course, grow more conscious of its nationalism, but after its "face" was regained, and she had won her place in the family of nations, she would become more accepting of others. Thus, there were to be new opportunities for Americans who had met the Chinese on their own terms and sought to understand the China of the present and the future.[5]

The Shanghai *Stripes* also presented several thoughtful, provocative editorials that manifested more than a casual interest in the Chinese world and its myriad problems. In one, appearing in the October 12, 1945, issue, written no doubt by Goodfriend, the editorialist asserted that he failed to understand certain hard-boiled so-called realists' talk about the current Chinese situation. These generally insisted that China was a fouled-up country, graft-laden and crippled by disease. The people were starving, and Chiang Kai-shek was surrounded by bandits and other miscreants. There would soon be a full-scale civil war between Chiang's Nationalists and the Communists, and therefore Westerners should depart or be consumed by the fire. The Chinese were sloppy and lazy, and needed the white man to keep them in line. These conditions would persist because China was incapable of ever righting itself. Though they were correct to a considerable extent, Goodfriend thought that the pessimists failed to take into account many essential truths about postwar China. One was that after eight years of playing for terrific stakes, China was still in the poker game and had a few chips left. In addition, China was now pulsing with new life; young people were disgusted with corruption and the old order of things and were determined to do something about them. Beyond this, the world was not blind to China's plight, and many talented people were busily at work trying to work things out. Certainly, China had a long, hard way to go, but was on its way, and with less of the old ways of thinking about her and a little faith, she had a chance of making the grade.

Another editorial appearing a week later in the October 19 issue, also presumably by Goodfriend, and titled "China for Chinese," was even closer to the mark. He first noted that many people could not get it into their heads that China now belonged to the Chinese. The pedestal had been kicked from under the white man, who was accustomed to dominating China. Many foreigners were now pining for the dear old days beyond recall when life was one long Shanghai holiday with no taxes, plenty of liquor, servants at their beck and call, and good "Westerners-only" clubs, where, if so inclined, one could play a "pukka chukker of polo." But "anyone who moans and groans about China's future — all because he personally has had a kick in the pants — is a barnacle on the backside of progress.... China may be in for a helluva headache. But the turn-back-the-universe-and-give-me-yesterday boys are not the aspirin China needs." Thus, the "century of shame," extending from the 1840s to the 1940s, when Western "rights" were mainly coerced or usurped, was over, and the China so beloved by the "Old China Hands" was consequently no more, and tears shed for its recall were unavailing.

Goodfriend's views were more accurate in the long run than in the short range, and were rather like one of Rudyard Kipling's assessments. The poet had famously written in his book *The Naulahka: A Story of East and West* that it was not good for the Christian's health to try to beat down the Asian because he would be worn down in the process, resulting only in a tombstone upon which was carved the epitaph that a "fool lies here," who "tried to hustle the East."[6] Kipling was certainly correct in the long view, though not in the shorter run, especially in the century from the 1840s to 1949. In those years, there was much hustling of the East, especially China, by the West. But now propelled by its one billion, three-hundred millions of people, and an altogether new spirit and set of circumstances, it is emerging into a new age, and Kipling in the future will undoubtedly be regarded as a prophet — the East will be increasingly difficult to "hustle."

Many of Goodfriend's opinions were in agreement with those of other knowledgeable observers of the Chinese scene, such as Pearl S. Buck. She developed them in her often neglected or ignored memoir, *My Several Worlds*, written shortly after the Communist takeover of China. Therein, we read that "the Chinese are a proud and envious people, as a nation and as individuals, and they do not love their superiors and never did, and the truth is they have never believed that their superiors could exist." This was one of the explanations of the present anti–Americanism, she wrote, coupled with the attitudes of white missionaries and traders and diplomats who considered themselves, whether consciously or unconsciously, superior to the Chinese. This smoldering fury, which white men could not or would not recognize, had lived on in Chinese hearts for more than a century. It was the chief reason why Chiang Kai-shek lost his country and the Communists won it. In fact, if he had been wise, he would have boldly expressed his own anti–Western feelings and thereby retained his leadership. He thought, however, that he could win by American power, and this his people could not forgive him. Accordingly, Mao Tse-tung seized the opportunity that Chiang threw away, and the power of history in Asia had therefore turned against the West. To reverse matters, Pearl Buck suggested that Americans in particular must prove to the Asians that they were not totally involved in suppressing the Chinese. They were therefore relatively innocent of much of the past. They were not to be confused with the British who once ruled India, and in China won the three Opium Wars and heavily taxed the people, nor with those officials in England who allowed Japan to remain in Manchuria, thereby establishing the basis for the Japanese imperial war. Americans should prove to Asia that they had not been as other white men had been. Nevertheless, this posed many difficulties because Americans were "only relatively innocent." Americans, for instance, in 1900, participated in suppressing the Boxer Rebellion, which was not a rebellion but rather a revolt against the white man. During this venture, Americans played a part in the destruction of palaces and the looting of incalculable quantities of the nation's treasure in Peking, Tientsin and elsewhere. Buck indicated that Americans did not heed nor understand — and do not yet understand — what the results of these actions would be, for they were numbered among the white men. After the storm and the defeat of the Chinese, the West went back again to China without a lesson learned. They returned to complacency, thinking that they had taught the Chinese a lesson by force, so that they would never again rebel against the white man's rule. They were allowed to come and go as they pleased in China, and their merchant ships and naval vessels could sail Chinese waters and dock at any port unhindered by rules and restrictions. Missionaries were given the freedom to live where they wished and to open schools teaching subjects foreign to the Chinese, though the schools were a boon as well. They could establish hospitals which practiced foreign medicine and surgery, though medical aid, as was true of education, was one of the positive sides of Western missionary intervention. Perhaps most devastating of all, missionaries were free to preach a religion entirely alien to the Chinese, insisting that their religion was the only true one, and declaring that those who refused to believe were condemned to hell. Buck, the daughter of missionaries, who had grown up in China and therefore possessed a first-hand knowledge of these matters, concluded that "the affrontery [sic] of all this still makes my soul shrink." Buck's tutor — a Mr. Kung — further warned her that there would surely be a reckoning "until justice is done," though he said it "gravely and with infinite pity."[7]

Significantly, the last issue of the *Magazine Supplement*, March 9, 1946, included an article on missionaries in the new era from the Western view. This noted that the Right Reverend Bartel Hilen Reinheimer, the Episcopal Bishop of Rochester, New York, among other churchmen, was of the opinion by 1946 that a more mature wisdom demanded that in China, native Christians would henceforth be in charge of their own religious affairs. Accordingly, while Western Christians would continue to assist the younger churches with funds and advice, they would only work under the leadership of native Christians. This was another case, however, of too little too late, a formulation that characterized the results of the Western stance and endeavors in China in the postwar years for many decades to come.

Indeed, a study of the immediate postwar months in China, which the Shanghai *Stripes* presents, provides a more detailed framework for projecting many dimensions of the Chinese puzzle as well as possibilities and probabilities for the West beyond the limited era of 1945–1946. Goodfriend's editorial views, which often reflected his longstanding international orientation, for example, can be seen as a trajectory projecting into the 21st century. In this regard, the paper also functioned as a transitional source, suggesting something beyond 1945–1946. To many Westerners, there have been perpetually varying policies in mind-boggling, confusing array, especially in the United States, concerning what role China was to play, both during the war and beyond. In most instances, the underlying assumption was always that whatever the policy, Asia in general, but China in particular, was as "clay in the hands of the West." At the heart of the West's wrong assumptions was the notion that China could be changed and reformed along Western lines. After all, the Japanese had progressed far along this road in the nineteenth century and had emerged as a world power to be reckoned with. But demands by the West for change such as prescribed by Christianity and democracy, offered by missionaries and foreign advisers, failed because they "were not indigenous demands of the society and culture to which they were brought." Those in America who, especially in the McCarthy era of the 1950s, so vociferously argued that many of their benighted countrymen had "lost" China, failed to grasp that China had never been "found" by the West; it was never the West's to "lose." The internal pressures between Chiang and the Communists were simply too intense and profound for the West to influence appreciably. Therefore, the concerns among many pundits and politicians that the return of the veterans amid so much clamor endangered the peace, at least in China, were ill-founded. There was simply too much "Chinese business" involved for any foreign intrusion to substantially alter matters. Certainly, the U.S. Marines, for instance, were far too few in number to turn the tide. Their final withdrawal was the only viable alternative. Beyond the years of World War II, attitudes still persist in many corners of the Western mind that contemplate how the West is to "'manage the rise of China,' [because] it gives us a sense of control and mastery, and of paternalistic superiority." Therefore, "with proper piloting and steady nerves on our part, the massive Chinese ship can be brought safely into harbor and put at anchor." But "isn't it possible," an American critic has recently asked, "that

XV. Conclusions

China does not want to be integrated into a political and security system that it had no part in shaping?" Indeed, "might not China, like all rising powers of the past, including the United States, want to reshape the international system to suit its own purposes, commensurate with its new power?"[8]

Also as to American views, James Lilley, a former U.S. ambassador to China, has observed in his memoirs something about a common American attitude toward that country: "For some reason, many Americans think their personal experiences in China are fascinating and unique, and, like the Ancient Mariner, they must tell their tale to the end. Their idea is: I have seen China, and, therefore, it now exists. But this is a static view, shaped by subjective interpretation and woefully narrow in scope." Later, he said, "I met American four-star generals who would get briefed on substantive issues before going into China. However, once they returned to the U.S. after their short trip, they would stop listening, thinking that they had China figured out. They became like one-way walkie-talkies that transmitted but didn't receive." He added, "This could be a harmless trait, but in generals it was dangerous." There were many Americans who desire to see "their" China, as opposed to the one that exists. They are impressed by the country, but they do not truly seek to know it.[9]

Other recent commentaries on trends and stances in our contemporary age also bear out some of Goodfriend's views expressed earlier in editorials in the Shanghai *Stripes*. Western attitudes that might be successful in meeting the 21st century regarding sound U.S.–Chinese relations, and Asia in general, are suggested as signposts for the future. A brief but cogent account by one sinologist, Mark Leonard, raises many pertinent questions about China and the West. He observes that the West knows little about contemporary Chinese thinkers and what they dream for their country, which, in turn, means a great deal of what the coming world will be like. As he asserts, "Europeans and Americans, in particular, are ill-equipped to answer these questions. Since the time when French and British missionaries first travelled to the East, the West has focused on what it wanted from China — and how to convert the Chinese to a Western way of life. People wrongly assumed that as China grew richer, it would also become more like us." Though they have become more Westernized regarding materialism and capitalism, they have not followed the West very far along the path of democracy.[10]

Leonard met many of China's intellectuals and watched fascinated as he "saw them take Western ideas and adapt them into a new Chinese approach for dealing with the world — joining an intellectual journey that China began when it first became entangled with the West in the nineteenth century." Leonard further notes that China in the past has often manifested an intellectual insecurity that resulted in massive swings from one extreme ideology to the next, as in the Cultural Revolution, for instance, and in Marxism, then maybe back, at least to some extent, to Confucius, then once more to the Western political and economic thought and practice. Certainly a case of the pendulum theory of history is in practice. What the Chinese are learning is that following the West too far leads to chaos and to China's falling between the two stools of extremism in ways not conducive to the development of the good life for all Chinese. Leonard quotes a Tsinghua University professor, Cui Zhiyuan, who wrote a seminal article calling for a new "Liberation of Thought," arguing that after Chinese intellectuals had freed themselves from orthodox Marxism, they now "should liberate themselves from their unquestioning admiration of Western capitalism. His goal was to break the boom and bust cycle that saw China embrace a new ideology every generation, and to encourage Chinese people to think for themselves." To these ends, China's New Left, "thirty years into China's reform process ... are challenging the philosophy of growth as the ultimate goal: Instead of hurtling towards nineteenth-century laissez-faire capitalism, they want to develop a Chinese variant of social democracy. And while, like magpies, they adapt ideas from all over the world to Chinese conditions, they feel that China's development should be built on Beijing's terms."[11]

The question in China today is "how quickly and competently will the new China manage to capitalize on its early, historical promise" and overcome and recede from its horrific "Century of Shame" contacts with the West? Can these be overcome and superseded? What will the new China look like? Will it be a danger to the West? Clearly, China is neither poor nor backward any longer. The Chinese language remains intact, essentially unaltered from its origins more than 3,000 year ago. While there was a hiatus of several hundred years, from about A.D. 1,500 to the present, China has now profoundly changed yet again, and within two decades has "become so rich, energetic, freewheeling, awesome, and spectacular," that "it seems abundantly clear that creativity, true inventiveness, is starting to flow in China once again, with the new prosperity of the country." Therefore, China is no longer "the sinkhole of decay and desuetude that it was. Nowadays, in every field—in science and technology on the one hand, in literature and the plastic arts on the other—the new China is entering a time of intense activity and entrepreneurial energy." Its new spirit is well exemplified by a giant billboard at the entrance to Jiuquan, one of China's massive space bases on the fringes of the Gobi Desert. The sign "simply and starkly, states: 'Without Haste, Without Fear, We Conquer the World.'" Therefore, "after 5,000 years of patient waiting, watching, and learning, this is at last China's appointed time."[12]

In another recent study of China, the American journalist James Fallows writes that "the United States should (and must) make a major effort to open itself to the Chinese, to develop the areas where mutual cooperation is feasible and valuable, to respect China's brainpower and do everything possible to recreate the United States in Chinese minds as a focus for research and a potential source of fruitful collaboration. The venues for this collaboration range from basic agriculture to banking, from global warming and the conservation of natural resources to the reconfiguring of Chinese views of their own future." Indeed, Fallows concludes, that such a meeting of the minds from both societies is essential to the well-being of all.[13]

Certainly Goodfriend would have applauded these prescriptions as mirroring his own views advanced more than a half-century earlier and developed further in the decades following. Were such a positive development of East-West relations now to ensue, Goodfriend would be happily reassured that his creation of the GI paper in Shanghai had not been in vain. Its existence, therefore, may well have accomplished more than simply its reportage of American involvement in the passing Chinese scene, which, on the whole, it did commendably, competently, and reasonably well.

Chapter Notes

Introduction

1. This document was also sent to the commanding generals of U.S. Army Air, Ground, and Service Forces. See in George Catlett Marshall, *The Papers of George Catlett Marshall*, Vol. 5, *The Finest Soldier, January 1, 1945 –January 7, 1947*, edited by Larry I. Bland and Sharon Ritenour Stevens (Baltimore: Johns Hopkins Press, 2003), 278–279. Hereinafter cited as Marshall, *Papers*.
2. See fact sheet concerning demobilization, in draft form, Washington, September 7, 1945, in ibid., 298–299.
3. There is a brief discussion of the points system in Stephen Ambrose, *Band of Brothers* (New York: Simon & Schuster, 2001), pp. 281–82, and Alfred Emile Cornebise, *Ranks and Columns: Armed Forces Newspapers in American Wars* (Westport, CT: Greenwood Press, 1993), p. 133, and note 88, p. 187.
4. See discussion in Cornebise, *Ranks and Columns*, pp. 159–168.

Chapter I

1. Much of the following account is drawn from Arthur Goodfriend's wartime memoirs, "I Want to Go Home, 1942–46," unpublished typescript, Goodfriend Papers, Special Collections,R00006, Box 14, University of Hawaii at Manoa Library. Hereinafter cited as "I Want to Go Home."
2. Another prominent paper in the CBI was the *Roundup*. It appeared in September 1942, and published its last issue as Vol. IV, No. 31 in Delhi, India, on Thursday, April 11, 1946.
3. For Wedemeyer, see his memoirs, *Wedemeyer Reports!* (New York: Henry Holt, 1958); Keith E. Eiler, *Wedemeyer on War and Peace* (Stanford: Hoover Institution Press, 1987); and two articles by Keith E. Eiler, "An Uncommon Soldier," a summary of Wedemeyer's career, and an account of an interview with him, "The Man Who Planned the Victory," both in the *Hoover Digest*, no. 4 (2001). Wedemeyer's papers are in the Hoover Institution at Stanford, California.
4. "I Want to Go Home," p. 315; Emanuel Goldberg, "G.I. Editors in China Given 'Magna Charta,'" *The Quill* 35 (March 1947): 9, 12; Cornebise, *Ranks and Columns*, pp. 144; 151–152.
5. "I Want to Go Home," p. 314. The "B-Bag" referred to a large clothing bag, commonly called the "barracks bag." An expression of the time was to advise anyone unhappy with his situation or condition to "blow it out your b-bag," thus to let off steam. The newspaper adopted this as the title of the complaints column, hence the "B-Bag." Such features were the most controversial of all those in the various editions of the *Stars and Stripes* and other service papers and often involved issues of censorship and freedom of the press in a military setting. See discussions in Cornebise, *Ranks and Columns*, pp. 149, 150, 154, 156, 162, 163, and *passim*. For other letters to the editors columns, apart from the "B-Bag," see ibid., pp. 119, 128, 130, 132, 149, and 162. The essence of Goodfriend's Magna Charta also appeared in an editorial in the first issue of the paper on September 28, 1945, titled "A Statement of Policy.
6. "I Want to Go Home," p. 315. For Wedemeyer's views, see also the *Stars and Stripes*, China Edition, Shanghai, September 28, 1945. Hereinafter cited by date of issue. The reference to Mauldin's cartoons concerned a celebrated encounter between Mauldin and General George Patton, who strongly deplored the cartoonist's depiction of slouchy, scruffy GIs, and the anti-officer tone of many of his creations. Patton failed to dissuade Mauldin, however, and he continued to draw as before. See his own account of the meeting in his memoirs, *The Brass Ring* (New York: W.W. Norton, 1971), pp. 245–264.

7. Staff Sergeant Edmund F. Hogan started his *Stripes* career in North Africa with the Algiers edition and migrated to Italy with the landings at Salerno. He served as managing editor of both the Rome and Naples editions, and was at one time managing editor of the 24-page Mediterranean Theater of Operations paper. He was succeeded as managing editor of the China edition by Staff Sergeant Franc Shor. He sailed home — on points — on the USS *Makin Island*. See account in the December 11, 1945, issue.
8. "I Want to Go Home," p. 315.
9. Ibid., pp. 315–316.
10. Ibid., p. 316. Additional details are in Arthur Goodfriend, *Rice Roots* (New York: Simon & Schuster, 1958), pp. 6–8.
11. "I Want to Go Home," p. 317. Lieutenant Maurice Pernod, production manager of the Shanghai *Stripes*, was later awarded a Bronze Star by Major General Ray T. Maddocks, deputy commander of China Theater, for work in transporting the *China Lantern* from Calcutta to China. See photo and account in the April 13, 1946, issue.
12. "I Want to Go Home," p. 317.
13. Ibid., pp. 318–319. Jessup had been a combat liaison officer with Chinese artillery units in Burma and South China before joining the staff of the *Stripes* (e-mail communication to the author). See also his article, "China Stripes — A brief but colorful run," *European-Pacific Stars and Stripes Association News* 16, no. 1 (January–February 2003): pp. 8–9.
14. Irene Corbally Kuhn (1900–1995) was a journalist and pioneer radio commentator in Paris and China in the 1920s and 1930s, and a war correspondent for NBC and various newspapers reporting from the China-Burma-India Theater during World War II and from Shanghai after the Japanese surrender in September 1945. See her memoirs, *Assigned to Adventure* (Philadelphia: J.B. Lippincott, 1938).
15. "I Want to Go Home," p. 319.
16. Ibid. It was noted that the eight pages put a severe strain on the mechanical resources available. The Chinese invented printing, and there were times when the staff thought that they had some of their original presses. October 8, 1945.
17. This detailed discussion of the paper's establishment, philosophy and early operations are to be found in "I Want to Go Home," pp. 319–320. For Wedemeyer's remarks, see the September 28, 1945, issue.
18. "I Want to Go Home," pp. 318–320.
19. Editorial, "For a Free Press," October 16, 1945. In this matter, Goodfriend was following precedents set by earlier editions of the *Stars and Stripes*. The World War I paper, for instance, justified its rather high price of a dime in U.S. currency by observing that Americans did not respect reading matter that appeared in the form of a store bulletin. See discussion in Alfred E. Cornebise, *The Stars and Stripes. Doughboy Journalism in World War I* (Westport, CT: Greenwood Press, 1984), p. 25.
20. See *China White Paper*, I, 36; 514–519, for the U.S.-Chinese treaty signed in Washington, January 11, 1943. It was ratified May 20, 1943. For the Jews in wartime Shanghai, see Howard M. Brotz, "Shanghai Ghetto Was Living Hell," *Stars and Stripes Magazine Supplement* 1, no. 2 (November 10, 1945).
21. Rana Mitter, *A Bitter Revolution. China's Struggle with the Modern World* (New York: Oxford University Press, 2004), p. 188.
22. September 28, 1945. See Huxley as quoted in Graham Earnshaw, ed., *Tales of Old Shanghai* (Hong Kong: China Economic Review Publishing, 2008), p. 108. Other sources pertinent to the Shanghai scene during 1945–1946 include a guide published by the 14th Air Force in Shanghai: *Flying Tigers' Guide to Shanghai* (Shanghai: Headquarters Fourteenth Air Force Information and Education Section, Special Services, November 1945). This discusses where to shop and dine, currency matters, expected conduct, and much else. It includes a detailed map of downtown Shanghai. See also the unpublished memoir, "One Pilot's Journey in World War II and the CBI Theater," by Flight Officer Kensley Robert Thompson located at: http://cbi-theater-4.home.comcast.net. From October to the end of November 1945, Thompson was stationed at Kiangwan Airfield, Shanghai, with the 330th Troop Carrier Squadron.
23. "I Want to Go Home," p. 313.
24. A U.S. Marine who served in Shanghai in those years recalled that they could purchase tailor-made civilian clothes and uniforms for a fraction of their cost at home. He noted that the "Chinese tailors custom made clothes from the finest chino khaki. Shirts, ties, camel-hair bathrobes (with dragon designs) ... and even silk underwear!" Ray Poppelman, "A China Marine: The Adventures of Ray Poppelman," *Leatherneck* (June 1992): 24.
25. September 28, 1945. For more on Shanghai, see Ralph Shaw, *Sin City* (New York: Time-Warner, 1992); Graham Earnshaw, ed., *Tales of Old Shanghai*, (Hong Kong: China Economic Review Publishing, 2008); and Stella Dong, *Shanghai: The Rise and Fall of a Decadent City* (New York: Harper, 2001).
26. For studies of the U.S. Navy in China between the World Wars, see Kemp Tolley, *The Yangtze Patrol: The U.S. Navy in China* (Annapolis, MD: Naval Institute Press, 1971); Dennis L. Noble, ed., *Gunboat on the Yangtze: The Diary of Captain Glenn F. Howell of the U.S.S.*

Palos, 1920–1921 (Jefferson, NC: McFarland, 2002). For the Marines, see Chester M. Biggs, Jr., *The United States Marines in North China, 1894–1942* (Jefferson, NC: McFarland, 2003); Alexander White, *The United States Marines In North China*. (Millbrae, CA: n.p., 1974). Specifically for Shanghai through the eyes of the 4th Marines who served there in the 1920s and 1930s, see Robert H. Williams, *The Old Corps: A Portrait of the U.S. Marine Corps Between the Wars* (Annapolis: U.S. Naval Institute Press, 1982); and Ray Poppelman, "A China Marine: The Adventures of Ray Poppelman," *Leatherneck* (June 1992). Williams was a junior officer; Poppelman was an enlisted man. Besides Shanghai, much of eastern China also knew the tread of U.S. Army soldiers between the world wars, a fact that is sometimes ignored if recalled at all. See this author's *The United States Fifteenth Infantry Regiment in China, 1912–1938* (Jefferson, NC: McFarland, 2004).

27. September 28 and 29, 1945.

28. A useful account about Shanghai as it emerged into the light of the postwar world appeared in *Fortune* magazine for February 1946. It described Shanghai's current conditions, business and governmental matters and financial forecasts. It was by Charles J.V. Murphy, a staffer of the magazine, and was published as "Shanghai: Reopened Under New Management."

29. September 28, 1945.

30. Ibid.

31. Ibid.

32. February 18, 1946.

33. October 29 and November 19, 1945.

34. February 6 and April 11 issues. There is an account of Crouch in the "Yank About China" column, by John Clift, in the February 6, 1946, issue.

35. October 5, 1945.

36. "I Want to Go Home," 320–321.

37. "I Want to Go Home," pp. 321–322; 330.

38. Ibid., p. 331.

Chapter II

1. George Weller, *Weller's War: A Legendary Foreign Correspondent's Saga of World War II on Five Continents*, ed., Anthony Weller (New York: Crown, 2009), pp. 505–510. To be sure, newsreels, movie documentaries, war movies, and such popular columnists as war correspondent Ernie Pyle did bridge some of the gaps. Pyle worked for the Scripps-Howard newspaper chain and his columns appeared in over 300 newspapers. He won the Pulitzer Prize for reporting in 1944. See his best-selling books: *Here Is Your War* (New York: Henry Holt, 1943); and *Brave Men* (New York: Henry Holt, 1944).

2. Editorial, "There's No Place Like Home," October 4, 1945. The editor noted that the GIs, with their distorted sense of reality about the home front, were perhaps thinking that there awaited them "a happy boss wooing them with oodles of dough. Wives lovelier by far than Hedy Lamarr." There was also perhaps the dream of a long vacation, "with America marking time until they are ready to lead it back to prosperity and peace." But in truth, "returning soldiers are already an old story. America has long since gone back to the business of peace." Bosses were paying men for their skills and knowledge, not their service ribbons. Wives, when the heat was off, would "turn out to have the same moles and wrinkles, and the same lipstick on their slips." As the paper matured, a sometime column, "Home is Where…" was devoted to unusual — even strange — events at home sometimes with the hint that the men were perhaps better off in China.

3. See editorial in the November 15, 1945, issue. The Committee, officially the "Congressional Joint Committee on the Investigation of the Pearl Harbor Attack," was convened on November 15, 1945, and continued its deliberations until May 31, 1946. See Records of the Joint Committees of Congress, 1789–1968, Record Group 128, in the National Archives.

4. October 4, 1945.

5. December 7, 1945 and February 1, 1946.

6. October 26, 1945.

7. September 28, and October 11 and 12, 1945. See also the *Magazine Supplement*, issue No. 10, January 5, 1946, for an article by Howard M. Brotz, "Full Employment — Or Bust!" He discussed the grave concerns in U.S. about the employment problem.

8. February 7, 1946, with apologies to Henley's "Invictus."

9. See Michener's *The World Is My Home: A Memoir* (New York: Random House, 1992), p. 263.

10. December 21, 1945, and January 14, 1946. By early 1946, some 125,000 veterans had enrolled with 207,000 more being processed. With a total enrollment of veterans projected to reach 600,000 by the fall of 1946, how to house them led to the moving in of temporary war and defense housing. These problems were compounded by the fact that thirty per cent of the veterans were married with ten per cent already with children and many more expected. Educational institutions had never coped with so many married students.

11. October 26 and 27, 1945.

12. See details of Walker's charges and appeals in the January 15, 1946, issue.

13. January 22, 1946.

14. Details of the Court's decision are in the February 7, 1946, issue.

15. February 16, 1946.
16. February 28, 1946.
17. March 1 and 4, 1946.
18. December 18, 1945.

Chapter III

1. See Austin C. Wehrwein, "China Lingo: Will Our GI Slang Live Stateside?" *Stars and Stripes Magazine Supplement* 1, no. 15 (February 9, 1946): p. vii.
2. Dong, *Shanghai: The Rise and Fall of a Decadent City*, p. 281.
3. October 2, 1945.
4. October 2 and 23, 1945. Some of the information about China was addressed in a box on the paper's front page called "Chinknowledge"—sometimes spelled as "Chinowledge"—one of which indicated that "when dining with a Chinese family, the fourth cup of tea is an invitation to leave." October 15, 1945.
5. February 26, 1946.
6. October 6, 1945.
7. October 18, 1945, and March 29, 1946. Thompson, "One Pilot's Journey." Franc Shor had his own highly favorable opinions of Chinese food. He discussed the attributes of both Szechwan and Peking duck and other culinary delights in some of his "Yank About China" columns. See, for example, a humorous article on eating duck in Kunming, in Yunnan Province, and another which included "An Ode to a Peking Duck," in the October 12 and 23, 1945, issues.

Chapter IV

1. April 3, 1946. See also letter in the November 14, 1945, issue regarding the officers' use of military vehicles. Therein, one critic put it bluntly. Officers could easily obtain jeeps to take their girls for a spin, which the rank and file could not normally do, and then send the vehicles back to some disgruntled GI to do the dirty work of cleanup and maintenance when their joyrides were over.
2. Austin C. Wehrwein, "But Don't Blame the GIs," *Magazine Supplement* 1, no. 13, January 26, 1946.
3. September 28, and October 2, 1945.
4. Ibid.
5. October 27, 1945.
6. November 5, 1945.
7. November 8, 1945. Another letter by a "confused and bitter ex-civilian," asserted that the continuation of military courtesies was simply the martinet's way of exacting a final measure of submission from the GIs under his yoke. For discussions pertaining to saluting in the Great War's edition of *Stripes*, see Alfred Cornebise, "The Great War Edition of *The Stars and Stripes*," *Relevance* 15, no. 2 (Spring 2006): pp. 22–23. The author Gertrude Stein once argued that if saluting were abolished worldwide, wars would cease. Probably not, but it is a novel notion.
8. October 26 and November 7 and 15, 1945.
9. November 17, 1945.
10. The paper was not above "stroking" the General on occasion. One instance was a short article in the March 4 issue which featured a photo of Wedemeyer playing an accordion. It was explained that he was taking lessons from the manager of the Capitol Theater, Sergeant Jim Klenes, the only man in the China Theater who could tell General Wedemeyer that he was "out of tune." While having little time to practice, he took three lessons per week, and had been doing so for about a month, usually just before supper. He preferred semi-classical selections and totally rejected jive. Another article featured the General's "Super Jeep" photographed in all of its glory. The men of 173rd Mobile Quartermaster Battalion had customized the vehicle in ways which were hardly regulation. It sported a bright green paint job, four white-walled tires, and a chrome grille complete with a statuette as a radiator cap. In addition, there were mud guards, a French horn, automatic windshield wipers, Plexiglas side visors, and three stars painted on both the front and rear lights. The leather upholstery had been installed earlier in Chunking. March 6, 1946.
11. November 22, 1945.
12. November 10 and 15, 1945.
13. November 16, 1945.
14. Letter, January 28, 1946, issue. "Pissed Off" or "Peter Oboed," was usually abbreviated "POed," This was derived from the commonly used radio alphabet code of the day, i.e., Able, Baker, Charlie, Dog, Peter, Oboe, etc.
15. November 14, 1945, and January 15, 1946. The Pentagon recognized that the entire Army was top-heavy with brass and moved to ease the problem, announcing that 1,054 generals were to be either retired or demoted, reducing their number to about 500. This was down from 1,540 as of July 1, 1945, the highest number attained during World War II. The situation in Shanghai had been pointed out to Wedemeyer by staffers of the Shanghai *Stripes* who explained that because some of the officers in Shanghai never had it so good, the China Theater Headquarters was having difficulty in clearing out all Stateside eligibles. Major Wendell Lockett of G-1 thereupon indicated that all eligibles should now ship out and further steps were to be taken to address the problem. February 1, 1946. A visiting journalist, John Hersey, also noticed the unusually high proportion

of officers in Shanghai at this time, and their conspicuous indulgence in luxury. See his "Letter from Shanghai," *The New Yorker* (February 9, 1946), p. 82.

16. See in Marshall, *Papers*, 278–279. The document was dated August 15, 1945, the day after the Japanese surrendered. It was ordered by the Secretary of War, and was also addressed to the commanding generals of U.S. Army Air, Ground and Service Forces.

17. December 27, 1945, and February 22, 1946. In Paris, some 500 disgruntled GIs formed a "GIs' Committee of Liberation" which demanded that the War Department address certain special privileges of officers and order elimination of officers' messes, introducing instead a system where all rations would be on a "first come, first served" basis; opening of all officers' clubs at all posts to officers and men alike; abolition of reserved sections for officers at recreational events; the elimination of all special officers' quarters; introduction of a requirement that all officers serve at least one year as an enlisted man except in time of war; and reform of the Army courts-martial system so as to include enlisted men.

18. March 21 and 30, and April 5, 1946. Hargrove's book was published in 1942 by Henry Holt, and was made into a movie in 1944. Also for the Board and its findings, see documents in Record Group 165, the War Department General And Special Staffs, and Record Group 334, Inter-Service Agencies, National Archives II, College Park, Maryland.

19. November 16, 1945. One solution to soothing EM seemed to be, as time evolved, to add stripes and ratings above those of master sergeants and chief petty officers, though always below officer ranks, creating a "zebra effect." The ideal officer was once poignantly depicted by Ernie Pyle in his book *Brave Men*. He was Captain Henry T. Waskow, a company commander in the 36th Infantry Division killed while fighting in the mountains of Italy. See Pyle, *Brave Men*, pp. 154–56.

20. March 26, 1946.
21. March 6, 1946.
22. November 3, 1945.
23. October 13, 17, and 31, and November 3, 1945.
24. November 20, 21, and 24, 1945.
25. October 6, 1945. The Race Course was also the site of a golf links. See in December 12, 1945, issue.
26. October 16, 20, 24 and 25; November 13, 1945.
27. December 17, 1945.
28. November 6, 1945.
29. Ibid.
30. October 4 and November 12, 1945.
31. October 11 and November 6, 1945.
32. November 24, 28; December 1, 6, and 8; February 1; April 12, 1946.
33. Discussions in November 5, 6 and December 6, 1945, issues. One of the films was titled *Your Job in Germany*. The tough-minded, controversial production had been created in part by Major Theodor Geisel, a.k.a. "Dr. Seuss." It warned that "the Nazi party may be gone, but Nazi thinking, Nazi training and Nazi trickery remains. The German lust for conquest is not dead.... You will not argue with them. You will not be friendly.... There must be no fraternization with any of the German people." Judith and Neil Morgan, *Dr. Seuss & Mr. Geisel: A Biography* (New York: Random House, 1995), pp. 110–115.
34. November 16, 1945, and editorial, "We Must Not Forget," in the October 24, 1945, issue.

Chapter V

1. November 7, 1945.
2. October 17, 22, 23, 1945.
3. November 9, 1945.
4. November 8, 1945.
5. Article in the *London News of the World*, republished in *Stars and Stripes*, January 1, 1946. Other evidence, written and pictorial, in the *Stripes* indicates that Noyes' report was essentially correct. See relevant photographs in the October 27 and 29, 1945, issues. Fraternization was also an issue in Japan and caused much controversy, especially in the United States. As to the fair sex in Japan, several China Marines, in a letter in the March 5, 1946, issue of the Shanghai *Stripes*, crassly observed that it was commonly recognized "to the victors belong the spoils. So why let them spoil?"
6. October 26 and November 8, 1945.
7. October 1, 1945.
8. October 25, 1945.
9. September 29 and October 1, 1945.
10. December 15, 1945.
11. November 12 and 27, 1945.
12. February 8 and 9, 1946.
13. March 14, 1946. Newby did record that the Japanese had maintained strict military discipline during the trip. The LSTs, i.e., "Landing Ship, Tank," and other types of landing craft, played pivotal roles in the many invasions in both Europe and the Pacific in World War II. (See illustration.) General Eisenhower is reported to have stated that such craft, together with the famous "jeep" and the workhorse transport aircraft, the Douglas C-47 *Skytrain*, were the three most important pieces of equipment that American forces used in the war. The LSTs were sometimes dubbed "Long, Slow Targets" by their crews.
14. September 29, 1945. See Robert Barr

Smith, "Japanese War Crimes Trials," *World War II Magazine* (September 1996).

15. FDR, in a letter dated in April 1942, had issued a stern warning to the Japanese of retribution for any executions of U.S. flyers engaged in the Doolittle raid. September 29 and October 10, 1945; March 22 and 27, 1946.

16. October 31, 1945. The eight American airmen were: Lieutenants Dean E. Hallmark, Robert J. Meder, Chase L. Nielsen, William G. Farrow, Robert L. Hite, and George Barr. There were two corporals, Harold A. Spatz and Jacob DeShazer. For the Doolittle raid, see Carroll V. Glines, *The Doolittle Raid: America's Daring First Strike Against Japan* (New York: Orion, 1988); and his *Doolittle's Tokyo Raiders* (New York: Van Nostrand Rinehold, 1968). For the Japanese trials, see January 19, and 21; February 5, 28; March 18, 20, and 21, 1946, issues. Details about the jail, the conduct and atmospherics of the trials, and the personnel involved, were presented by *Stripes* reporter Jim Becker in an article, "'Beast of the East' and His Guilty Pals," in the *Magazine Supplement* 1, no. 19 (March 9, 1946). A sketch of the courtroom is included.

17. See January 19 and 21, 1946, issues and Carroll V. Glines, *Four Came Home* (New York: Van Nostrand Reinhold, 1966). There had been confessions from the airmen but these were written only in Japanese and were not translated into English. Those whose sentences were commuted were later informed that their fate had resulted from a direct order from Emperor Hirohito.

18. January 21, 1946. Other accounts give the time and date of their execution as 4:30 P.M. on October 16, 1942.

19. Details of the Japanese court martial are in Glines, *Four Came Home*. What is forgotten, especially in the U.S., was that the Japanese proceeded brutally against the Chinese for assisting some of Doolittle's men to get to safety after they had crash-landed or parachuted from their aircraft. They burned hundreds of villages and killed many Chinese wholesale. Some estimates of the numbers slain, both soldiers and civilians, are as high as 250,000. One scholar has concluded that "the Chinese paid a terrible price for the Doolittle raid, but they never complained." Dick Wilson, *When Tigers Fight: The Story of the Sino-Japanese War, 1937–1945* (New York: Penguin, 1983), p. 207.

20. November 24 and 30, 1945; January 22, 23, 25; February 11, 12, 13, 14, 15, 16, 19, 20, 25, 27, 28; March 1, 1946.

21. April 5, 1946.

22. October 31 and November 1, 2, 3, 5, 6, 7, 8, 9 10, 12, 13, 14, 15, 16, 17, 1945.

23. November 9, 14, 16, and 17, 1945, issues. Major George F. Guy, one of the Allied Defense Council members, presented a memorandum on the proceedings and conduct of the general's trial for distribution to the Japanese home press in which he assured the Japanese people that the Yamashita case would be a full, fair and complete trial, regardless of what the outcome might be. He concluded that the defendant was being afforded every legitimate defense that could be presented in his behalf. Revelations in the trial indicated much that was done in the name of the emperor, resulting in an editorial in the *Stripes* issue of November 17 that asserted that the most infamous war criminal in all of Japan was the emperor and yet he was still on the throne.

24. November 22, 23, 24, 30, 1945.

25. November 26, 28, 1945.

26. December 5, 1945.

27. December 7, 8, 1945.

28. January 8, 10; February 6, 8, 9, 1946.

29. February 25, 27, 1946.

Chapter VI

1. October 17, 1945.
2. October 17, 18, and December 7, 1945.
3. November 7, 1945.
4. For some details regarding the 14th, see Charles R. Bond, Jr., and Terry Anderson, *A Flying Tiger's Diary* (College Station: Texas A&M University Press, 1984), p. 216 and *passim*, and Daniel Ford, *Flying Tigers* (Washington: Smithsonian Institution Press, 1991), pp. 377–78.
5. December 3, 1945.
6. October 15 and November 16, 1945. The latter article contains much information about the road, something of its history, and a discussion as to what its detractors thought of it.
7. October 23, 1945.
8. For Tunner's career and accomplishments in China and later his management of the Berlin Airlift in 1948–49, see Andrei Cherny, *The Candy Bombers: The Untold Story of the Berlin Airlift and America's Finest Hour* (New York: Putnam, 2008), pp. 324–342, and *passim*. Tunner's own account was published as *Over the Hump: The Story of General William H. Tunner* (New York: Duell, Sloan and Pierce, 1964). Tunner retired as a Lieutenant General. October 20 and November 16, 1945. For statistics, see *The India-Burma Last Roundup*, Delhi, India, April 11, 1946. For details of all aspects of operations over the Hump, see the Hump Pilots Association, "*China Airlift—The Hump.*" (Dallas: Taylor Publishing, 1980).
9. December 7, 1945.
10. April 2 and 8, 1946.

Chapter VII

1. There is a large collection of Lieutenant Colonel Arthur Goodfriend's papers catalogued as the Papers of Arthur Goodfriend, in Special Collections, University of Hawaii at Manoa Library. There is a finding aid, Manuscript R00006, prepared by Richard H. Perrine, July 2000. The collection is housed in ninety-six numbered boxes. It includes copies of the author's several published books and periodical articles, his sketchbooks, notebooks and, most importantly, fifty-one of his holographic journals, the first dating from 1928. These journals are copiously illustrated with the author's drawings in various media — pencil, pen, watercolor, felt pen and crayon — and reveal his skills as illustrator and artist.

There is also a six-page Oral History Finding Aid, as Goodfriend recounted much about his life on tape to Shari Tamashiro, Jason Yamashita, and Ihsia Hu. This consists of two parts: a series of fifteen 100-minute audiocassette tapes, and another seven taped sessions containing discussions of Goodfriend's World War II experiences, recorded August 5, 7, 18–21, and September 5, 1997, and transcribed by Jason Yamashita. Goodfriend's Ed.D. dissertation is in Box 70, together with his diploma and other pertinent documents. His dissertation is titled "The Education of Arthur Goodfriend: A Case Study of Autobiography in an Educational Metaphor" (1988). It has been published as *The Education of a Survivor: From the School of Hard Knocks to a Doctoral Degree* (Honolulu: University of Hawaii Press, 1989). Another important manuscript is an unpublished account of his military service in World War II titled "I Want to Go Home, 1942–1946." It is in Box 14. Other important sources are his books *Rice Roots* (New York: Simon and Schuster, 1958), and *The Only War We Seek* (New York: Farrar, Straus and Young, 1951).

2. Much of the following account is based on Goodfriend's published dissertation: *The Education of a Survivor*.

3. *Education of a Survivor*, pp. 39–40. Frank Shor later borrowed this story for one of his "Yanks About China" columns for the occasion identifying Goodfriend as "Colonel Gideon." This is in the November 16, 1945, issue.

4. For Geisel's wartime activities, see Judith and Neil Morgan, *Dr. Seuss & Mr. Geisel: A Biography* (New York: Random House, 1995), pp. 101–117. See also Arthur Goodfriend Oral History Project; *The Education of a Survivor*, pp. 61–62. See also his "official" EM ID card for "Pvt. Arthur Goodwin," which he signed with an "X." This is in a leather-bound journal, "Ticket to Invasion, 1944," which recounts and illustrates, with copious drawings, his service during the war years, culminating with a short account of his being in China. It is in Box 13 of the Goodfriend Papers.

5. Goodfriend, Oral History Project.

6. Discussions in ibid. On the problem of infantry replacements as viewed from the War Department, see Marshall, *Papers*, 74–76; 145–147.

7. Goodfriend, Oral History Project.

8. *Education of a Survivor*, pp. 64–66.

9. There was much controversy about editorials in the paper, especially after Goodfriend became editor-in-chief. See discussions in Bud Hutton and Andy Rooney, *The Story of The Stars and Stripes: A Paper for Joe* (New York: Farrar and Rinehart, 1946), pp. 66, 127, 230–233, and Andy Rooney, *My War* (New York: Crown, 1995), p. 93. These two deplored the new approach, charging that it was transforming the *Stars and Stripes* into an official propaganda sheet. Some of these matters even reached Eisenhower's ears. For Goodfriend's assessment of the uproars that some of his editorial writing caused, as well as other shortcomings of his views and actions, see Goodfriend, Oral History Project.

10. "I Want to Go Home," pp. 192–193. Also in these memoirs, Goodfriend devoted an entire chapter to the subject to the gripes column. See ibid., pp. 192 ff. For his numerous accomplishments Goodfriend was awarded the Bronze Star, specifically for his *Army Talks* series. He also received the Legion of Merit, a high award rarely given, mainly for his work as editor-in-chief of European editions of the *Stars and Stripes*. The French awarded him the Croix de Guerre for reasons that were unclear, though he surmised that the U.S. had decorated some Frenchmen and his was a matter of reciprocity. He could also wear the coveted Combat Infantryman's badge. For an account of his awards, see Goodfriend, Oral History Project. Citations for the awards are in the journal, "Ticket to Invasion, 1944," in Box 13, The Goodfriend Papers.

11. *Education of a Survivor*, pp. 97 ff.

12. Details are in *Rice Roots*, pp. 10–13, and in numerous documents and illustrations of his efforts in China, 1949, in Box 19, The Goodfriend Papers.

13. It was published by Farrar Straus in 1951.

14. *Education of a Survivor*, pp. 101 ff; *Rice Roots*, pp. 13–19; letters to and from President Truman in untitled folder, Box 81, The Goodfriend Papers.

15. For these adventures, which included his wife Eadie, son Arthur, and daughter Jill, see his book, *Rice Roots*.

16. Hutton and Rooney, *The Story of The Stars and Stripes*, p. 236; statement, Oral History Envelope, Box 81, The Goodfriend Papers;

and interviews by the author of members of the library staff at the University of Hawaii, especially Karen Peacock and Bronwen Solyom.

17. Questionnaire in Box 81, The Goodfriend Papers.

18. October 23, 1945. Something of the magnitude of what the United States contributed to the casualties and destruction of war can be ascertained in American war production statistics. In the October 11, 1945, issue of the *Stripes* an announcement released in Washington, October 10, by Chairman A.J. Krug, of the War Production Board was published. He reported that American munitions works had produced 2,700,000 machine guns, more than 315,000 rockets for bazookas and more than 24,000,000 land mines. In the last five years, enough guns and mortar ammunition and aircraft bombs to load 210,000 freight cars in a train 1,800 miles long had poured out of the factories. By the end of July 1945, 534 Victory and 2,710 Liberty Ships to transport this massive production had been launched. In addition, the Maritime Commission had built 479 cargo vessels, 297 dry-cargo vessels and 700 standard tankers.

19. See Hutton and Rooney, *The Story of The Stars and Stripes*, p. 120.

20. "I Want to Go Home," n., p. 318.

21. October 12 and 18, 1945.

22. November 1, 1945.

23. November 2, 1945.

24. November 27, 1945.

25. October 13, 1945.

26. October 31, November 10, and December 15, 1945; January 12, 1946.

27. January 15, 1946.

28. January 16, 1946. Later in life Shor became an associate editor of the *National Geographic* magazine and wrote and edited both books and articles for the publication and its Foundation. He toured the world, often accompanied by his wife, coauthor and professional photographer Jean Bowie Shor.

Chapter VIII

1. "I Want to Go Home," p. 322.

2. October 2, 1945.

3. September 28, 1945.

4. See Draft of a Speech delivered to the Academy of Political Science in New York on April 4, 1945 in Marshall, *Papers*, 119–126; and his Remarks at Annual Conference of Supervisory Chaplains, in Washington, April 5, 1945, in ibid., pp. 128–132.

5. Ibid., 200–204; note 2, 260.

6. Radiogram, Marshall to Eisenhower and McNarney, Washington, August 10, 1945, in ibid., 264.

7. "Draft Statement for the Secretary of War," Washington, August 13, 1945, ibid., 272–273. Early in September, Marshall prepared a document to provide information for members of Congress to use in replying to constituent mail on demobilization plans. Since the surrender of Japan, he wrote, "the demobilization of long service veterans in the fairest, fastest, and most understanding manner is now the governing policy of the War Department." There were always, however, vexing conditions: this had to be done "without lowering the quality of the troops on duty in Europe, in Japan, and the Pacific islands." See draft fact sheet, Washington, September 7, 1945, in ibid., 298–299.

8. October 8, November 22, and December 28 and 31, 1945. As to decorations, an article in the April 11, 1946, issue of the *Stripes* noted that the Army had awarded 1,725,344 decorations and awards from Pearl Harbor through November 30, 1945, not including the Purple Heart given to all men wounded in action. The Medal of Honor went to 240 Army men; Distinguished Service Cross, 4,036; Distinguished Service Medal, 987; Silver Star, 69,027; Legion of Merit, 12,285; Distinguished Flying Cross, 124,827; Soldier's Medal, 11,345; Bronze Star, 340,510; and Air Medal 1,162,087. PFCs outnumbered all other ranks in winning decorations. The Air Forces received the largest number of decorations, 1,304,399, including 1,147,635 Air Medals, which were routinely awarded for successful completion of five combat missions. One is reminded of Napoleon's remark that "it is with baubles that men are led," but at this juncture U.S. soldiers were obviously more interested in the points that these medals represented than recognition of their exploits on the battlefield.

9. November 19 and December 18, 1945; February 26, 1946.

10. October 4, 1945.

11. See photos and articles in the October 31 and November 9, 1945, issues.

12. October 26, 1945. Joe Palooka, the comic strip hero, was a Private First Class when he was discharged.

13. Mickey Rooney, *Life Is Too Short* (New York: Villard, 1991), pp. 211–217.

14. March 8 and 26, 1946.

15. See photo of sixteen returning war dogs from CBI in November 3, 1945, issue. Bob's photo, revealing his smoking proclivities, is in the November 24, 1945, issue.

16. January 11, 1946.

17. October 19, 1945.

18. No change however, was to be made in critical lists of scarce categories for both officers and men for whom the point system did not apply, certainly an ongoing matter of concern among those affected. October 5 and 12, 1945.

19. October 6, 20 and 30, and November 22, 1945.
20. October 8, 1945.
21. Ibid.
22. October 9, 18 and November 20, 1945.
23. The USS *Makin Island* was a 7,800-ton escort carrier, a light ship with relatively few aircraft aboard.
24. October 4 and November 14, 1945.
25. November 13, 1945. The *Annabelle Lykes* also soon arrived. Rather at odds with the overwhelming desires so often expressed to return home, the *Stripes*, no doubt with a clucking of the tongue and in a chiding tone, reported that some men, scheduled to return home on the USS *Hocking*, had checked into their bunks aboard ship and then promptly had gone AWOL, wishing to sample just once more the attractions of Shanghai's Bubbling Well Road. If they failed to get on board in time to sail, they would not be assigned another homebound ship anytime in the near future, the paper sternly warned. There was no indication of their fate. November 12, 1945.
26. November 22, 1945.
27. The first public performance of the song, however, also by Crosby, was on the NBC radio show *The Kraft Music Hall*, on Christmas Day, 1941. Berlin won an Oscar for the song in 1943.
28. Among the souvenirs were firearms. These, however, became a problem of some dimension. See Marshall's Memorandum for General Surles, Washington, August 1, 1945, in Marshall, *Papers*, 254–255. Marshall, in talking to Patton in late July, asserted that Patton was greatly shocked to receive the statistics of his Headquarters showing that in a single week in the Third Army seventy soldiers had been killed and 500 wounded in "fooling with the German machine pistol." The guns had subsequently been confiscated and tagged with the men's names. The *War Department Circular 155* (May 28, 1945) was amended to prohibit an individual from bringing into the U.S. more than one serviceable authorized type of enemy firearm. This was to meet some of the misgivings of the FBI about weapons flooding the country.
29. November 23, 1945.
30. This was no doubt written by Goodfriend. He left in a few days. His last editorial was in the November 12, 1945, issue.
31. November 16, 1945.
32. This speech is in Marshall, *Papers*, 336–343. General Wedemeyer agreed, later charging that "America had fought the war like a football game, after which the winner pulls up stakes and goes off on a celebration." "Consequently," he continued, "there was no realization that it would be disastrous to demobilize our armies until we had ensured that the aims for which we fought would be implemented...." *Wedemeyer Reports!*, p. 356.
33. November 14 and December 27, 1945. There is a discussion of Rankin's views by Edmond J. Nouri in "This Week in Review," *The Stars and Stripes Magazine Supplement* 1, no. 12, January 19, 1946.
34. December 14, 1945.
35. Ibid. *China White Paper*, II, 607–609.
36. December 18, 1945.
37. December 21, 1945.
38. Another temporary difficulty as to getting men home was a glut of personnel arriving at West Coast ports. Army estimated that 110,700 troops were scheduled to be on the West Coast by December 24, and at least 80,000 were expected to spend the holidays there unless rail transport was speeded up. The Office of Defense Transportation immediately ordered trains to be operated on accelerated schedules faster than those of regular passenger trains. A following report indeed noted that stranded men usually waited no longer than about six days on the West Coast and many would be moved out by New Year's Day. Numbers arriving had also declined, so the problem was on the way to a solution. December 21, 28, 1945.
39. December 28, 1945.
40. December 31, 1945.
41. January 8, 1946.

Chapter IX

1. A GI letter to "B-Bag" a bit later, in the January 17, 1946, Shanghai *Stripes* firmly and forthrightly explained the unrest as it pertained to China. What had forced the issue, its author wrote, was the announcement that 4,000 additional troops were required to help send the Japs home and help move the Chinese armies wherever the faction in power wanted them. He wanted to know what treaty, agreement or pact required this of the Americans. In addition, why did those in power stall and try to flimflam the men stuck overseas and their folks at home? Why did they not admit that the Chinese could repatriate the Japs themselves and acknowledge that it would be less dangerous for the Nationalists to move their own men? Finally, soldiers and Marines should simply be told that they were mere political trump cards in the total scheme of things in the China Theater.
2. January 7 and 14, 1946. Wedemeyer, writing later in his book *Wedemeyer Reports!*, p. 357, is remiss, however, when he states, regarding the pressures being brought to bear on officials, that "all of this was part of the postwar hysteria which the Communists so cleverly and widely exploited." The "hysteria"

hardly required Communist involvement. The drive to get everyone home had sufficient impetus of its own.

3. The Mead Committee was organized by Senator James M. Mead of New York, and was headed by Senators James M. Tunnell, Democrat of Delaware, and Robert R. Knowland, Republican of California. Six Army and Navy officials and civilians were also included. It had originally been formed to study the disposition of surplus materiel with special reference to reports of wanton destruction of surplus materiel and installations. It was also to ascertain the quantities of stocks required for occupational forces, and the costs of guarding and disposing of this materiel. For one report of destruction, see the account in the January 15, 1946, issue of a Manila GI's charges that the Army had destroyed millions in surplus goods.

4. January 9, 1946.
5. Ibid.
6. January 10, 1946.
7. January 11, 1946.
8. Ibid.
9. January 9, 1946.
10. See in *Magazine Supplement* 1 no. 13, January 26, 1946. Von Steuben served as Inspector General in General Washington's Continental Army. He played a major role in the drill and training of the Colonial forces, among other things, writing a basic training manual for their use.
11. January 12, 1946.
12. January 12, 14, and 15, 1946.
13. January 10, 1946.
14. January 10, 1946. Also at the press conference, the journalist Drew Pearson gave Truman a six-inch stack of papers which he said listed 30,000 GIs in the Philippines protesting Army's demobilization policy under the slogan: "No boats, no votes." This was similar to another circulating in the States, together with baby shoes and booties arriving in Senators' offices in large numbers with the demand to "Send Daddy Home," or the warning "No dad, no votes." January 22, 1946.
15. The U.S. Dock workers of the National Maritime Union, CIO, struck on December 3, only unloading troopships and vessels carrying relief supplies in a 24-hour work stoppage to protest the slow return of servicemen from abroad. Joseph Curran, president of NMU, charged the government with bungling the redeployment of GIs, and indicated that 90,000 workers were involved in the strike. December 4, 1945.
16. January 7, 10 and 11, 1946. An editorial noted that the points system in place counted points as of September 2 — V-J Day. But the system needed to be constantly updated so that overseas service credits would still accrue. If not, all service personnel, even those in the States, would receive the same point credits.

Robert P. Patterson, an attorney, was appointed Under Secretary of War under Henry L. Stimson in late 1940. On September 27, 1945, he became the Secretary of War succeeding Stimson, remaining in that office until July 18, 1947. In World War I, he served as a captain in the 360th Infantry Regiment of the 77th Division. He was decorated with the Distinguished Service Cross for heroism and the Purple Heart for wounds received. In 1919, he was promoted to major and soon left the service to resume his law career. See the study by Keith E. Eiler, *Mobilizing America: Robert P. Patterson and the War Effort, 1940–1945* (Ithaca: Cornell University Press, 1998).

17. In response, China Theater commanders noted that surplus low-point China GIs had always been sent home as soon as possible. January 11, 1946.
18. January 12, 1946.
19. January 8 and 12, 1946.
20. Also at the meeting with Wedemeyer, EM antipathy toward officers — especially colonels, who were charged with using every means at their disposal to retain their rank — was especially obvious. Wedemeyer noted that he had been alerted to this problem and would act on it. January 14, 1946.
21. January 12, 1946.
22. January 14, 1946.
23. At this juncture, Representative Hugh Emerson Delacy, a Democrat from the state of Washington, released a cablegram from 362 servicemen in Vienna asking why there were then fourteen generals, forty-three colonels, ninety light colonels, and 133 majors in Vienna. A good part of the 12,000 EM in Vienna were mainly engaged in maintaining this heavy load of brass. January 14, 1946.
24. January 14 and 15, 1946.
25. January 15 and 16, 1946.
26. Ibid.
27. December 17, 1945; January 15 and 16, 1946.
28. January 16, 1946.
29. January 17, 1946.
30. General Eisenhower's reference to firemen produced a "B-Bag" letter which argued that many officers were not firemen because firemen choose their career, while most officers were not career soldiers and should not be discriminated against. January 17, 1946. Navy officials had earlier noted that according to current schedules, all of the sixty-pointers would be afloat by December 15. December 10, 1945.
31. January 18, 1946.
32. January 18 and 19, 1946.
33. January 18, 23 and 28; February 5; and March 5, 1946.

34. January 22, 1946. McKenzie also understood that there were inequities in the discharge system, and that some high-point men had been retained wrongly. But it was only natural that when handling millions of men some degree of unfairness would result. His views were shared by the editor of the Marine Corps paper, the *North China Marine*. In an editorial in the paper's January 30, 1946, issue, he took servicemen to task for wanting to return home before the peace had been won. Certainly, others were likewise guilty: the American people in the last six months had taken initial steps toward losing the peace. Those chiefly to blame were numerous anxious parents and homesick servicemen, who refused to consider the consequences that a too-rapid demobilization might have on the future of American foreign policy, and similarly of the deleterious effect it was having on the ideals for which men had so recently fought and died. January 31, 1946.

35. See Eric Bergerud, *Touched with Fire: The Land War in the South Pacific* (New York: Viking, 1996), p. 153, and discussion in Alfred Emile Cornebise, *The CCC Chronicles. Camp Newspapers of the Civilian Conservation Corps, 1933–1942* (Jefferson, NC: McFarland, 2004), pp. 239–242.

36. October 27, 1945; Thompson, "One Pilot's Journey."

37. *Wedemeyer Reports!*, pp. 345–46; 348. See November 3, 1945, issue for a list of the units involved.

38. November 22, 1945.

39. Studs Terkel, *"The Good War": An Oral History of World War Two* (New York: Ballantine, 1985), pp. 171–175.

40. January 15, 1946.

41. January 9, 11, 31 and March 12, 1946.

42. November 3 and 7, 1945.

43. November 3 and 19, 1945.

44. November 19, 21 and 22, 1945.

45. February 28, 1946.

46. The *Scott* was manned by a Coast Guard crew on this occasion. March 5 and 6, 1946.

47. March 25, 1946.

48. April 2, 1946. General George Marshall, who had recently arrived as Truman's special envoy seeking to bring an end to the Chinese civil war, had selected May 1 as the day when this would occur. He had hopes that the lower American military profile might help him to accomplish his mission. See in Marshall, *Papers*, 514.

Chapter X

1. There are substantive discussions of these matters in Cornebise, *Ranks and Columns*, pp. 149–157.

2. December 27, 1945, and January 12, 1946. See also, Cornebise, *Ranks and Columns*, pp. 150–151.

3. "Over The Desk" editorial page in *Magazine Supplement* 1, no. 19, March 9, 1946. For censorship problems in general in World War II, see George Weller, *Weller's War: A Legendary Foreign Correspondent's Saga of World War II on Five Continents*, ed., Anthony Weller (New York: Crown, 2009), pp. 191–199. He asserted that "the American and British peoples were fighting to be informed. They did not want to be fooled. They wanted to hear the truth. They could take it." Indeed, he concluded, "it is through knowing the truth that the people discover their hidden will." p. 199.

4. Editorial and "B-Bag" letter in the January 14, 1946, issue.

5. January 14, 1946.

6. February 12, 1946.

7. February 3 and 15, 1946.

8. February 18, 1946.

9. Ibid.

10. January 24, 1946.

11. March 4, 6, 8, 11, and 20, 1946. One result of these proceedings was the request of transfers from other members of the Tokyo *Stripes*' staff. In Tokyo, a Mutual Broadcasting System correspondent, Don Bell, reported that the Army was contemplating replacing the Pacific edition of the *Stars and Stripes* by a Japanese-owned, edited and written paper, the *Nippon Times*, a change that was apparently in the works before the latest developments had ensued. In the event, this change was not implemented, and the Tokyo *Stripes* continues to the present, published as the Pacific Edition.

12. March 9, 1946.

13. March 19 and 21, 1946. In civilian life, Kestler had been on the staff of the *Des Moines Register Tribune*. In the ETO, Lee commanded SHAEF's Services of Supply (SOS), and as of January 1944, he was the Deputy Commander of U.S. Forces in Europe. Widely regarded as a martinet of the first order, because of his initials, "J.C.H.," he was called "Jesus Christ Himself" Lee.

14. March 29, 1946.

15. April 2, 1946.

16. Mauldin appeared before the board on March 31, 1946. See an account in the April 1, 1946, issue. See also Carl W. Larsen, "Twenty years ago with the *Stars and Stripes*," *The Quill* (December 1964), 8–14, in which he observed that the *Stripes* was generally famous for taking on "the 'whole blasted Army' in fighting for 'truth not propaganda.'"

17. *The Story of the Stars and Stripes*, page xi. For a discussion of the status of the *Roundup*, and some of the issues involved, see its last issue, styled "*The Last Roundup,*" Delhi, India, April 11, 1946.

Chapter XI

1. Cleverly titled "The Marine ... Hmm [Hymn]," the poem was published in the February 28, 1946, issue.
2. November 12, 1945. See also Henry I. Shaw, Jr., *The United States Marines in North China, 1945–1949* (Washington: Headquarters, U.S. Marine Corps, Historical Branch, 1960, and revised edition, 1962).
3. See Shaw, *The United States Marines in China*, pp. 6, 10, and *passim*. According to Shaw, Marine losses in China totaled ten killed and thirty-three wounded in action with an additional twenty-two flyers killed in operational accidents between 1945 and 1949. See Appendices A, B and C.
4. Ibid. p. 5. On at lease one occasion, at Chiang's request, Japanese artillery opened up on Communist positions near Tientsin. There is an account in the October 4, 1945, issue. The numbers of the Japanese remaining in China were not known with any certainty, and the estimates of these varied widely in various sources addressing the matter. Shaw, *The United States Marines in China*, pp. 3–4.
5. Article by Austin Wehrwein, staff correspondent in the November 8, 1945, issue. Also at Peiping, on November 11, 1945, the Marines celebrated the 170th anniversary of their Corps by a parade of units of the 5th Marine Regiment. There, on the polo field outside the Legation quarter, infantry units of the 5th Marine Regiment were reviewed by Brigadier General Louis R. Jones, commander of Marines in Peiping. November 12, 1945.
6. October 27 and November 14, 1945.
7. Wedemeyer's press release in Chungking, November 11, in the November 12, 1945, issue. Details of these and other encounters are in Shaw, *The United States Marines in North China*, passim.
8. "I Want to Go Home," pp. 326–329. Goodfriend based an editorial on this incident for which see the November 13, 1945, issue.
9. October 8, 1945, issue; Shaw, *The United States Marines in North China*, p. 2.
10. November 8, 1945.
11. February 14, 1945.
12. October 31, December 11, and 17, 1945.
13. Also present was Major General Keller E. Rockey, commanding general of III Amphibious Corps.
14. In a letter in the December 31 issue, "Disheartened SeaBees" also weighed in, noting that they had arrived in Tsingtao from the Philippines, had been there for several weeks, and were still living under lousy conditions in a wrecked garage while their officers lived in a beautiful apartment house. "Words fail us," they could only conclude.

15. This sally was also to refute Dick Wilson's article in which he indicated that Marine morale was low because the postwar tasks in China should be done by professionals and not by battle-weary Leathernecks who only wanted to return home to their civvies. January 1, 1946.
16. December 3, 1945; January 4, 15 and 16, 1946.
17. A personal emissary from Major General Keller E. Rockey of the 1st Marines was to be sent and leaflets would also to be dropped over the village warning of the impending attack if it were to be launched. November 12, 17; December 7, 1945.
18. December 18, 1945.
19. December 27, 1945; February 1, 13 and 25, 1946.
20. January 5, 1946.
21. January 24, 1946.
22. February 7, 1946.
23. Shaw, *The United States Marines in North China*, pp. 14–15; February 25, 1946.
24. December 20, 1945.
25. January 21, 1946.
26. February 20 and 27, 1946. See also Shaw, *The United States Marines in North China*, pp. 9, 13–14. Wedemeyer, in his capacity as military advisor to Chiang, had warned him as early as November 1945, however, that he should first consolidate his grip on North China before moving into Manchuria. Some commentators hold that Chiang's actions here were pivotal to what followed in China, resulting in the Communist takeover in 1949. February 1, 13, 25, 1946.
27. February 9, 1946.
28. January 18, 1946.
29. February 5, 1946.
30. November 21, 1945; January 4, 1946.
31. A large, well-patronized club was also established in Tsingtao. See article and photo in the February 6, 1946, issue. The author of two books, Camp had been with the Fourth Marine Regiment in Shanghai in 1929. February 6, 14, 19, 25, 26 and March 20, 1946.
32. February 7; March 12, 18, 1946.
33. April 11, 1946. Meanwhile, the Navy indicated that its final point score of twenty-three for enlisted men and thirty for officers would go into effect on June 15, and that on July 1, the points score system for naval reservists would be scrapped. Finally, it would have completed its demobilization by September 1, 1946.
34. See, for example, Shaw, *The United States Marines in North China*, pp. 16–17.
35. Ibid., p. 15.
36. Ibid., pp. 23–25.
37. Ibid., pp. 25–26.

Chapter XII

1. See the remarkable collection and commentary by an American missionary, Arthur Henderson Smith, who understood as much about the Chinese as any missionary ever did, published as *Proverbs and Common Sayings from the Chinese* (New York: Dover, 1965. Reprint of 1886 edition).
2. See Stella Dong, *Shanghai*, p. 281; and John Hersey, "Letter from Shanghai," *The New Yorker* (February 9, 1946), p. 82.
3. November 17 and December 12, 1945.
4. December 10, 1945. A recent study on the conduct of U.S. servicemen during World War II, while concerned mainly with the ETO, could be applied to the China Theater. See J. Robert Lilly, *Taken by Force: Rape and American GIs in Europe During World War II* (New York: Palgrave Macmillan, 2007). This adds other dimensions to the "Band of Brothers" ideals so often stressed in studies of World War II. See also Andrew J. Huebner, *The Warrior Image: Soldiers in American Culture from the Second World War to the Vietnam Era* (Chapel Hill: University of North Carolina Press, 2008).
5. September 29, 1945.
6. October 11, 1945. The officer mentioned by Ziegfield hardly merited a Legion of Merit, Stegor went on. Instead, perhaps all the men in the Army should get a Medal of Honor for what they accomplished. Ziegfield, who was accused of bucking for corporal by writing the letter, was rather clearly in line for a "Yard Bird medal."
7. Unpublished memoirs of Flight Officer Kensley Robert Thompson, "One Pilot's Journey in World War II and the CBI Theater," at http://cbi-theater-4.home.comcast.net. Thompson was a member of 330th Troop Carrier Squadron of the 513th Troop Carrier Group based at Shanghai's Kiangwan Airfield. November 5, 28, 1945.
8. November 9, 10, 1945; January 10, 1946.
9. See "B-Bag" letter in the January 10, 1946, issue. The complaints that Kilroy answered were in two letters in the "B-Bag" column in the January 9, 1946, issue. Later, the China Theater Headquarters awarded the Legion of Merit to Kilroy. The sergeant-major to the headquarters commandant, he had received the distinction for founding, organizing and operating the EM club from December 10 to February 18. Kilroy had served 27 months in China after earlier service in North Africa and India. He was a veteran of seventeen years in the Army, and had come overseas with the 857 Ordnance seeing action in the interior China when the action was hot around Chanyi and Chengtu. He also headed the GI gripe committee that Wedemeyer had set up in January of 1946. He had earlier earned a Bronze Star, four battle stars and the Chinese order of Yun Hui. These details are in an article in the March 7, 1946, issue.
10. January 18, 1946.
11. January 23, 1946. To be sure, not all American conduct was bad. A situation arose which was addressed by the British Consul General Alwynne Ogden in Shanghai. He warned GIs not to make loans to former British prisoner-of-war camp internees whom they might encounter in Shanghai bars. Their hard-luck stories were often accompanied by plaintive pleas for loans, which often had been given by gullible GIs and sailors. But these kind gestures were misplaced, and the Americans were advised not to trust the British in these matters but should contribute to more deserving causes. In any case, Ogden concluded, there were British national agencies which were available to assist the needy former prisoners. November 17, 1945.
12. December 14, 1945; February 22; March 1, 23, 1946. Sometimes, however, Chinese specifically attacked sailors, adding to the problems. See article in the January 23, 1946, issue.

Chapter XIII

1. For details of these matters see U.S. Department of State, *The China White Paper, August 1949*, 2 vols. Reissued with an introduction by Lyman P. Van Slyke (Stanford: Stanford University Press, 1967). For relations between Chiang and the Communists see ibid., I, 38–58.) This will be cited hereinafter as *China White Paper*. As to Chiang's views as to the relative threats of the Japanese and the Maoists, he allegedly once said, "The Japanese are a disease of the skin, while the Communists are a disease of the heart." There is a brief discussion in David C. Wright, *The History of China* (Westport, Connecticut: Greenwood Press, 2001), p. 135.
2. See in Wedemeyer, *Wedemeyer Reports!*, pp. 267–301.
3. For this treaty and the Yalta Agreement, see *China White Paper*, I, 113–126; II, 585–596.
4. Ibid., II, 596–604.
5. For Hurley's ambassadorship, see ibid., I, 59–112; II, 561–584.
6. November 16, 17 and 29, 1945.
7. For Hurley's charges against the State Department and its officials, see his letter of resignation to Truman of November 26, 1945, in *China White Paper*, II, 581–584. On a further note, General Claire L. Chennault stated that the career diplomats charged by Hurley should be tried by a civil court. There is a discussion in the December 1, 1945, issue.
8. See Marshall, *Papers*, 372, for details. He

was asked to retain his military uniform as seemed appropriate for this mission. It was thought in some circles that Marshall was a novice regarding China. He, however, had served there. As a lieutenant colonel, he was the executive officer of the 15th U.S. Infantry Regiment, which had been stationed in Tientsin since 1912. Marshall arrived in September 1924 and departed in May of 1927. While there, he was in command of the regiment on two occasions in the absence of the commanding colonel. He also acquired a tolerable knowledge of Mandarin Chinese and had met prominent personalities of the day. See this author's study, *The United States 15th Infantry Regiment in China, 1912–1938* (Jefferson, NC: McFarland, 2004), pp. 76–82, and *passim*. Generals Stilwell and Wedemeyer had also served in the 15th Infantry in China. See in ibid.

9. Details of Stuart's ambassadorship are in *China White Paper*, I, 230–310. See also radiogram, Marshall to Under Secretary of State Dean George Acheson in Marshall, *Papers*, July 5, 1946, pp. 620–621, and notes 1–4, pp. 621–622, for Stuart's appointment. For Wedemeyer's views on these events, see his *Wedemeyer Reports!*, pp. 366–367. While he insisted that he did not really want the post, nonetheless he objected to the Communists' exercising "power to determine who might be appointed to positions of responsibility within the United States Government." While Marshall had originally supported Wedemeyer for the position, there were also strong differences between them, and Wedemeyer later asserted that the course "followed by General Marshall, first as Special Envoy to China and subsequently as Secretary of State," was "dangerous." Ibid., p. 367.

10. December 7, 8 and 12, 1945.

11. December 10, 1945. Hurley later unaccountably revealed some uncertainty, when in Albuquerque, on April 7, 1946, he asserted that the Communists held out more hope than imperialism to a billion oppressed people, who were then under imperialism's rule. April 8, 1946.

12. December 12, 1945. See lengthy article by Walter G. Rundle, of the UP, datelined Shanghai, December 14, published in the December 15, 1945, issue. Also for Marshall's appointment and his mediation mission, see a memoir by an American journalist under contract with the Chinese Government as an adviser on public relations who was closely involved with the proceedings, John Robinson Beal, *Marshall in China* (Garden City, NY: Doubleday, 1970). Another memoir written by a member of the U.S. Embassy Staff when Marshall was in China, John F. Melby's *The Mandate of Heaven: Record of a Civil War, China 1945–49* (Garden City, NY: Doubleday, 1971), also contains much insight. See also Marshall, *Papers*, 371–776, and Larry I. Bland, ed., *George C. Marshall's Mediation Mission to China, December 1945–January 1947* (Lexington, Virginia: George C. Marshall Foundation, 1998).

13. November 29, 1945. Byrnes's appearance before the Foreign Relations Committee is discussed in *China White Paper*, II, 606–607.

14. November 29 and December 1, 1945.

15. Truman's statement is in *China White Paper*, II, 607–609. There is also a discussion in the December 17, 1945, issue.

16. Marshall, *Papers*, 397. There is further discussion in the December 18, 1945, issue.

17. Marshall, *Papers*, 396. Stimson, who had been Secretary of War from 1940 to 1945, had been replaced by Patterson in September 1945.

18. Ibid., 398.

19. Ibid., 398–99 ; *Wedemeyer Reports*, p. 363.

20. Marshall, *Papers*, pp. 404–405.

21. Letter, Bernard M. Baruch, August 21, 1946, Nanking, China, in ibid., 660–662, and Marshall's Personal Statement, Washington, January 7, 1947, ibid., 772–776.

22. Melby, *The Mandate of Heaven*, p. 241.

23. *China White Paper*, from the Introduction. See also Thomas D. Lutze, *China's Inevitable Revolution: Rethinking America's Loss to the Communists* (New York: Palgrave Macmillan, 2007).

24. See essay, "The American Mission," by John T. Bookman, in *The Mythology of American Politics* (Washington, DC: Potomac Books, 2008), pp. 119–138.

25. Goodfriend's editorial is in the November 5, 1945, issue. See also *Magazine Supplement* 1, no. 3, November 17, 1945, for a major article by Howard Brotz titled "China's Time for Decision," which was a brief history of Chiang's China and Communist China. Brotz discussed the differences between them, how they got where they were by 1945, and the responsibility of both sides to compromise in the name of peace for China, as well as the rest of the world.

Chapter XIV

1. November 21, 1945.

2. December 14, 1945; February 19, 1946. A soldier, Corporal Don R. Hearner, similarly praised the editorials and wished that the people back in the States could read them, especially those regarding attitudes towards the Japanese who should not be let off too easily. December 3, 1945.

3. January 4, 1946.

4. December 19, 1945.

5. February 19, 1946.

6. December 3, 1945.
7. January 7, 1946.
8. Goodfriend, Oral History Project.
9. Vol. 1, No. 167, Special, Saturday, April 13, 1946.
10. April 13, 1946.
11. "Yank About China" article in the March 25, 1946, issue, about the artists. Pernod was known by his nickname, "Stubby."
12. See article about nicknames of staff by Jim Becker, and other features in the April 13, 1946, issue.
13. Ibid.
14. Ibid.
15. Ibid.
16. "I Want to Go Home," p. 323; editorials in October 8 and 9, 1945, issues, and numerous notices and articles in *passim*. Goodfriend was a lifelong proponent of education. See his book, *Survivor*.
17. February 13, 27, 28 and March 1, 1946. See also letter in "B-Bag" from some officers who saw nothing remiss in the taxes.
18. November 6 and 17, 1945.
19. November 1, 1945.
20. January 3, 1946.
21. January 29, 30, February 1 and 2, 1946.
22. *Magazine Supplement* 1, no. 1, November 3, 1945, and no. 19, March 9, 1946.
23. See especially the issues for November 16, 19–22, 27–30 and December 1 and 3, 1945.
24. November 27, 1945.
25. November 27 and 30, 1945.
26. November 3, 5, 8, 10, 27, 28, 29, and 30, 1945. The game was also broadcast by Roland Cooper direct from the Canidrome by the Armed Forces radio station XMHA in Shanghai.
27. For details and photos of the events of the packed day in Shanghai, see the December 3, 1945, issue. There was an addendum to the Derby proceedings. Goodfriend had departed China two weeks earlier, but a colleague sent him a note regarding the contest. After the game and the Derby, a huge cocktail party was held at the staff's residence. There ensued a commotion at the door and the Derby winner arrived, complete with the horseshoe of flowers that had been bestowed on him in the winner's circle. His problem was that he thought the winner's purse ought to be more. This had amounted to about $20 American and he deemed it too small. The staffer agreed and gave the winner ten dollars out of his own pocket, which greatly pleased him. He recognized that he could have argued the point, much as pedicab drivers and rickshaw boys always haggled over the fare, and it was a matter of "face" to them to win something extra. "But Hell," he concluded, "we'd had a great day, and I didn't want one scene to ruin it." "I Want to Go Home," note, p. 328.

28. Jessup could only ruefully conclude: "The revenge of a nerd." See his "China *Stripes*—A brief but colorful run," p. 9.
29. April 13, 1946. As to their hostess, Christine England, she had been an old Shanghailander of twenty-five years, and after the *Stripes* lost their palatial quarters, she was not out of a job for long. Personnel of the Army 172nd General Hospital asked her to open a club, which she did, at Rivers Courts in the former private quarters of the CO of the hospital. She turned it into a games room for bridge, poker and mahjong, and a reading and writing room, and also provided hot snacks. See in "Yank About China," by John Clift, March 7, 1946, issue. "No Momma, No Poppa" referred to a familiar chant at the time, part of the chatter and patter on the street intoned by Chinese children beggars seeking "*cumshaw*"—a handout. It was derived from the poem "Shanghai Waif," from Shamus A'Rabbitt, *China Coast Ballads* (Shanghai: A.R. Hager, 1938), n.p. A typical verse concluded: "No whiskey soda/ No chow."
30. See Bill Jessup, "China *Stripes*—A brief but colorful run," p. 8; March 23, 1946.
31. March 4, 1946.
32. "I Want to Go Home," p. 313.

Chapter XV

1. As to the atom, see editorial in October 15, 1945, issue arguing that there seemed to be too much fuss in Stateside papers about atomic energy. What mattered was the way that humans used all things at their disposal, including atomic power. All else was of little consequence. The paper did, however, publish a feature, "Atomic Secrets," in the form of single-panel cartoons presenting rudimentary facts about atomic energy. There were six in all. The coming Bikini Atoll atomic bomb tests also merited some space. The two planned atomic explosions—"Operation Crossroads"—were announced in December 1945. They were carried out in July 1946, after the paper had ceased publication. For the "Atomic Secrets," see December 19, 20, 21, 22, 24, and 25, 1945, issues. For the Bikini Atoll tests, see editorial in December 15, 1945, issue and articles in March 4, 18, 19, 20, 22, and March 25, and April 1, 1946, issues. The article on the upcoming Bikini Atoll tests in the March 22 issue recorded that the government had summarily rejected offers of certain persons volunteering to stay aboard the ships to be subjected to the atomic bombs during the tests.
2. Wilson, *When Tigers Fight*, pp. 254–255.
3. Barbara Tuchman, *Stilwell and the American Experience in China, 1911–45* (New York: Bantam, 1972), p. 678.

4. Shaw, *The United States Marines in North China*, p. 24. See also U.S. Department of State, *United States Relations with China*, 2 vols. (Washington, 1949), I, 336.

5. *Magazine Supplement* 1, no. 19, March 9, 1946.

6. Rudyard Kipling, *The Naulahka: A Story of East and West* (London: William Heinemann, 1892), chapter 5. This novel was written in Vermont, in collaboration with Kipling's brother-in-law, Wolcott Balestier.

7. Pearl S. Buck, *My Several Worlds* (New York: John Day, 1954), pp. 52–54.

8. Robert Kagan, in the *Washington Post*, Sunday, May 15, 2005, as quoted in Mark Leonard, *What Does China Think?* (New York: Public Affairs, 2008), p. 115.

9. James Lilley, *China Hands: Nine Decades of Adventure, Espionage, and Diplomacy in Asia.* (New York: Public Affairs, 2004), pp. 170–171.

10. Leonard, *What Does China Think?*, p. 7.

11. Ibid., pp. 9, 14, 32 and 34.

12. Simon Winchester, *The Man Who Loved China: The Fantastic Story of the Eccentric Scientist who Unlocked the Mysteries of the Middle Kingdom* (New York: HarperCollins, 2008), pp. 257–265.

13. See James Fallows: *Postcards from Tomorrow Square: Reports from China* (New York: Vintage, 2009), and a review of the book by Jonathan Spence in the *New York Times Book Review*, March 8, 2009, p. 14. Fallows is a correspondent for *Atlantic Monthly*.

Selected Bibliography

Documents and Archival Sources

This study is substantially based on the *China* (Shanghai) *Edition* of the *Stars and Stripes*, September 28, 1945, to April 13, 1946. A microfilm of this edition is in the New York Public Library, as is a complete file of the paper's *Magazine Supplement*, which appeared on Saturdays, in nineteen issues, from November 3, 1945 to March 9, 1946.

Another major source is the large collection of Lieutenant Colonel Arthur Goodfriend's papers catalogued as the Papers of Arthur Goodfriend, in Special Collections, University of Hawaii at Manoa Library. There is a finding aid, Manuscript R00006, prepared by Richard H. Perrine, July 2000. The collection is housed in ninety-six numbered boxes. It includes copies of the author's several published books and periodical articles, his sketchbooks, notebooks and, most importantly, fifty-one of his holographic journals, the first dating from 1928. These journals are copiously illustrated with the author's drawings in various media — pencil, pen, watercolor, felt pen and crayon — and reveal his skills as illustrator and artist.

There is also a six-page Oral History Finding Aid, as Goodfriend recounted much about his life on tape to Shari Tamashiro, Jason Yamashita, and Ihsia Hu. This consists of two parts: a series of fifteen 100-minute audiocassette tapes, and another seven taped sessions containing discussions of Goodfriend's World War II experiences, recorded August 5, 7, 18–21, and September 5, 1997, and transcribed by Jason Yamashita. Goodfriend's Ed.D. dissertation is in Box 70, together with his diploma and other pertinent documents. His dissertation is titled "The Education of Arthur Goodfriend: A Case Study of Autobiography in an Educational Metaphor" (1988). It has been published as *The Education of a Survivor: From the School of Hard Knocks to a Doctoral Degree* (Honolulu: University of Hawaii Press, 1989). Another important manuscript is an unpublished account of his military service in World War II titled "I Want to Go Home, 1942–1946." It is in Box 14.

Other important documentary sources used include *The Papers of George Catlett Marshall*, vol. 5, *The Finest Soldier, January 1, 1945–January 7, 1947*, edited by Larry I. Bland and Sharon Ritenour Stevens (Baltimore: Johns Hopkins Press, 2003). Also: U.S. Department of State, *The China White Paper, August 1949*, 2 vols., reissued with an introduction by Lyman P. Van Slyke (Stanford: Stanford University Press, 1967). In addition, for U.S. foreign policy as to China, see U.S. Department of State, *United States Relations with China*, 2 vols. (Washington: U.S. Government Printing Office, 1949).

Other relevant documentary sources are: Record Group 165, the War Department General and Special Staffs, and Record Group 334, Inter-Service Agencies, and Records of the Joint Committees of Congress, 1789–1968, Record Group 128, in the National Archives.

Books

Abend, Hallett Edward. *My Life in China, 1926–1941*. New York: Harcourt, Brace, 1943.
Ambrose, Stephen. *Band of Brothers*. New York: Simon & Schuster, 2001.
A'Rabbitt, Shamus. *China Coast Ballads*. Shanghai: A.R. Hager, 1938.
Beal, John Robinson. *Marshall in China*. Garden City, New York: Doubleday, 1970.
Bergerud, Eric. *Touched with Fire: The Land War in the South Pacific*. New York: Viking, 1996.
Biggs, Chester M., Jr. *The United States Marines in North China, 1894–1942*. Jefferson, NC: McFarland, 2003.
Bland, Larry I., ed. *George C. Marshall's Mediation Mission to China, December 1945–January 1947*. Lexington, Virginia: George C. Marshall Foundation, 1998.
Bond, Charles R., Jr., and Terry Anderson. *A Flying Tiger's Diary*. College Station: Texas A&M University Press, 1984.
Bookman, John T. *The Mythology of American Politics*. Washington, D.C.: Potomac Books, 2008.
Brook, Timothy. *Vermeer's Hat: The Seventeenth Century and the Dawn of the Global World*. New York: Bloomsbury Press, 2008.
Brownell, Susan. *Beijing's Games: What the Olympics Mean to China*. Lanham, Maryland: Rowman and Littlefield Publishers, 2008.
Buck, Pearl S. *My Several Worlds*. New York: John Day, 1954.
Cherny, Andrei. *The Candy Bombers: The Untold Story of the Berlin Airlift and America's Finest Hour*. New York: Putnam, 2008.
Coble, Parks M. *Facing Japan: Chinese Politics and Japanese Imperialism, 1931–1937*. Cambridge: Harvard University Press, 1991.
Condit, Kenneth W., and Edwin T. Turnbladh. *Hold High the Torch: A History of the 4th Marines*. Nashville, TN: Battery Press, 1989.
Cornebise, Alfred Emile. *The CCC Chronicles: Camp Newspapers of the Civilian Conservation Corps, 1933–1942*. Jefferson, NC: McFarland, 2004.
_____. *Ranks and Columns: Armed Forces Newspapers in American Wars*. Westport, CT: Greenwood, 1993.
_____. *The Stars and Stripes: Doughboy Journalism in World War I*. Westport, CT: Greenwood, 1984.
_____. *The United States 15th Infantry Regiment in China, 1912–1938*. Jefferson, NC: McFarland, 2004.
Dong, Stella. *Shanghai: The Rise and Fall of a Decadent City*. New York: Harper, 2001.
Dreyer, Edward L. *China at War, 1901–1949*. New York: Longman, 1995.
Earnshaw, Graham, ed. *Tales of Old Shanghai*. Hong Kong: China Economic Review Publishing, 2008.
Eiler, Keith E. *Mobilizing America: Robert P. Patterson and the War Effort, 1940–1945*. Ithaca: Cornell University Press, 1998.
_____. *Wedemeyer on War and Peace*. Stanford: Hoover Institution Press, 1987.
Fallows, James. *Postcards from Tomorrow Square: Reports from China*. New York: Vintage, 2009.
Ford, Daniel. *Flying Tigers*. Washington, DC: Smithsonian Institution Press, 1991.

Glines, Carroll V. *The Doolittle Raid: America's Daring First Strike Against Japan.* New York: Orion, 1988.
_____. *Doolittle's Tokyo Raiders.* New York: Van Nostrand Reinhold, 1968.
_____. *Four Came Home.* New York: Van Nostrand Reinhold, 1966.
Goodfriend, Arthur. *The Education of a Survivor: From the School of Hard Knocks to a Doctoral Degree.* Honolulu: University of Hawaii Foundation, 1989.
_____. *The Only War We Seek.* New York: Farrar, Straus and Young, 1951.
_____. *Rice Roots.* New York: Simon & Schuster, 1958.
Gould, Hunter Thomas. *An American in China, 1936–1939: A Memoir.* New York: Thomas and Sons Books, 2004.
Huebner, Andrew J. *The Warrior Image: Soldiers in American Culture from the Second World War to the Vietnam Era.* Chapel Hill: University of North Carolina Press, 2008.
Hump Pilots Association. *China Airlift—The Hump.* Dallas: Taylor, 1980.
Hutton, Bud, and Andy Rooney. *The Story of The Stars and Stripes: A Paper for Joe.* New York: Farrar and Rinehart, 1946.
Kaplan, Robert D. *Hog Pilots, Blue Water Grunts: The American Military in the Air, at Sea, and on the Ground.* New York: Random House, 2007.
Kates, George N. *The Years That Were Fat: Peking, 1933–1940.* New York: Harper, 1952.
Kingsbury, R. Richard. *The Eighteen-Year-Old Replacement Facing Combat in Patton's Third Army.* Columbia: University of Missouri Press, 2008.
Kipling, Rudyard. *The Naulahka: A Story of East and West.* London: William Heinemann, 1892.
Kuhn, Irene Corbally. *Assigned to Adventure.* Philadelphia: J.B. Lippincott, 1938.
Leonard, Mark. *What Does China Think?* New York: Public Affairs, 2008.
Lilley, James. *China Hands: Nine Decades of Adventure, Espionage, and Diplomacy in Asia.* New York: Public Affairs, 2004.
Lilly, J. Robert. *Taken by Force: Rape and American GIs in Europe During World War II.* New York: Palgrave Macmillan, 2007.
Lutze, Thomas D. *China's Inevitable Revolution: Rethinking America's Loss to the Communists.* New York: Palgrave Macmillan, 2007.
Mauldin, Bill. *The Brass Ring.* New York: W.W. Norton, 1971.
McCarthy, James. *A Papago Traveler: The Memories of James McCarthy.* Tucson: University of Arizona Press, 1985.
Melby, John F. *The Mandate of Heaven: Record of a Civil War, China 1945–49.* Garden City, New York: Anchor Books, 1971.
Meyer, Robert, Jr., and Omar N. Bradley, eds. *The Stars and Stripes Story of World War II.* New York: David McKay, 1960.
Michener, James A. *The World Is My Home: A Memoir.* New York: Random House, 1992.
Mitter, Rana. *A Bitter Revolution: China's Struggle with the Modern World.* New York: Oxford University Press, 2004.
_____. *The Manchurian Myth: Nationalism, Resistance, and Collaboration in Modern China.* Berkeley: University of California Press, 2000.
Moran, Daniel. *Wars of National Liberation.* Washington, DC: Smithsonian Books, 2006.
Morgan, Judith, and Neil Morgan. *Dr. Seuss & Mr. Geisel: A Biography.* New York: Random House, 1995.
Noble, Dennis L. *The Eagle and the Dragon: The United States Military in China, 1901–1937.* Westport, CT: Greenwood, 1990.
_____, ed. *Gunboat on the Yangtze: The Diary of Captain Glenn F. Howell of the U.S.S. Palos, 1920–1921.* Jefferson, NC: McFarland, 2002.
Paxton, Robert O. *Vichy France: Old Guard and New Order, 1940–1944.* London: Barrie and Jenkins, 1972.

Power, Brian. *The Ford of Heaven*. New York: Michael Kesend, 1984.
Power, Desmond. *Little Foreign Devil*. Vancouver, Canada: Pangli Imprint, 1996.
Pyle, Ernie. *Brave Men*. New York: Henry Holt, 1944.
_____. *Here Is Your War*. New York: Henry Holt, 1943.
Rooney, Andy. *My War*. New York: Random House, 1995.
Rooney, Mickey. *Life Is Too Short*, New York: Villard, 1991.
Shaw, Henry I., Jr. *The United States Marines in North China, 1945–1949*. Washington, DC: Headquarters, U.S. Marine Corps, Historical Branch, 1960; revised edition, 1962.
Shaw, Ralph. *Sin City*. New York: Time-Warner, 1992.
Sheridan, James E. *China in Disintegration. The Republican Era in Chinese History, 1912–1949*. New York: Free Press, 1975.
Shunxun, Nan, and Beverly Foit-Albert. *China's Sacred Sites*. Honesdale, Pennsylvania: Himalayan Institute Press, 2007.
Smith, Arthur Henderson. *China in Convulsion*, 2 vols. New York: Fleming H. Revell, 1901.
_____. *Chinese Characteristics*. Norwalk, Connecticut: Eastbridge, 2002. Reprint of edition: Edinburgh: Oliphant, Anderson and Ferrier, 1900.
_____. *Proverbs and Common Sayings from the Chinese*. New York: Dover, 1965. Reprint of 1886 edition.
_____. *Village Life in China: A Study in Sociology*. New York: Fleming H. Revell, 1899.
Stimson, Henry L. *The Far Eastern Crisis: Recollections and Observations*. New York: Harper and Brothers, 1936.
Terkel, Studs. *"The Good War": An Oral History of World War Two*. New York: Ballantine, 1985.
Tolley, Kemp. *The Yangtze Patrol: The U.S. Navy in China*. Annapolis, MD: Naval Institute Press, 1971.
Tuchman, Barbara. *Stilwell and the American Experience in China, 1911–45*. New York: Macmillan, 1970.
Tucker, Spencer, and Priscilla Roberts. *Cold War: A Student Encyclopedia*. 5 vols. New York: ABC-Clio, 2007.
Tunner, William H. *Over the Hump: The Story of General William H. Tunner*. New York: Duell, Sloan and Pierce, 1964.
Waln, Nora. *The House of Exile*. Boston: Little, Brown, 1933.
Wedemeyer, Arthur Coady. *Wedemeyer Reports!* New York: Henry Holt, 1958.
Weller, George. *Weller's War: A Legendary Foreign Correspondent's Saga of World War II on Five Continents*, Anthony Weller, ed. New York: Crown, 2009.
White, Alexander. *The United States Marines in North China*. Millbrae, CA: n.p., 1974.
Williams, Robert H. *The Old Corps: A Portrait of the U.S. Marine Corps Between the Wars*. Annapolis: U.S. Naval Institute Press, 1982.
Wilson, Dick. *When Tigers Fight: The Story of the Sino-Japanese War, 1937–1945*. New York: Penguin Books, 1983.
Winchester, Simon. *The Man Who Loved China: The Fantastic Story of the Eccentric Scientist Who Unlocked the Mysteries of the Middle Kingdom*. New York: HarperCollins, 2008.
Wright, David C. *The History of China*. Westport, CT: Greenwood, 2001.

Articles

Cornebise, Alfred. "The Great War Edition of *The Stars and Stripes*." *Relevance* 15, no. 2 (Spring 2006).
Eiler, Keith E. "The Man Who Planned the Victory." *Hoover Digest*, no. 4 (2001).

———. "An Uncommon Soldier." *Hoover Digest*, no. 4 (2001).
Flint, Roy Kenneth. "The United States Army on the Pacific Frontier, 1899–1939." *The Proceedings of the Ninth Military History Symposium, United States Air Force Academy* (October 1980): 139–59.
Frank, Benis M. "Shanghai's 4th Marines: The Glory Days of the Old Corps." *Shipmate* (November 1979): 16.
Goldberg, Emanuel. "G.I. Editors in China Given 'Magna Charta.'" *The Quill* 35 (March 1947).
Hersey, John. "Letter from Shanghai." *The New Yorker* (February 9, 1946), p. 82.
Jessup, Bill. "China *Stripes*—A brief but colorful run." *European-Pacific Stars and Stripes Association News* 16, no. 1 (January-February 2003).
Larsen, Carl W. "Twenty years ago with the *Stars and Stripes*." *The Quill* (December 1964): 8–14.
Morton, Louis. "Army and Marines on the China Station." *Pacific Historical Review* 29, no. 1 (February 1960): 51–73.
Murphy, Charles J.V. "Shanghai: Reopened Under New Management." *Fortune* (February 1946).
Poppelman, Ray. "A China Marine: The Adventures of Ray Poppelman." *Leatherneck* (June 1992).
Smith, Robert Marr. "Japanese War Crimes Trials." *World War II Magazine* (September 1996).

Pamphlets

"History of the 31st Infantry Regiment," n.p., n.d., Folder: The Joseph B. Longuevan Papers, United States Army Military History Institute, Carlisle, Pennsylvania.

Online sources

"Breckinridge, James C. Collection. Personal Correspondence, 1929–1933" at: http://www.mcu.usmc.mil/MCRCweb/ftw/files/pap2933.txt.
Gluckman, Ron. "From Shanghai to Vegas," *Wall Street Journal*, September 1996, reproduced online at http://www.gluckman.com/ShanghaiJews2.html.
Library, California State University, Northridge. Introduction to a discussion of the Old China Hands Archive, at http://library.csun.edu/Old China Hands.
Thompson, Kensley Robert. "One Pilot's Journey in World War II and the CBI Theater," a flight officer's unpublished memoirs, at: http://cbi-theater-4.home.comcast.net.

Index

Acheson, Dean (U.S. secretary of state) 70, 141
Adams, Franklin Pierce 73
Air Transport Command (ATC) 62, 63
Alger, Horatio 72
American Red Cross 41, 57, 76, 156
American Volunteer Group (AVG; "Flying Tigers") 62, 168–169
Anderson, Ernie 116
USS *Annabelle Lykes* 88
Armed Forces Radio System 46, 114, 129
Army Post Office (APO) 45
Army Talks (training pamphlets) 67, 68
Arnold, Gen. "Hap" 108
Associated Press 16, 114
Atcheson, George, Jr. 140
atomic bomb 8, 13, 32, 72–73

"B-Bag" (letters column) 7, 14, 25, 32, 40, 41, 69, 78, 80, 83, 85, 93, 101, 103, 107, 113, 115, 116, 125, 148
Barkley, Sen. Alben 29
Barr, Maj. Gen. David 162
"Barracks Bards" (column) 16, 24, 25, 74, 81
Baruch, Bernard M. 144
Becker, Jim (news desk) 16
SS *Benjamin Brewster* 64
Bergerud, Eric 105
Bergson, Henri Louis 22
Berlin, Irving 88
Berry, Brig. Gen. Robert 86
Blew, John (cartoonist) 16, 151
Blitzkrieg 12
Blondie (cartoon strip) 25
"Books for the Kids of China" 152
Boxer Rebellion 165
Boyle, Hal (correspondent) 73, 96–97, 124, 128
Bradley, Gen. Omar N. 69
Bridge House Jail (Shanghai) 55
Bridges, Harry 99
Brotz, Howard 16
Buck, Pearl S. 164, 165

Bureau of Educational and Cultural Affairs (ECA) 69
Byrnes, James F. (U.S. secretary of state) 89, 110, 139, 142

Cairo Agreement 91, 143
Calcutta, India 11
Camp Edwards, Massachusetts 67
Camp Kilmer, New Jersey 67
Camp Lee, Virginia 66
Caniff, Milton 25, 85
Capitol Theater 41, 45
Capp, Al 25
Cathay Hotel 15, 42
CBI Roundup 118
Century of Shame 21, 161–169
Chaney 152
Chennault, Brig. Gen. Claire 62, 137
Chiang Kai-shek 8, 15, 92, 136, 137, 163, 165; U.S. support of 26, 100, 101, 106–107, 125, 127, 136–140, 142, 143, 144, 145, 146, 162–163; Wedemeyer and 92, 106–107, 110
China: attitudes toward in the Shanghai *Stars and Stripes* 149; civil war 131, 137, 163, 165; civilization 34, 35, 161–169; Communism 8, 26, 69–70, 92, 110, 136, 137, 142, 144, 145, 165; currency 19, 22, 75; food 37; language 34, 35; and the West 9, 161–169
China Air Service Command 62
China-Burma-India Theater (CBI) 11, 12, 34
China-India Pipeline 62–63
China Sketches (book by Crouch) 25
China Theater of Operations 12, 14, 21, 42, 63, 81, 87, 92, 97, 100, 106, 110–111, 120, 137
China Theater Replacement Service (CTRS) 94
China Theater war crimes trials 55–60
Chinese Democratic League 144
Chinese Lantern 15
Chinwangtao 120, 125, 130
Chou En-Lai 136
Chungking 11, 12, 13, 14, 16, 19, 22, 41, 61–62, 63, 74–75, 111, 142
Churchill, Winston 5, 12

Index

CIO Longshoremen's Union 99
Clare, John 95
Clark, Lt. Col. A.D. 117
Clarke, Col. Harry 58, 59
Clausewitz, Carl von 141
Clift, SSgt. John 14, 16, 151, 158, 159
Cold War 9, 146, 161
College of the City of New York 64
Combat Infantry Badge 41
Communist 8th Route Army 123
Convair B-36 *Peacemaker* 108
Cooke, VAdm. Charles M. 110, 135
Council on Cultural and Economic Affairs 70
Crosby, Bing 88
Crouch, Lt. A.L. (poet) 25, 80, 148, 151, 158
Curtiss C-46 *Commando* 47, 106

D-day 11
Daily Pacifican 114
Davies, SSgt. John O., Jr. 151, 158
Dempsey, Cdr. Jack 84
Dick Tracy 25
Dickens, Charles 36
Ding How (book by Crouch) 25
Dittmore, Col. H.P. 115
Domei (Japanese news agency) 53
Dongworth, Eddy 150
Doolittle, Gen. James 43
Doolittle flyers 54, 55–56
Douglas C-47 14–15, 76
Dyke, Col. Ken 50

Eaker, Lt. Gen. Ira C. 108
East Asia Co-Prosperity Sphere 52, 137
Edmonds, Brig. Gen. James 66
Eisenhower, Gen. Dwight David 9, 68, 69, 82, 99–100, 102, 103, 104, 117, 118
Emery, Pvt. Stewart Mackie 64
England, Christine 16
Esquire (magazine) 31
Euripides 49
European Theater of Operations (ETO) 5
"Excelsior" (poem) 109
Extraterritorial rights 20, 21

Fallows, James 168–169
Ferdinand the Bull (book by Leaf) 67
15th U.S. Infantry Regiment 11–12, 21
1st Infantry Division 67
1st Marine Air Wing 128
Fisher, Ham 25
Forrestal, James (U.S. secretary of the Navy) 44
Fort Belvoir, Virginia 66–67
Fort Benning, Georgia 12, 66
Fort Lawton, Washington 110
Fort Leavenworth, Kansas 12
14th U.S. Air Force 16, 62
Freedom of the soldier press 112–119

Gallup polls 6
Gauss, Clarence E. 138
Geiger, Lt. Gen. Roy S. 102
Geisel, Theodor 67
USS *General Eltinge* 93, 94
USS *General Hugh L. Scott* (AP-136) 109, 110
G.I. Bill of Rights 31, 105
G.I. slang 34, 35
Gillem, Lt. Gen. Alvin D. 63, 130
Goddard, Paulette 32
Goebbels, Joseph 49
Goode, Ham (staff photographer) 16, 151
Goodfriend, Col. Arthur 11, 12, 13, 14, 15, 16, 17, 18, 22, 26, 64–73, 122–123, 147, 158, 169; characteristics 71–72, 80; editorials 27, 146, 163–164, 166; life 64–72
Gould, Chester 25
Grable, Betty 67
Graham, TSgt. Mary "Sunny" 150

Hall, Lt. Gen. Charles P. 99
Hall, Maj. Gen. R.R. 115
SS *Hamburg* 65
Hanggi, Marie (staffer) 150
Hangkow 14
Hargrove, Sgt. Marion 43
Harris, Larry ("B-Bag" editor) 151
Hearst papers 113, 149
Hegenbarger, Maj. Gen. Albert F. (commander, 10th U.S. Air Force) 61, 106
Henley, William Ernst 30
Hirohito, Emperor 50, 54, 59–60, 90, 116, 153–154
Hitler, Adolf 66
Hitler, S1c William Patrick (Adolf's nephew) 83
HMHA (U.S. Armed Forces radio station, Shanghai) 46
USS *Hocking* (APA-121) 88
Hodge, Lt. Gen. John R. 97
Hogan, SSgt. Edmund (managing editor) 14, 15, 16, 87, 158
Holdridge, Brig. Gen. H.C. 43
Holiday Inn (movie) 88
Holmes, Burton 36
home front 9, 28, 29, 30, 33, 80–85, 88–89, 93
Homer 133
Honolulu Star Bulletin 16
USS *Hornet* 55
House Appropriations Committee 86
House Un-American Activities Committee 116
Howard, Maj. Gen. A.F. 129
Huebner, Gen. Clarence Ralph 66, 68
The "Hump" 35, 63, 87, 106
Hurley, Maj. Gen. Patrick J. 138–139, 140–141, 143
Hutton, Bud 73, 118–119
Huxley, Aldous 22

Index

Iliad 133
Information and Education Section 45–47, 113, 114; headquarters, U.S. Forces in China (USFCT) 19
International Settlement (Shanghai) 16
It Sez Here! (sports column) 26

SS *James Duncan* 85
Japan: civilians 8; home front 8, 53–54; repatriation 49, 54, 92, 93, 100, 101, 102, 127, 128, 137; troops 8, 52, 121, 122, 124; war crimes trials 8, 55–60
"Japan Today" (column, Tokyo edition of the *Stars and Stripes*) 114
Jensen, Sgt. Charles 151
Jessup, Alpheus ("Bill") 16
Jews 20
Joe Palooka 85
Joint Commission on Rural Reconstruction 69, 73
Jones, Brig. Gen. Louis R. 126
Joy, RAdm. C.T. (commander of the Yangtze Patrol) 155, 156

K-9 Service Corps 85
Kamikaze pilots 53
Katsumo, VAdm. Minoro 52
Kennedy, John Fitzgerald 70
Keppel, Francis 67
Kerr, Maj. Robert M. 59
Kestler, Maj. Hal 117, 118
Kiangwan Airfield (Shanghai) 15, 19, 155
Kinkaid, Adm. Thomas C. (commander of U.S. Seventh Fleet) 23
Kipling, Rudyard 132, 163, 164
Kriegsacademie 12
Kuhn, Irene (correspondent) 16, 17, 18, 22, 74
Kunming 11, 22, 61, 62, 63, 74, 87, 102, 149

La Havre, France 97
Lamarr, Hedy 84
Landis, Carole 32
Lantham, Brig. Gen. Charles T. 113
Leaf, Munro 67
Lee, Lt. Gen. Clifford Hodges 117
Lee, Lt. Gen. John C.H. 68
Lee, Lt. Terry 85
Leonard, Mark 167, 168
Leong, Charlie 16
Levine, Sgt. A.P. 115–116
Life (magazine) 107
L'il Abner 25, 151
Lilley, James 167
London News of the World 51
Longfellow, Henry Wadsworth 109
Louis, SSgt. Joe 83–84
Loyalty check for GIs 115, 116, 117
LST (landing ship, tank) 54, 101, 127, 128
Luce, Henry 107

MacArthur, Gen. Douglas 5, 13, 41, 50, 51, 59, 101, 114, 115, 116, 153
Macbeth (play) 38
Magic Carpet Fleet 87
Magna Charta 13, 14
Mahoney, Col. Charles A. 99
"Mail Call" (column) 117
USS *Makin Island* (CVE-93) 87
Manchuria 137–138, 139, 154
Mao Tse-tung 136, 137, 146, 165
Map Reading for the Soldier (book) 67
USS *Marine Phoenix* 130
Marshall, General George Catlett (Army chief of staff) 6, 7, 8, 9, 12, 42, 81, 82, 83, 90, 110, 130, 131; mission to China 136–146
Mauldin, Bill 14, 25, 42, 43, 118, 148, 149
McCarthy, Joseph 116, 166
McClellan, John 99
McGrath, J. Howard (U.S. solicitor general) 59
McNarney, Lt. Gen. Joseph T. (occupation commander in the ETO) 82, 96, 102, 104
Mead Committee 96, 100, 101
Medea (play) 49
Michener, James A. 31
Middleton, Brig. Gen. John W. 55–57
Military caste system 7, 38, 39, 112, 118
Miller, Lou (sports editor) 16
Milton, John 78
Milwaukee Journal 16
USS *Missouri* 85
Moon Mullins 25
Mountbatten, Adm. Lord Louis Francis 12
Moynihan, John C. (feature editor) 25, 44, 151
Murrow, Edward R. 70
My Several Worlds (Buck memoir) 164–165

Nanking 61, 63, 106, 131, 162
National Maritime Union 91
The Naulahka: A Story of East and West (Kipling novel) 164
New China Daily News 139
New Delhi, India 12
New York Herald Tribune 54, 65, 90
New York Times 93
New Yorker 73
Newsweek 107
Nielson, Capt. Chase J. 55
Nikitin, Alexander P. 150
Nimitz, Adm. Chester 13, 40, 102, 104
North China Daily News 15
North China Marine 159
Northcliffe, Lord 112
"Not Fit to Print" (Goodfriend editorial) 27
Noyes, Thomas 51
Nuremberg Tribunal 48

O Henry 78, 149
O'Brien, Capt. T.J. 52

196 Index

Officer-Enlisted Relationships Board ("Gripe Board") 43, 44
Old China Hands 37, 164
Olmstead, Brig. Gen. George 30
O'Neil, Hugh (staffer) 151
The Only War We Seek (Goodfriend book) 70
Opium Wars 20
Orwell, George 8

Paris Herald Tribune 15
Park Hotel 45, 157
Patterson, Robert P. (U.S. secretary of war) 43, 95, 99, 100, 102, 103, 117
Patton, Lt. Gen. George C. 41, 69
Peace Corps 71
Pearl Harbor 12
Pegler, Westbrook 115–116
Peiping 5, 19, 120, 121, 129, 130
People to People Health Fund (Project HOPE) 71
Percival, Lt. Gen. Arthur C. 57
Pernod, Lt. Maurice 15, 16
Pettuis, T-3 L. 114, 115, 117
Philadelphia Inquirer 16
Philippines 11
Pittsburgh Press 16
points system 6, 7, 81, 82, 83, 85–86, 87, 93, 95, 99, 101, 102
Potsdam Agreement 91
Potsdam Declaration 89, 143
Powell, John W. 15
Power, Tyrone 83
Prince of Wales 65
"Private Arthur Goodwin" 67, 68

Radtke, Tom (staffer) 151
Randolph, Bob 16
Rankin, John 90
Recreation and Amusement Association (RAA) 51
Recruiting Act of 1945 108
Reinhardt, Siegfried (cartoonist) 25, 151
Revercomb, Chapman 91
Reynolds, Maj. Gen. Russell B. 57
Rice, Grantland 73
Richardson, Lt. General Robert C., Jr. 97, 113
Rockefeller, John D., III 70
Rockey, Gen. Keller E. 126, 130
Rockwell, Norman 88–89
USS *Rocky Mount* (AGC-3) 19, 23
Rooney, Andy 73, 118–119
Rooney, Mickey 84
Roosevelt, Franklin Delano 12, 105; attitude toward China 136–137, 138
Rosen, Abe (columnist) 16, 151, 156
Ross, Harold 73
Royall, Kenneth 96
Ruark, Robert C. 44
Rubin, TSgt. Barnard 114, 115, 117

St. Cyr, Lili 32
St. Louis Post-Dispatch 16
San Francisco Chronicle 129
USS *Saratoga* 87
Saturday Evening Post 88
Schulz, Peter (circulation) 151
Scripps-Howard papers 113
"Seabees" 30, 148
See Here, Private Hargrove! 43
Selznick, David O. 88
"Semester at Sea" 71
Senate Foreign Relations Committee 140, 141
Senichenko, Victor 15
Service, John S. 140, 141
Services of Supply 68
Shakespeare, William 38
Shanghai 5, 11, 14, 15, 16, 19, 20, 23, 46, 60, 61, 2, 91; history and characteristics 20–21, 23, 24, 25, 26; symphony orchestra 46; U.S. Navy 23, 24
Shanghai Air Depot 62
Shanghai Bund 15, 19, 20
Shanghai Evening Post and Mercury 15, 18, 19
Shanghai International Settlement 21
Shanghai Municipal Council 21
Shanghai *Stars and Stripes*: attitudes toward veterans 28, 29, 30; campaigns 149, 152–154; career 158–159; distribution 19; editorials 27, 49–51, 71, 72–73, 89–90, 93, 98, 103, 107, 117, 118, 146, 163–164, 166; launching 11–20; operations 13, 14, 15–16; philosophy 13–14; policies 17–18, 19, 20, 147–148, 152–153; Rickshaw Derby and Army-Navy football game 155–156; staff 16, 150–151; supplements 154
Shanghai Volunteer Corps 21
Shanghailanders 20
Shaw, Merv (cartoonist) 151
Shelley, Percy Bysshe 11
Shepherd, Maj. Gen. Lemuel C., Jr. 103, 124–125
Shor, Franc 16, 22, 52–53, 73–39, 148, 151, 152
Shreve, Levan 16
Siccawei Creek 23, 60
Sikhs 15, 16, 133
Since You Went Away (movie) 28, 88
Skeezix 85
Skelton, Red 84
Smart, Gino 74
Smock, Bill 16
soldier press: characteristics 9; freedom 147–148; uses, Southeast Asia Command (SEAC) 12
Stand By for Music (Marine touring show) 129
Stars and Stripes: European editions 69; Honolulu edition, 112–113; Mediterranean edition 117–119, 158, 159; Tokyo edition 114–115, 117; World War II editions 5, 7, 9, 11, 14, 69, 117–119

Sternberg, Lt. Jonathan 46
Steuben, Maj. Gen. Friedrich Wilhelm von 97
Stilwell, Lt. Gen. Joseph 12, 137, 162
Stilwell Road 62
Stimson, Henry (U.S. secretary of war) 6, 7, 143
The Straight Scoop (radio program) 129
Stratemeyer, Lt. Gen. George E. (commander of U.S. Army Air Forces in China) 40, 61, 98, 147
Stuart, Dr. J. Leighton 140
Stuka 87
Sturdevant, William 16
Styer, Lt. Gen. Wilhelm D. 96

Taylor, Robert 83
10th U.S. Air Force 62, 106
Terry and the Pirates 25, 85
Theater Education and Recreational Tours (TERT) 47
3rd Amphibious Corps 128
Thompson, Dorothy 66
"Three Little Girls" (poem) 77–78
Through Chinese Eyes (Goodfriend book) 69
Tientsin 5, 19, 120, 122, 123, 126, 130, 131, 159
Time (magazine) 107
"To a Skylark" (poem) 11
Tojo, Gen. Hideki 49
transitional aspects of the era, 1945–1946 2–3, 8, 9, 161–169
Trawick, Lt. John D. 128–129
"Treaty of Friendship and Alliance Between the Republic of China and the U.S.S.R." 138
Treaty Ports 20
Troop Carrier Command 47, 62
Troop Carrier Groups 106
Truman, Harry S 59, 69, 70, 91, 92, 99, 117, 130, 136; Chinese policies 139, 142–143; policies 92–93, 94
Truscott, Lt. Gen. Lucian K. 47–48
Tsingtao 5, 120, 124, 125, 129, 131, 148
Tuchman, Barbara 162
Tunner, Brig. Gen. William H. 63

Union of Soviet Socialist Republics (USSR) 138, 139, 154
United Nations 90, 139, 142
United Nations Relief and Rehabilitation Administration (UNRRA) 30, 130
United Press 114
United States Army Airway Communications System 62
United States Army Command and General Staff School 12
United States Army Criminal Investigation Division 133
United States Army Forces in China (USAFC) 111, 130
United States Congress 69, 70, 90–91, 94, 96, 102, 103–104, 115

United States Information Agency 70
United States Marine Corps 19, 21, 23, 26, 32, 92, 111, 113–114, 120–131; and Communism 121, 122, 123–124, 125, 131; morale in 120, 121, 122–131; and Shanghai *Stars and Stripes* 113–114, 148, 151, 158–159
United States Marine 1st Division 123, 126
United States Marine Third Amphibious Corps 123, 126, 159
United States Marine 4th Regiment 21, 121
United States Marine 6th Division 111, 124, 125, 129
United States Marine 9th Battalion 131
United States Military Advisory Group in China 92–93, 94, 100, 112, 162–163
United States Military Commission 55–57
United States Navy Asiatic Fleet 21
United States Navy East India Squadron 21
United States Navy 7th Fleet 19, 125, 134
United States Supreme Court 31, 32, 59
United States Third Army 47–48
United States troops: attitudes 28, 29, 30, 38–47, 48, 51–52, 60–61, 80–85, 96–97, 98; conduct 132–135; discipline 40, 41
United States War Department: plans and policies 6, 7, 12, 42–43, 81–83, 85, 86, 90, 97, 114–117
SS *Universe* 71
University of Hawaii 71

Vargas, Alberto 31, 32
"Vargas Girls" 31, 32
V-E Day 5, 86, 88
Victory Plan 12
V-J Day 5, 6, 85, 88, 89, 95, 98, 99

Walker, Col. John E. 87
Walker, Frank 31, 32
Walters, Col. W.E. 114
War Area Service Corps 47
Ward Road Prison 16
Washington Daily News 44
Weart, Maj. Gen. D.L. (commander, Shanghai Base Command) 16–17, 25, 26, 40, 46
Wedemeyer, Lt. Gen. Albert Coady (commander, China Theater of Operatons) 6, 9; attitudes toward troops 98, 99, 100–101, 102–103, 104, 113; life and career 11–13; plans and policies 11, 12, 13, 14, 15, 16, 17, 40, 41, 63, 91, 92, 94, 98, 100–101, 110, 111, 122, 125, 131, 137, 140, 147, 155, 156, 158; role in founding Shanghai *Stars and Stripes* 11–14; views of Chiang 106–107
Wedemeyer Reports! (memoir) 106
Wehrmacht 12
Wehrwein, Austin C. (columnist) 16, 34, 39
West, Maj. Willis A. 55
West Point 11
Western missionaries 20, 165–166
Whangpoo River 19, 23
"White Christmas" (song) 88

Whitehead, Don 112
Why We Fight (film series) 67
Williams, Sgt. Henrietta 76–77
Williard, Frank 26
Wilson, SSgt. Dick (correspondent) 103, 114, 125, 126, 128, 150, 151, 154, 162
Wittman, Col. R.C. 91
Woods, Maj. Gen. Louis E. 104
Woollcott, Alexander 73

XABU (U.S. Marine Corps radio station, Tsingtao) 129
XBOR (U.S. Marine Corps radio station, Tientsin) 129
XUSF (U.S. Armed Services radio station, Chungking) 114

Yalta Agreement 138
Yamashita, General Tomoyuki 57–60
Yangtze River Patrol 134, 155
Yank (magazine) 9, 25, 67
"Yank About China" (column) 16, 52–53, 74, 75, 78–79
Yenan (Chinese Communist capital) 26, 136, 142, 143
Yenching University (Peiping) 140
YMCA 45, 46, 76, 77, 100, 156–157

www.ingramcontent.com/pod-product-compliance
Lightning Source LLC
Chambersburg PA
CBHW032100300426
44116CB00007B/822